BUILDING EFFECTIVE BOARDS FOR RELIGIOUS ORGANIZATIONS

BUILDING EFFECTIVE BOARDS FOR RELIGIOUS ORGANIZATIONS

*A Handbook for Trustees,
Presidents, and Church Leaders*

Thomas P. Holland

David C. Hester

Editors

Jossey-Bass Publishers
San Francisco

The case example concerning Worshipful Work on page 114 is included herein by kind permission of Charles M. Olsen, executive director of Worshipful Work, Inc.

The case example concerning Daughters of Charity National Health System (DCNHS) on pages 114 and 115 and Figure 6.2 on page 116 are included herein by kind permission of Donald A. Brennan, president and CEO of DCNHS.

Jossey-Bass books and products are available through most bookstores. To contact Jossey-Bass directly, call (888) 378–2537, fax to (800) 605–2665, or visit our website at www.josseybass.com.

Substantial discounts on bulk quantities of Jossey-Bass books are available to corporations, professional associations, and other organizations. For details and discount information, contact the special sales department at Jossey-Bass.

TCF Manufactured in the United States of America on Lyons Falls Turin Book. This paper is acid-free and 100 percent totally chlorine-free.

Library of Congress Cataloging-in-Publication Data

Building effective boards for religious organizations: a handbook for trustees, presidents, and church leaders/Thomas P. Holland, David C. Hester, editors.—1st ed.
     p.   cm.
   Includes bibliographical references and index.
   ISBN 0-7879-4563-3 (alk. paper)
   1. Church management Handbooks, manuals, etc. 2. Religious institutions—Administration Handbooks, manuals, etc. 3. Executive advisory bodies Handbooks, manuals, etc. I. Hester, David C. (David Charles), date.
   BV652.B765   1999
   254—dc21   99-39404
                                                        CIP

FIRST EDITION

HB Printing 10 9 8 7 6 5 4 3 2 1

CONTENTS

LIST OF FIGURES, TABLES, AND EXHIBITS

FIGURES

TABLES

EXHIBITS

PREFACE

BECAUSE THIS BOOK is the result of two very personal journeys of faith, we are taking the unusual liberty of beginning it with some introductory remarks about who we are and what brought us to the creation of this book.

To begin with, religious organizations are not simply a topic of professional interest for either of us. Both of us are committed to a living religious tradition—in our case, the Christian Church. Both of us take the work we do on behalf of more effective governance of religious organizations to be a faithful extension of our commitment to the Christian tradition. We believe that our tradition, our faith, calls us to attend carefully and thoughtfully to the structures of governance by which organizations dedicated to the faithful work of teaching, worship, healing, or social services provide their services. If we are to experience God's love in our world at all, it must be through human agency and by means of human institutions. Our hope is that this book may enable the practice of better, more faithful governance so that religious organizations may more successfully be bearers of God's love, as they intend to be.

You should also know that we have come to our work as editors of this volume from very different places. Thomas Holland is a professor of social work at a large public university who has spent more than thirty years observing and working with boards of nonprofit institutions, most recently including those of congregations and theological schools. A committed Episcopal layman, Holland is currently involved in a major research project on questions of governance in the Episcopal Church. He has led countless workshops for boards of colleges, seminaries, congregations, social service agencies, and hospitals. With colleagues Richard Chait and Barbara Taylor, he has written about effective governance and compiled a list of characteristics that define effective boards. That work is woven into his chapters in this volume and, more implicitly, into the volume as a whole.

David Hester is a professor of Christian education at a small Presbyterian Church (USA) seminary and an ordained minister in the Presbyterian Church (USA) who has worked in congregations in Maine, North

Carolina, and Kentucky. He has come to this project with a particular concern that trustees or leaders of governing boards in congregations should learn to think theologically about the issues they face and the decisions they make. He wants to find ways to help leaders practice governance faithfully, which means reflecting critically and creatively and in dialogue with the institution's history, present context, and religious commitments and values. From his point of view, board education is theological education, because it is equipping a board for the mission God has given it. This perspective has generated his chapter on practicing governance in the light of faith (Chapter Four) and motivated his involvement in the editorial formation of the book.

We want to offer you, the reader, an invitation to make your own whatever you find here that may be of interest or use to you. Don't adopt it—adapt it! We know that every context is different—remarkably and wonderfully different. If there is one thing we know about religious institutions it is that one-size governance solutions do not fit all. We hope that pastors, leaders of congregations, seminary trustees, church-related college and hospital trustees, and others will find this book a helpful resource. But if it is to be useful, you will have to translate and transport and transform what is said here so that it makes sense in your own setting and circumstances. In that way, we believe, our book will be useful. It is not a utility piece that you may simply apply and twist in order to fix the problems you face. We make no apology for this. We believe that the significant resources provided in this book's chapters are far more lasting and adaptable than any one-time repair kit. We believe they get to the heart of hard issues that boards must face. But the presenting name of these issues is "Legion" (Mark 5:9). As in the New Testament story, we have tried to see through the clanging chains and noise of the instant to the soul of the board's work, to help it find the freedom and joy in which it was intended to live and serve.

A Brief History of Religious Boards

Organizations that serve religious purposes are among the oldest ways in which people have come together for cooperative efforts. From loosely structured local worship groups to multinational denominational systems, religious organizations have taken many forms and served a wide variety of needs for millions of people. Many of these organizations came into existence because of the heroic efforts of missionaries, lay and ordained clergy, and other leaders who worked to bring their faith into new regions of the world. Local congregations were established, with both indigenous leaders and representatives of the parent organization overseeing them. Over time, additional forms were created, including seminaries to provide educated ministers for local congregations, hospitals to provide health care to the sick, orphanages to provide shelter and care for children without parents, schools to educate children and young adults, and social service agencies to serve the poor and needy in many communities.

Most of these organizations grew under the watchful eye and financial support of those in leadership positions in religious institutions of people sharing a faith tradition. While these affiliations adapted to local circumstances, their participants sought to remain faithful to the beliefs and practices of their larger religious body. Sustaining commitment to the costly process of developing new, local organizations required the continuing involvement of many people, at both the sponsoring level and the local level.

Involvement in the development of religious organizations usually included both providing financial support and having a voice in policies and practices. Some denominations relied on persons in authoritative positions to make decisions about issues and policies facing all their organizations (for example, bishops in the Roman Catholic and Episcopal Churches) but over time came to value greater involvement of local representatives in governance, especially regarding policies that most directly affected the local organization. Other denominations took a more democratic or congregational approach. Early American congregational meetings to address the concerns shared by members of the local church were as common as community or town meetings of citizens. In later years, faculties of seminaries met together to work on policies to guide their efforts, as did physicians in hospitals.

As religious organizations grew larger, both the more centrally controlled denominations and the more congregational ones moved to greater reliance on their organizations' local governing boards. Bishops invited parishes to select representatives to advise priests on local matters. Congregations that had only loose ties to their larger denomination began selecting representatives to periodic regional or national assemblies, where they worked on issues of concern to all congregations and brought back recommendations for consideration by the local congregation. Almost every religious organization has come to have a specific group of persons, whether chosen by central appointment or local vote, who meet regularly to address the needs of the organization and its participants. This trend can be traced in most denominations, including in their constituent congregations, as well as in a wide variety of religiously affiliated organizations, such as seminaries, hospitals, and other philanthropic efforts. Both lay and ordained participants serve in such roles.

By the middle of the twentieth century, most of these oversight groups had developed into governing boards for their organizations. Whether called the board of elders, the vestry, the overseers, the board of trustees, or some other title, these governing bodies shared many features. Within the guidelines developed by their judicatory or denominational structures, the boards of these local organizations began developing local policies, advising or even supervising the minister or the chief executive officer, and maintaining communications with others in the wider association. The responsibilities and duties of these boards evolved over time, often with little guidance or critical examination of changes in the environment, organizational needs, or constituents' expectations. As a result, the quality of their performance of their governance responsibilities varied widely.

The Present Situation

In recent years, leaders of many national and international religious bodies as well as leaders of their local organizations have become increasingly concerned about the performance of their governing boards. Ineffective governance stems from many sources, including ambiguities or unresolved conflicts about such vital matters as the appropriate differentiation of the roles and responsibilities of paid, professional staff (such as clergy in congregations, deans and faculties of seminaries, or physicians in hospitals) from the roles and responsibilities of the voluntary and often lay members of governing boards. Other challenges include questions about the appropriate extent of local autonomy in relation to national denominational policies, traditions, or the mission of the founding body; how to deal with budgetary decisions and with imbalances between the financial needs of the local organization and funds provided by the denomination; qualifications for and authority to decide on who holds various roles in the organization; and other critical matters of policy.

Few denominational bodies have addressed such questions of governance clearly, leaving the boards of most local religious groups to struggle with them alone. In turn, many board members are unsure how to resolve such complex challenges and unclear about the impacts of their efforts on the quality of performance of their organizations. There are few educational resources to which they can turn for help. Some ecumenical works directly address issues in the governance of religious organizations (a notable example is Charles M. Olsen's *Transforming Church Boards into Communities of Spiritual Leaders,* Alban, 1995). Publications on the general topic of leadership have long been available, but they seldom address the particular concerns of governing boards. Although boards need skilled individual leaders as members, the essential *group* character of governance requires further resources and capacities that have received little attention in the religious literature. Religious organizations are mentioned only in passing by the authors of most volumes on management, leadership, and teamwork in nonprofit organizations, despite the fact that religious organizations constitute by far the majority of all nonprofits.

The Lilly Endowment is among the few foundations to sponsor research and training projects for the leaders and trustees of many denominations and religious organizations. Its support of projects addressing governance of seminaries and congregations has allowed several of the authors of the present volume to work in this area, from studies of congregational leaders to the development and testing of learning resources for seminary trustees. Growing out of those experiences was a shared concern to bring together a range of resources specifically targeted at this long-neglected group—those who serve as members of the governing boards of religious organizations. The support and encouragement of Craig Dykstra and Fred Hofheinz of the Lilly Endowment's Religion Division are heartily acknowledged.

Members of governing boards of religious organizations face multiple, complex issues and ambiguous, sometimes inconsistent expectations. They are told to be enthusiastic advocates for the organization, yet not to get caught up emotionally in their own agenda for it. They are supposed to oversee carefully the use of all the organization's human and material resources, but to remain focused on the nonmaterial purposes they serve. They are supposed to set clear priorities for moving forward in the organization's mission, even when its purposes are unclear or defined in divergent ways by various participants. They are supposed to formulate thoughtful plans for the future, even when that future is largely unpredictable and understood in different ways by members. They are to resolve conflicts without alienating those whose positions are not accepted. They are told to focus on the "big picture" while not ignoring the important details of organizational quality. They are expected to be independent thinkers, yet not to act without the group's direction. They are to maintain strong leadership and clear focus while maximizing opportunities for staff members and consumers to pursue their own interests. Little wonder that one observer of these organizations described them as having only loosely linked parts, and another wryly likened their efforts to the futility of trying to herd cats!

Although many board members wish that their efforts were more evidently productive and satisfying, few know where to begin or how to proceed with steps of change toward improvement. In most discussions of what a board should do in the months ahead, there are as many views as there are participants in the discussion. The pressures of already overloaded agendas leave members with little time or inclination for attention to *how* the board is doing its work.

A major premise of this volume is that such attention is crucial if a board is to add value to its organization. We address the challenges of understanding how and why boards of religious organizations operate as they do, and we discuss a variety of practical steps that boards can take to strengthen their performance. Understanding the key components of governance and learning about how effective boards implement them can serve to stimulate motivation to change. Drawing on the experiences of many boards of a variety of religious organizations, the authors provide practical guidance to boards that want to improve the quality and impacts of their work as well as to increase their satisfaction in knowing they make a difference in the lives of their organizations.

Organization of the Book

We have organized the chapters written for this volume around two themes. The chapters in Part One provide foundational insights into the meaning and practice of faithful governance. The chapters in Part Two offer a treasury of more specific and detailed discussions of special issues that boards face. We have carefully avoided any division between theory and practice. All of the chapters contain *theory in practice,* and all represent *practice observed and reflected in theory.*

Part One begins with Malcolm L. Warford's search, in Chapter One, for a scriptural model for organizing the board's work to replace the hierarchical management model that is currently standard. He suggests an image of trustees as "prophetic inquirers" and proposes a cooperative model of trusteeship that encourages faithful practice of governance. Thomas Holland follows in Chapter Two with a primer on the basic duties and responsibilities of the board. New board members especially, as well as new presidents or clergy, should find this a particularly helpful chapter; but because it is a definitive chapter, trustees and leaders of various years of experience will also find it refreshing and informative. In Chapter Three, William L. Sachs explores the mission of religious governance, looking at it particularly through an historical prism. The concern with mission continues in Chapter Four with David Hester's proposal that the mission statement of a congregation or theological institution proclaims the values and commitments that must inform the board's conversation and decision making. The work of the board, Hester argues, is nothing less than the work of practical theology, because the trustees are stewards of a faith tradition that finds particular expression in the institution's mission statement.

Part Two begins in Chapter Five with Holland's proposals for developing a more effective board. This chapter reflects Holland's insights from years of research and consulting with boards. It may serve as something of a plumb line for boards to see themselves at various stages of development. Chapter Six considers the issue of the distribution of power and authority on a board. Thomas J. Savage provides a series of case examples of non-hierarchical restructuring that represents the purpose and identity of the particular organization more faithfully than current structures. From each case Savage draws a lesson for governance and concludes the chapter with a series of recommendations aimed at helping boards reflect on ways they might move beyond hierarchies and toward greater flexibility.

In Chapter Seven, Christa R. Klein explores the unique role of boards as they span the boundaries between the institution and the social and religious context of which the institution is a part. What Klein dubs the "boundary work" of the board, far from being negative baggage, has the exciting yet awesome potential of enabling the board to participate in the reshaping of the present religious landscape.

In Chapter Eight, David J. Nygren, Julie Hickman Burg, and Dennis A. Ross discuss the challenges an organization faces when joining or merging with another organization. In an academic and health care marketplace, where competition for students and patients is fierce, merger or closure is a crucial issue. This is no less so for small churches, where shifting population trends and aging members have left congregations economically vulnerable and depleted of institutional energy. Merging two small churches seems an obvious answer; but how to do so with integrity—that's the question that Nygren and his colleagues explore.

Richard P. Chait in Chapter Nine leads the reader through the maze of arguments about the board's proper role in the strategic planning of a religious institution. Is the board, session, or vestry the body responsible for strategic planning? Or does that role belong entirely elsewhere, with administration, faculty, or a special task force in a congregation? Chait suggests that the board has a particular and a particularly important role: it is neither all nor nothing.

Chapter Ten, by Lawrence M. Butler, perhaps the most technical chapter in the book, may also be one of the most useful. It provides suggestions for gathering information that allow leaders to read the current health of the institution quickly and easily. When that is done, the board becomes free to devote itself and its precious time to other issues of importance.

Finally in our Conclusion, rather than trying to tie all the threads together neatly, we point toward the work that needs to be done in the future. We suggest that every religious governing board faces the persistent task of interpreting the present in light of the past while being called toward an envisioned future. We use the term *turning point* to describe where we are now in our ongoing search for practical wisdom, understanding, and methods to carry out the work of building effective boards for religious organizations.

In all of these efforts, our intended audience has been those board members whose energy and dedication sustain these invaluable organizations in this nation and around the world. Their leadership has brought us this far, and their examples warrant our respect and honor. They are the truly unsung heroes of our religious history, regardless of tradition. If this volume helps any of them or their successors to do a better job and gain greater satisfaction from their efforts, we will have succeeded.

August 1999

THOMAS P. HOLLAND
Athens, Georgia
DAVID C. HESTER
Louisville, Kentucky

THE EDITORS

DAVID C. HESTER holds a B.A. degree in Philosophy from the University of Maine, Orono. He earned an M.Div. degree at Bangor Theological Seminary, Bangor, Maine. While there he served small churches throughout the state. He subsequently attended Duke University, Durham, North Carolina, earning a Ph.D. degree in religion, with a major in biblical studies.

While in North Carolina, Hester served as pastor to a rural congregation and later as associate minister to a large, downtown congregation, which included responsibilities for church education and urban ministry. He has taught at Berea College and for the last fourteen years has served as Christian education professor at Louisville Presbyterian Seminary. He is the author of numerous reviews, articles, and chapters in *How Shall We Witness? Faithful Evangelism in a Reformed Tradition* (1995) and *The Presbyterian Presence: The Twentieth Century Experience* (1992). Along with Thomas P. Holland, he was the recipient of a Lilly Endowment grant to evaluate theological school trustee education projects at sixteen seminaries and theological schools. Hester and his wife, Gale, live in Louisville, Kentucky; they are the parents of four adult children and have five grandchildren.

THOMAS P. HOLLAND is professor and director of the Institute for Nonprofit Organizations at the University of Georgia and also serves as director of the University of Georgia School of Social Work's Center for Social Services Research and Development. Over the past thirty years he has published extensively on management and governance of nonprofit organizations, including recently *Improving Board Effectiveness: Practical Lessons for Nonprofit Health Care Organizations* (1997), *How to Build a More Effective Board* (1996), and "Self-Assessment by Nonprofit Boards," which appeared in *Nonprofit Management and Leadership* (1991). He is coauthor (with Richard P. Chait and Barbara Taylor) of *Improving the Performance of Nonprofit Boards* (1993) and "The New Work of the Nonprofit Board," published in the *Harvard Business Review* (1996). Holland consults nationally with executives and governing boards of nonprofit organizations and teaches graduate courses about the nonprofit field.

THE CONTRIBUTORS

JULIE HICKMAN BURG has a consulting practice located in Seattle, Washington. Formerly a consultant with William M. Mercer, Incorporated, Burg focuses on designing change processes that link individual performance and development to the overall goals and culture of the organization. Her consulting experience has focused on performance management, management development, competency profiling, training, and organizational assessment and change. Burg received her Ph.D. degree in organizational psychology from DePaul University. She and her colleagues were recently awarded the Peter Drucker award for their efforts in competency modeling in health care.

LAWRENCE M. BUTLER is a Senior Fellow of the Cheswick Center, a charitable trust dedicated to improving the governance function in nonprofit institutions. He was principal investigator of the multiyear project funded by the Lilly Endowment that demonstrated in a variety of settings (including a theological seminary) the value of specially designed board information systems for enhancing institutional governance. As an outgrowth of that work, he has established a specialized consulting service through which he assists colleges, universities, and a broad variety of organizations in enhancing the communicative power of board information. Butler is cofounder and principal of Institutional Strategy Associates (ISA), a management consulting firm specializing in strategic and program planning for nonprofit institutions in higher education, health care, philanthropy, and the arts. Prior to establishing ISA, Butler was a senior manager with The Boston Consulting Group. He holds an M.B.A. from Harvard Business School and a B.A. magna cum laude from Harvard College.

RICHARD P. CHAIT is professor at the Harvard Graduate School of Education, with a special interest in the governance of nonprofit organizations. With Thomas Holland and Barbara Taylor, he has written two books on governance: *The Effective Board of Trustees* (1993) and *Improving the Performance of Governing Boards* (1996). He is also coauthor of two *Harvard Business Review* articles on the subject: "Charting the Territory

of Nonprofit Boards" (1989) and "The New Work of Nonprofit Boards"
(1996). He is a member of the board of directors of the National Center
for Nonprofit Boards and a frequent consultant to governing boards.

CHRISTA R. KLEIN is dean of the Center for Continuing Formation at
St. Mary's Seminary and the University of Maryland at Baltimore. Klein
serves on the governing boards of Valparaiso University and In Trust, Inc.,
and is seminar director for In Trust's educational programs for theological
school presidents and trustees. For more than a decade, Klein was a program consultant to the Religion Division of Lilly Endowment Inc., where
she specialized in theological school governance and worked with more
than one hundred theological schools across the Christian denominational
spectrum. Klein holds a master's degree and a doctoral degree from the
University of Pennsylvania in the field of American civilization. Her specialization is the history and governance of American Protestant and Roman Catholic religious institutions.

DAVID J. NYGREN is global leader of the Performance and Development
segment for William M. Mercer, San Francisco, in the Performance and
Reward Practice. He joined Mercer from DePaul University, where he was
executive vice president. A distinguished academician, he earned a Ph.D.
in social and organizational psychology from Boston University in 1988,
where he taught organizational behavior, mergers and acquisitions, leadership, and the management of change in the Graduate School of Management. He also graduated from Harvard University's Institute for
Educational Management in 1995. Nygren is currently global leader and
intellectual champion for BoardWorksSM, a distinctive consulting service
designed to align the structure and process of board governance with
organizational strategy.

DENNIS A. ROSS is the president and owner of Data Analysis and Research, a research and consulting firm located in San Francisco.

WILLIAM L. SACHS is an Episcopal priest, historian, and foundation consultant. Currently rector of St. Matthew's Church in Wilton, Connecticut,
he has served churches in Virginia and Chicago. In addition to a Ph.D. degree in the history of Christianity from the University of Chicago, he holds
degrees from Baylor, Vanderbilt, and Yale Universities. He is the author
of two books, most recently *The Transformation of Anglicanism* (1989)
and more than one hundred articles and reviews. He is codirector (with
Thomas P. Holland) of the Zaccheus Project, a study of the Episcopal

Church that is one of the largest studies of grassroots commitment in mainline Protestant denominations. He has been a consultant on religious leadership for the Lilly Endowment and the Episcopal Church Foundation. He is a frequent lecturer, conference leader, and teacher.

THOMAS J. SAVAGE, S.J., died on May 10, 1999. He was a member of the Society of Jesus and, until his death, served as a senior consultant for William M. Mercer, San Francisco, in its Performance and Reward Practice. He joined Mercer from Rockhurst College, where he was president from 1988 to 1996, and from Rockhurst's National Seminars Group, where he was president from 1991 until 1999. As an adjunct professor at the Haas School of Business, University of California, Berkeley, Savage taught strategic planning in the MBA program. In his consulting experience and executive management roles, he emphasized strategic thinking and leadership, board development, and organizational effectiveness. Savage studied architecture at the Catholic University of America and philosophy and sociology at Boston College, where he graduated summa cum laude. He held graduate degrees in city planning from the University of California, Berkeley, and in public policy and administration from Harvard University, where he earned his doctorate. His *Seven Steps to a More Effective Board* (1994) is widely used by boards of trustees and directors seeking to improve their performance.

MALCOLM L. WARFORD is professor of the practice of ministry at Lexington Theological Seminary in Lexington, Kentucky. He is an ordained minister in the United Church of Christ and has served congregations in New York and Vermont. Warford has been a member of the faculties of St. Louis University and Union Theological Seminary in New York. He has served as president of Eden Theological Seminary in St. Louis, Missouri, and Bangor Theological Seminary in Bangor, Maine. He serves often as a consultant to foundations, schools, and church organizations. For more than a decade he was a trustee of the Maryknoll School of Theology in New York.

To Henry Sherrill, Robert Lynn,
and Craig Dykstra—
true pioneers who showed us
the way and inspired our efforts
to explore the territory further—

and to the memory of Thom Savage,
who passed away just a few months after
preparing his chapter for this book

PART ONE

PRACTICING FAITHFUL GOVERNANCE

I

STEWARDS OF HOPE

THE WORK OF TRUSTEES

Malcolm L. Warford

Called to the one hope of your calling.

—Ephesians 4:4

SEVERAL YEARS AGO, a tourist, Erwin Kreuz, arrived at the Bangor, Maine, airport on a charter flight from Europe. The plane was headed to San Francisco and stopped over in Bangor to refuel and to permit passengers to go through customs. Kreuz, however, who was from Germany and spoke no English, thought he had arrived in California. He left the airport, checked into a hotel, and for a couple of days walked around Bangor thinking he was in San Francisco, until someone he met discovered the confusion. He was then interviewed by Nancy Remsen, a reporter from the *Bangor Daily News* (1977), with the help of an interpreter and

The figures used in this chapter have been created over several years. They have been changed and modified with the assistance of participants in the various gatherings where they have been presented. I want to express my thanks to John Frazer, former head of the Association of Independent Kentucky Colleges and Universities, for his thoughtful reading and observations during the development of this chapter.

became something of a local hero. Some townspeople actually collected enough money to put him back on the plane to San Francisco.

At first it is hard to conceive of someone confusing a small town like Bangor with a large city like San Francisco. (I am grateful to the staff of the *Bangor Daily News* for confirming this account and to Barbara McDade, librarian, and Cindy Todd, reference librarian, at the Bangor Public Library for assistance in verifying the details of the story.) Bangor is a wonderful community, but it is not especially known for its cosmopolitan lifestyle. You might bump into Stephen King on the sidewalk, but celebrities are usually hard to find. Can you imagine those few days as Kreuz walked around Bangor trying to fit what he was seeing into the image of San Francisco in his mind? As he walked past the local Chinese restaurant he must have thought, "Chinatown is not as large as described in the guidebook." He may have wondered why the streetcars were not running or why the town felt smaller than he expected it would. In the interview the reporter asked, "Wasn't there any moment in which you were suspicious that you were not in San Francisco?" "Well," Kreuz replied, "I was a bit disappointed in the bridge."

We often have the same problem as the tourist: we keep trying to fit what is actually going on into an image in our mind of what we want to see. We think we are in San Francisco when we are really in Bangor. In this regard, Max De Pree's (1989, p. 9) familiar words ring true: "The first responsibility of a leader is to define reality." In this regard, it is the responsibility of the board to ensure that an organization knows the reality of its situation and is guided and informed in all its various tasks by this shared sense of truth. For organizations standing within a religious tradition, not only should this sense of reality be defined by the facts and values of institutional life, but it should also be understood within the particular angle on the nature of reality that is formed by their tradition's religious or theological perspective. Within the Christian tradition, this perspective is shaped by the themes of servanthood, stewardship, and fidelity.

Servanthood, Stewardship, and Fidelity

The gospel of Luke (22:27) is clear about the pattern of Christ's leadership: "But I am among you as one who serves." It is this sense of leadership that transforms the usual hierarchical images of authority and turns upside down the primary modes of governance in society. A commitment to serve is the prerequisite for leading. Without this essential motivation, leadership easily becomes self-serving, turned in on itself and its own needs. Most of all, this service is a form of commitment to a vision that calls an institution into being and nurtures and guides its life.

As stewards, trustees are called to remember that the institution they serve does not ultimately belong to them. Institutions standing within theological and ecclesial traditions cannot define themselves simply on their own terms. If such institutions lose sight of their essential vocation as communities ultimately accountable to the gospel, then they have lost their reason for existence. It is the task of trustees to remember this calling and to care for the life of the organization in light of this commitment. In particular, trustees hold in trust the vision of the organization and the contemporary nature of that calling (Greenleaf, 1980).

Steward is a primary image for leadership and governance in the Christian community. Essential to understanding the office of steward is the recognition that it originates in something beyond itself. At the center of stewardship is the management of resources belonging to God. "Think of us in this way, as servants of Christ and stewards of God's mysteries" (1 Cor. 4:1). The hallmark of stewards is "that they be found trustworthy" (1 Cor. 4:2). This means that there are multiple criteria for the practice of stewardship, and not simply the bottom line of economic profit, which drives most corporate structures. In fact, the fiduciary responsibility of trustees is not just to keep an institution solvent; it is most of all to keep the institution faithful. The primary work of stewardship is to build up relationships, to nurture the connections among all Earth's creatures, and to live with a sense of humility in the face of the mystery of God.

In Luke 12:42–46, Jesus connects servanthood and stewardship in drawing attention to watchfulness as an essential characteristic of faithful disciples. In this parable of household stewards, the point is made that they are to care for the well-being of the whole house. They are reminded that they are held accountable to the head of the house and, though that head might be away, they are not to act independently but to remain faithful to the owner's interests (Hall, 1990).

Thus, to think of governance in a religious perspective is to consider organizational life within the practices of fidelity. Faithfulness is the essential category for determining the quality and adequacy of a trustee's service as a steward. Though often confused with belief, faith is actually something quite different. We can believe anything we want, and we often do, without necessarily ever having to demonstrate the truth of those beliefs. Faith, conversely, is fundamentally defined by the connection between what we profess to believe and what we actually do. It is consistency between belief and practice. What makes such consistency possible is the vision that lies at the center of fidelity. As Wendell Berry (1975, p. 157) writes, "The test of faith is consistency—not the fanatic consistency by which one repudiates the influence of knowledge, but rather a consistency between principle and behavior." Northrop Frye (1989, pp. 52–53) affirms, "Faith, then, as distinct from professed faith, is the activity of realizing a visionary model in the mind suggested by hope."

The Christian vision is shaped by the life, death, and resurrection of Jesus, in whom we see the promise of a new humanity and a new heaven and Earth. As we dwell in Christ, we participate in a new creation where God "makes all things new" (Rev. 21:1–4). It is a world in which injustice, hunger, and suffering no longer exist. It lies within the eternity of God but now and then reveals itself in this time and place. This promise informs institutions that stand in the Christian tradition, and it establishes the criteria by which such institutions are measured against a society whose values often collide with this vision.

Rethinking Trusteeship

For too long trusteeship has been viewed as the work of custodians whose primary task is the maintenance of the organization as it is or has been. We have often gone forward by looking through a rearview mirror. Conversely, we just as often have seen trusteeship as the work of referees who sort out conflicts and step in when harmony falls too far out of balance. Trustees have often presided as a court of last resort without acknowledging or accepting responsibility for the overall well-being of the organization.

Another existing image of trusteeship is that of a lobbyist who represents a constituency or interest group. In this sense, the board is understood as a kind of parliament or a general assembly in which particular claims on the institution are made. What often happens in this arrangement is that some demands are met but everyone loses sight of the whole in the process. The organization is lost in its particularities and no connections are made so that its center or core may be understood, supported, and advocated.

When trustees view themselves as custodians, referees, or lobbyists, they give up the most important task of trusteeship, which is responsibility for the vision of the organization. Though trustees cannot arbitrarily make decisions about that vision, they are fundamentally responsible for seeing that the vision is articulated and that it informs all operations of the organization. The vision should shape the institution's mission and its programs. Ultimately, trustees are the only group in an institution who have primary responsibility for seeing that the vision does not get lost in the details of daily life.

As the holders of that ultimate responsibility, trustees need to help every member of the organization's community raise the question, What does the vision of this organization require of me? (This was a question that

Robert Greenleaf raised in various ways throughout his life and writings; see Greenleaf, 1998, pp. 24–26.) In this question reside hope and imagination for religious service. An organization's vision calls everyone to an uncommon level of service. The organization's challenge is not so much a matter of finding extraordinary people as it is being committed to the promise of a great vision that can make the difference in the organization's character and performance (Greenleaf, 1980).

Trustees should look at institutional life through their religious or theological resources of tradition, memory, and hope. Various organizational techniques and strategic planning models have been tried. But instead of relying on these derivative business and management models, religious organizations need to pursue the fundamental question of who is calling them and what they are called to be. It is through attention to these questions that they will be able to deepen their understanding of their history, mission, and distinctive ways of sorting out the various claims that are made on their resources.

One of the key responsibilities of trustees is therefore to help executives remember that their office is a teaching office, not just a managerial one. Teaching should be the primary role of the executive. Essentially this is the calling expressed in Ephesians 4:12–13: "to equip the saints for the work of ministry, to build up the body of Christ." Though the popular definition of the executive is that of chief administrative officer, a religious perspective on "organization" will help to illuminate the extent to which this person is essentially a teacher, an educator of the board (McCarter, 1996). Obviously this is a call to mutual learning; in seeing teaching as a fundamental calling, the executive also acknowledges herself or himself to be one, like Chaucer's (1958, p. 10) clerk, who "gladly wolde . . . learne and gladly teche." Such an understanding of the executive and trustees defines the board as a community of faith and learning; it begins to change the style of trusteeship, moving the board toward levels of trust and mutual inquiry that best serve the organization.

My experience is that an institutional vision cannot be contained in any document or statement of mission, no matter how impressive, for it is primarily through stories and symbols that this vision is understood. Though we may design institutional logos or corporate seals, symbols arise out of the life of a community and cannot be manufactured. They represent the promise and the spirit that sustain the mission and character of the organization. The teaching office of the executive is embodied in the activities of evoking the metaphors, symbols, and stories that are attached to the vision out of which the organization lives, by which its mission is shaped and its specific programs are formed.

An essential point in the executive's teaching of the board is in the orientation of new trustees. Here it is crucial for the executive to convey the style and content of the board's culture. This involves describing the organization's tradition, its distinctive elements of belief and way of doing things, and the primary activities of trusteeship. Many new trustees will come to a board with experiences of trusteeship that are contrary to the spirit and forms of trusteeship held by the institution they are now to serve. Thus it is important for the executive and trustees to initiate their new colleagues into seeing trusteeship as a mode of inquiry, a way of leading that calls trustees to the deepest levels of thought and commitment.

Trustees and executives have to keep central their organization's vision of what it is and who calls it to life. The hard work of management will not disappear. In fact, the energies needed by trustees, executives, and senior professional staff members to deal with fiscal pressures and program or service commitments will probably increase in the coming years. But nothing that organizations achieve will make any real difference if they are not empowered by a compelling vision and if their mission and programs are not sustained by the hope that such a vision makes possible. Thus, at the center of a trustee's vocation is the task of keeping the vision in sight and responding to the new duties and responsibilities the vision reveals in the organization's contemporary and perhaps changing mission.

It is important to recognize that trusteeship is vested in the board as a whole. It is the board of trustees that is granted authority, not any single trustee. This means that trustees are not authorized to act individually; it is not a singular office. The board alone is granted power and authority to act. Some of the most disruptive and ultimately fatal moments in trusteeship occur when a single trustee or small group of trustees acts as if it has the authority to function outside the whole board.

This notion is sometimes difficult for trustees to understand because many trustees hold professional positions in which they are granted power to operate essentially on their own. The corporation executive who is now a trustee may forget that as a trustee he or she does not have the singular authority of office he or she might assume in some business organizations. Even well-intended efforts by individual trustees can complicate the life of the organization. For example, a trustee of one school developed the custom of coming to the campus a day or two before the board meeting to engage in his own inspection tour, dropping in to see selected faculty, staff, and students. He indicated to those he met that he wanted to get the real story and be receptive to news he intimated would never come to the board through regular channels. Although he may not have intended to imply that something was wrong, this trustee's behavior suggested that the president and the board could not be trusted. Though his interest in the school's life was on target, the method in which he carried it out suggested a very different agenda.

The Practice of Thoughtful Questions

One central aspect of trusteeship is sustaining a conversation about things that matter in the life of the organization. Instead of being fearful that discussion about issues will be disruptive, trustees need to affirm argument as a significant practice that lies at the center of institutional life. (I am, of course, using *argument* here in the classical sense of persuasion. It is civil argument, not quarrelsome confrontation.) When issues of institutional life are simply reduced to politics, the pursuit of truth is subsumed beneath efforts to exercise power, engage in mutual threats, and circumvent the needed inquiry in covert ways. If argument is denied by such maneuvering, then conversation is trivialized to the level of gossip, where there is little accountability for what is said and little effort is made to correct or revise portrayals of truth when they are challenged by new facts or perspectives. The problem that presents itself to trustees is establishing the rules, protocols, and manners of argument within the institution. Senior professional staff (such as physicians in hospitals or faculty in schools) play a particularly crucial role in this conversation with trustees, and other members of the organization's community are also partners in the debate at crucial points.

As institutional pressures, financial issues, and legal questions intensify in theological seminaries, for example, the trend is to follow the problematic model of universities and colleges, which have restructured higher education along corporate lines. "You will find universities that ten years ago were run in a collegial fashion," Bartlett Giamatti (1988, p. 41) once wrote, "are now completely structured to look from the outside as if they were manufacturing or banking firms, with tables of organization replete with executive vice-presidents, vice-presidents, lawyers: all the appurtenances of a major profit-making corporation." Such restructuring is not simply a matter of shifting responsibilities; rather, it represents a fundamental realignment of the academic community itself. "What I fear most in the universities and colleges in America," Giamatti added, "is that those who are responsible for the legal processes and those who are responsible for the daily life of the mind will see themselves as somehow engaged in different things" (p. 43).

When any organization is defined by an arbitrary division between the so-called facts of institutional life and the institution's values, the institution's basic identity is eroded. British philosopher Michael Oakeshott (1989) maintains that a university (and by extension a seminary or another kind of school) is "a home of learning, a place where a tradition of learning is preserved and extended, and where the necessary apparatus for the pursuit of learning has been gathered together" (p. 97). At the center of such a community are "the manners of the conversation" (p. 99). This sustained conversation stands in contrast to the kind of highly politicized market or ideologically driven activities of some places that still call themselves schools. Oakeshott would insist that where the manners of conversation cannot be sustained, that is, where the various members of an academic community cannot carry on over time a conversation about things that matter, then essentially the school no longer exists.

Conversation about things that matter is not just inquiry among those who share common interests; it also includes and takes place among all those who are involved in discussion about the nature of the organization itself. It is in such conversation that an institution expresses its fidelity to sustained inquiry into what should claim the institution in the present moment and in years to come. This is the familiar point made by Alasdair MacIntyre (1997), that a lively institution is characterized by a continuing argument about who it is and what it ought to be doing to express its primary purpose: "So when an institution—a university, say, or a farm, or a hospital—is the bearer of a tradition of practice or practices, its common life will be partly, but in a centrally important way, constituted by a continuous argument as to what a university is and ought to be or what good farming is or what good medicine is. Traditions, when vital, embody continuities of conflict" (p. 222).

A primary task of trusteeship, then, is to attend to the *rules of argument* that will be the form by which the organization engages institutional issues. At the center of this concern is the recognition that various parts of the organization have unique contributions to make to the development of institutional policies and programs. Moreover, it is the practical necessity of how institutions really work.

Part of what gets in the way is that the formal model of governance does not express the actual or hoped-for model of shared governance. In the usual institutional chart of organization, a hierarchical pattern is obvious. The organizational chart in Figure 1.1 reflects the legal definitions of institutional responsibility. It shows how the board of trustees has ultimate fiduciary responsibility for the life of the organization. From the board flow all other delegated tasks and responsibilities to the executive, staff, and members of the organization. The difficulty with this model is that while it describes adequately the legal structure of governance and re-

Figure 1.1. Formal Model of Governance.

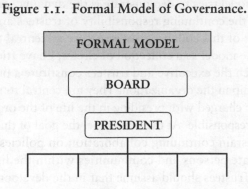

sponsibility, it does not express how an institution actually works, and in the case of religious institutions, how it is expected to work in light of biblical and theological norms for servanthood, stewardship, and fidelity.

In contrast to the formal structure of governance, the functioning model (Figure 1.2) attempts to express the commitments to caring for individuals and remaining faithful to a vision that lie at the heart of institutions called into being by religious commitments. The specific roles identified in this model are taken from seminaries (the type of religious organization with which I am most familiar), but they can be readily translated into appropriate terms for other types of religious organizations.

Figure 1.2. Functioning Model of Governance.

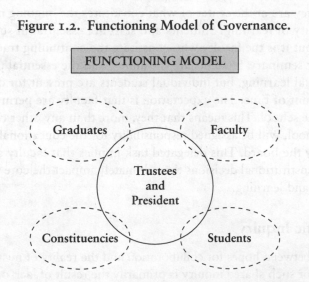

Note: *Faculty have a particular collaborative relationship in shared governance.*

What this model tries to demonstrate is the dynamic quality of institutional life and the continuing responsibility of trustees and executives to see the nurture of this collaborative structure as central to their calling. In designing the model as a collection of circles, I have tried to describe a process in which the executive and trustees constitute a primary community of leadership in the organization. They are central to institutional life in that they are charged with presiding in the life of the organization; they are ultimately responsible. At the same time, the goal of this presiding is to initiate and sustain continuing collaboration on policies and programs with appropriate persons and communities within the life of the whole organization. Trustees should assume that in the development or consideration of any policy or program, the first question is how to create a plan of consultation and collaboration that involves the persons most affected by the policy or program. This means that at various times, depending on the nature of the specific policy or program, a community within the life of the organization will be closely tied to the trustees in a collaborative inquiry. In creating and implementing such structures, the board of trustees does not abdicate any of its constitutive responsibilities, but it acknowledges that it cannot make adequate or faithful decisions without collaboration.

In this collaborative model, the senior professional staff (such as faculty of a school or physicians in a hospital) especially are recognized in the distinctiveness of their responsibilities in the life of the organization. In a school or seminary, for example, faculty are not just another interest group; they are at the center of what constitutes the ongoing nature of a community of learning. Students and staff are essential in such a community, but it is the faculty who constitute the continuing tradition of a school or seminary. Students are the aim of and the essential partners in this mutual learning, but individual students are present for only a limited amount of time. The expectation is that faculty are permanent officers of the school. This means that they, more than any other community of the school, will be assigned responsibility for the educational life of the school by the board. This delegated task implies that faculty are central to other institutional decisions that ultimately impact the core identity of teaching and learning.

Prophetic Inquiry

The gap between hopes for collaboration and the reality of missed opportunities for such shared inquiry is primarily the result of lack of attention to developing the means by which such collaboration may be implemented. In particular, trustees are responsible for creating this process of inquiry; it is their fundamental religious task in overseeing, evaluating, and reviewing the relationships among the idea the organization holds of itself, the way the organization actually functions, and what it might be called to do and be in light of the vision that gives it life.

One way of understanding this responsibility is to see it as a prophetic office to help the organization deepen and recall its fundamental vocation, remember its history, care for its common life, and carry out its mission and programs. Although trustees cannot take on this prophetic task by themselves—indeed, as I have suggested, part of their responsibility is to involve as many communities of the organization's life as possible in this continuing inquiry—they alone are charged with the responsibility for this task. In the standards of the Association of Theological Schools (ATS) in the United States and Canada (1997, p. 75, Standard 8.1.8.3), this obligation of seminary boards is made quite clear: "As fiduciaries, they [the governing board] should commit themselves loyally to the institution, its purpose, and its overall well-being. They should lead by affirming the good that is done and by asking thoughtful questions and challenging problematic situations."

In particular, the practice of this kind of responsibility is expressed in the fundamental style of trusteeship, that is, by "asking thoughtful questions and challenging problematic situations." The ATS standards at this point pick up a fundamental point made by Greenleaf (1980), who often reiterated that raising thoughtful questions was the essential practice of trusteeship. This style is very different from the mode of judging, refereeing, or lobbying for one point of view. It assumes that the essential work for trustees is discerning how God is calling the organization to rethink and redefine the nature of its mission and the allocation of its resources. The fundamental vocation of a seminary, as H. Richard Niebuhr (1956) once suggested, is to express the love of God and neighbor in the form of an intellectual center serving the church's life. The actual form of that calling will continue to change, and the particular missions and programs that focus its energies in any given time are subject to redefinition in response to this prophetic inquiry.

The visible expression of the trustee's vocation is the development of policies that guide the relationships, practices, and programs within an organization. The term *prophetic inquiry* calls attention to the deep need in our society for the development of thoughtful policies that serve human needs and address issues of alienation and brokenness in social structures through the articulation of hope and the passionate pursuit of justice and compassion (Underwood, 1969; see also Shriver, 1971). In an organization, this comes down to inquiring into how the organization fulfills its vision in what it claims to be and do. This work of inquiry is prophetic because it calls for watchfulness and thoughtful criticism; it requires imagination and patience (Wehrli, 1992; see also Brueggemann, 1978). It is the work of stewards who know they are called to serve the vision, the gospel, that should inform the organization's life and programs. This is not the same as strategic planning, in which various issues are isolated and analyzed in pursuit of solving a particular set of problems. Instead, it is a style of institutional governance that attempts to evoke as a regular occurrence, and not as an episodic enterprise, thoughtful questioning of the quality of the organization's programs, the nature of its common life, and its service to the vision that gave it birth.

The work of prophecy is the practice of discerning the Spirit in the midst of our common life. It is not a matter of a charismatic prophet speaking a lone word; instead, prophecy results from a community working together to discern what the Spirit might be saying in the issues and questions of organizational life. This inquiry comes out of our unblinking critique of our own lives and institutions in light of the new life and new creation announced in Christ (Wehrli, 1992).

Trustees are called to watch (to care for) the institution they serve and to discern God's presence in the midst of institutional life. If this sense of an institution being claimed by God's new reign is not part of the consciousness of trusteeship, then all of our rhetoric about faith and values really makes no difference at all, and God becomes simply a distant reference in the opening devotional of the meeting, which quickly moves on to other issues. We replicate the dreary pattern of separating facts and values, and by default assume the superiority of the quantitative "facts" that are presumed to be true. I am suggesting that instead of doing things this way, we should consider that at the center of trusteeship is the basic question of what God calls the organization to be and to do, and the complex issue of how we discern this calling in the muddle of issues, events, conflicts, and trends that make up institutional life. This is the work of raising thoughtful questions, cultivating and sustaining covenants of relationship within the various communities of the organization, providing financial support for its programs and services, and making decisions in light of the Spirit's guidance.

Most of all, trustees are called to pray for the organization they serve, to offer hope, and with imagination and love to provide a centered community of leadership in the life of the organization.

A Practical Model

Exhibit 1.1 presents the inquiry model of governance. In this model, inquiry (the practice of asking thoughtful questions) is most of all expressed

Exhibit 1.1. Inquiry Model of Governance.

June
- Presidential review (also an occasion for reviewing the work of trustees) and definition of issues for the coming year in light of the mission statement
- Definition of responsibilities and research
- Creation of plan of work—envisioning how to deepen inquiry and move toward decisions
  Fall Meeting
- Initial work of the board committee and consultative groups
  Winter Meeting
- Preliminary report on research, development of models and options
  Spring Meeting
- Board action, commitment to further inquiry, or creation of planning process
  June
- Process ends and begins again

in settings called *meetings*. Many times, trustee meetings are not so much occasions of conversation, inquiry, and relationship as they are platforms for already determined outcomes. They are often made up of one committee report after another. As an alternative to this usual way of doing things, the meeting of the board of trustees should be considered an event within which there are different kinds of meetings and occasions. These meetings flow from the board's work in determining the issues that are most important in the life of the organization—the issues that must be researched, discussed, and addressed by the board and by other communities of institutional life that share the activities of governance. This determination is so central to the work of trustees and executives that it should become their essential focus. The vehicle for this work is the executive's office; its beginning is the annual review of the CEO and trustees, which in this model is conducted each year in June by the executive committee of the board. At this review session, the executive presents a memo that discusses the current year—the goals that were set, the work that was done. In this memo, the executive frames the emerging issues that will be most important for the organization and the work of the board of trustees in the coming year.

The work that lies behind this memo involves extensive research and consultation with staff and board committees, who should continually review the issues that are their main responsibility and try to anticipate as part of their continuing work the new issues emerging in the institution or coming onto the horizon in the external context. Each committee should maintain its own plan of work that names issues and questions, develops a schedule for research and consultation, and considers the way these issues need to go to the board for inquiry and action.

In this meeting of the CEO and the board's executive committee, agreement is reached on the issues that are to be the work of the whole board for the coming year. This point of decision making is the key to inquiry in the whole institution because it requires a plan of work, a schedule of collaboration with those most directly involved with and affected by the issues, and the creation of a series of meetings and tasks that will make possible the trustees' inquiry and possible decision making.

Each issue should be developed in regard to the kind of data required to generate usable information, the necessary process of collaboration and consultation, and the schedule of board meetings in which these various steps will be taken. Thus the nature of the year's meetings will be shaped by the issues the board needs to address and the kinds of decisions it will have to make, if appropriate. This type of process requires the development of priorities and the designation of key issues. Though there are always unpredictable issues arising in the life of the organization, this process aims at sustaining a more intentional way of working. Most of all, however, it encourages trustees to think about their responsibilities for the care of the institution. It moves them to greater involvement in leadership at an appropriate level. In looking ahead and trying to discern the kinds of trends and factors that are shaping the organization, the trustees have a chance to anticipate and respond to the issues they will face; they can shape the ways in which questions about these contextual factors can be posed, instead of letting some other group or some other pressure frame the question for them by default.

Example: Inquiry into a Trend

One of the key issues in theological education is the trend toward part-time students, which extends the amount of time a student takes to complete his or her academic program. Trustees who recognize this trend should seek information about it and other characteristics of the student body, about credit hours being taken per semester, about graduation profiles, and about other issues that depict what is happening in the life of the school, rather than simply wait until such a trend turns into a major change in patterns of enrollment or in the ways students attend seminary. The trustees should ask the faculty and administration to research these issues and articulate the educational and institutional questions being shaped by these issues, then they should ask themselves whether the school is moving in a direction in which it wants to move; or if the school cannot do anything to affect these trends, the trustees should ask what is required of the seminary to respond to these changes in light of its basic commitments. The basic question is, In light of changing circumstances, how does the school claim the most important commitments of its life before those commitments are forever modified by forces and factors beyond the school's control?

The president of a particular seminary determines in his June review, after consultation with faculty and staff, that the issue of changing enrollment patterns should frame much of the work of the board for the coming year. In his planning memo for the trustees, the president outlines the various aspects of the issue and develops a plan for research and inquiry that deepens understanding of the issue. At this point, it is not clear what the full extent of the issue will be or what kinds of questions the school will have to address in dealing with the issue. The main goal at this stage is for the president and the trustees to agree on the primary issue and frame a way of thinking about it in the board and in other appropriate communities of the school. The work for the summer will be to identify the research needed to provide the background data for this inquiry. This work will require researching the external context as well as the internal context of the school, assigning responsibility for the research, and designating the schedule of work. The goal is to have this preliminary material ready for the board's meeting in the fall.

At the fall meeting, the issue is described, the larger context is defined, and the effort is made to transpose various data into usable information. At this point, the aim is to deepen the question and develop a base of information that accurately describes the issue. This information will be conveyed to the trustees in readable form that does not overwhelm with minutiae but helps frame the questions. The development of this briefing paper is the primary work of a board committee or an ad hoc committee made up of staff and faculty, students, and alumni and alumnae who are invited to help the board think about the issue.

During this first trustee meeting of the academic year, specific time is focused on deepening the board's understanding of the issue with the help of someone knowledgeable about the issue in its larger context. The seminar leader has provided background material for the trustees to read ahead of the meeting, with the aim of making this a time to explore the broader nature of the specific institutional issue with which the trustees are dealing. The leader could be a theologian who helps trustees think about biblical and theological foundations for ministry and about the kind of education needed to equip the ministry of pastors, teachers, and leaders; or the board could seek assistance in understanding the context of contemporary church life and how this context provides a larger context for understanding the issue of students' patterns of completing degrees. Just as appropriately, the leader of the seminar could be someone from higher education who traces the ways in which the trends facing theological education have been part of the recent history of colleges and universities. Again, the aim of this time of teaching and learning within the board is to enhance the trustees' understanding of the issue at hand and to help them think about the question out of their particular commitments as a school and as an institution of the church.

Another way of deepening the board's understanding of the designated issue would be to hold an evening dinner and program in which various members of the organization's community could look at the issue together. In small groups composed of faculty, students, staff, and trustees, the members of the board could hear stories from students who feel that the nature of their lives requires part-time study and extension of the time it takes to complete their degree programs. These students could be joined by faculty and staff giving their perspectives on how these student patterns affect courses and institutional life.

Before the end of this fall meeting, the trustees will clarify the next steps that will be taken to consider the issue, identify the kind of research and consultation that might still need to be done, and affirm or modify the original schedule for considering the issue. If appropriate, the trustees will focus their next meeting on the consideration of options or models that respond to the dynamics of the issue, and at the third trustee meeting of the year they will actually make a decision on a policy direction or decide that no decision will be made as they continue to think about the matter. Again, the mode of inquiry is a continuing style of trusteeship. Sometimes it will result in decisions that emerge out of the board's careful delineation of issues and questions. Other times it will permit the board to realize the complexity of the issues and recognize that they cannot be resolved quickly by some kind of technical fix. If the board does decide that it needs to act on an issue, it can move toward a more formal planning process designed to lead to a decision.

An Alternative Way of Structuring Board Meetings

To follow the kind of model I have described for the work of the board and to have the flexibility to adapt and redesign similar models for your own organization, it is important to shift your basic understanding of the nature of meetings. Many boards meet three or four times a year in a business meeting that is essentially structured by committee reports. Often there are social gatherings with senior professional staff and other members of the organization's community, but essentially the trustees' time is devoted to a meeting composed mostly of hearing reports, taking votes, and engaging in itinerant discussion. In contrast to this model, I suggest that the board meeting be conceived as a series of events and settings that are shaped by the current commitments and priorities of the board. A model of what I have in mind looks something like this:

FIRST DAY

1:30—Worship. Begin the meeting of the board with worship that provides time for thanksgiving, prayer, meditation on the Word, and as appropriate, celebration of the Eucharist. This should be more than a brief devotional period that feels ornamental. Instead, it should be a substantive moment of gathering in the name of Christ that establishes the context of the meeting.

2:00—Plenary Session. This session is really the business meeting of the board. It is the occasion for the executive's report, financial reports, and action on designated issues. Though committees might use this meeting as a time to discuss their work, generally this session would take the form of sharing information that the board needs to know and checking on the directions in which it is going. The important thing is not to replicate the usual pattern of committee reports that are inert and deadening. The assumption is that committees are created to equip the board for its continuing inquiry and the decisions it has to make. This means that each committee should pay attention to the crucial issues and questions for which it has particular oversight. In a sense, committees function best when they are perceived as the antennae of the board. This moves the reports of committees from being inert summaries toward being deliberative support for board inquiry and action.

3:00—Break.

3:30—Seminar. This is a serious educational time in which trustees meet as a seminar to understand more fully a theological, institutional, or policy issue. In particular, this is an occasion for the board members' own continuing education to inform their work as trustees and their understanding of the issues they face. Moreover, this is a setting in which religious reflection is a direct objective. Such reflection undergirds the life of the board and provides ongoing education in the gospel, which is one of the key reasons that many people agree to serve on the board of a religious organization in the first place.

5:00—Dinner with Community Representatives. The board could invite the whole community of the organization or representatives of its larger groups to a dinner and seat them at tables with trustees; or trustees could arrange for representative groups to be invited to dinner at others' homes. Senior professional staff and trustees should be brought together on a regular schedule at meals where they would have a chance to get acquainted. These meals could be held in the executive's home or arranged as smaller gatherings in senior staff members' homes or at other local sites.

6:30—Evening Program. This program consists of a presentation on a current issue or some other kind of program related to questions about religious or church life. The program could be enhanced by formation of small groups to discuss specific questions that could then be shared with the whole assembly. On other occasions, a member of the senior professional staff might be invited to speak on a topic that is the subject of his or her research. Sometimes a person from outside the organization's community could be invited to address the gathering. Periodically it might be good for the whole organization to be convened at an artistic or musical event. This could be a program presented by either organization members or outsiders, or it could be a community project in which a choral piece such as Handel's *Messiah* could be sung by the entire organizational community.

SECOND DAY

8:30—Committee Meetings. Committees may have met at other times before the board meeting, but the committee session within the board meeting occurs at this time in order to emphasize the long-term planning and inquiry of committees. Sometimes committees that meet just before a business meeting will make decisions or suggest courses of action without adequate time for reflection.

10:00—Break.

10:30—Collegium. The collegium is a gathering of the executive and trustees for candid conversation. It is a time for reflecting on the issues raised in the meeting, for looking ahead to the next meeting, and for discussing with the executive questions that would not be appropriate in a more public gathering. It is also a time for the board to act on an issue that needs immediate attention. Most importantly, it is an occasion for formative evaluation of the meeting itself, the work of the trustees, and the functioning of the board. At some designated point, the executive should leave the conversation and let the trustees meet alone. The executive should then rejoin the group before the session concludes. This session is a crucial time for developing trust, emphasizing the particular work of trustees, and discussing issues that are often talked about in the corridors but not brought to the table.

My expectation is that a board will meet three or four times a year, but if it only meets twice each year this format can still be followed. Also, it is important to maintain the flexibility and adaptability of the schedule so that it can be changed as suggested by any particular meeting.

Finally, many boards have found it helpful to meet annually in some kind of retreat setting for a weekend, during which trustees can gather without the press of immediate business, take time to get to know one another in greater depth, and discuss some primary issues in detail. Boards have often found such retreats to be of value in establishing the foundation on which the continuing work of the board may be based.

Summary

In this chapter I have tried to describe a way of thinking about trusteeship that is shaped by the theological themes of servanthood, stewardship, and fidelity, which are expressed most of all in the practice of prophetic inquiry. It is this model of inquiry that suggests a way of defining the work of trustees and offers a flexible pattern for designing processes and occasions for carrying out this basic responsibility of caring for, overseeing, and reviewing the life of an organization. This model of trusteeship assumes that trustees lead by posing thoughtful questions about the life of the institution. These questions emerge from the trustees' commitment to the vision that has called the organization into being, and they recall the institution to faithfulness in each generation as it reconsiders its statement of mission, allocates resources, and initiates, sustains, or ends programs.

In many theological schools, for example, one finds uncertainty about the roles and responsibilities of the various members of the seminary community. Faculty, students, and administrators seem to negotiate their respective relationships on each issue that arises in the life of the institution. Boards of trustees have had to sort out their own sense of authority and responsibility—key issues for any kind of organization. What we need now is an understanding of the nature of the organization as an institution shaped by and accountable to traditions of faith and practice. This is basic conceptual work; it is not a matter of simply changing existing institutional components.

Although organizational politics are always involved with individual and group interests, we need to address the substantive questions of polity, that is, the meaning and structure of our life together. There can be no responsible political life removed from questions of polity, and there can be no polity without continuing inquiry into the nature of the central commitments that nurture the life of the entire community. In the theological community, this center is defined by the image of Jesus Christ as the servant of God who calls us to embody a ministry of service in the world. Trustees are stewards of the hope of this calling (Eph. 4:4).

REFERENCES

Association of Theological Schools in the United States and Canada. *Bulletin 43, Part 1, ATS Constitution and Dues Structure, Procedures Related to Membership and Accreditation, Standards of Accreditation, Policy Statements.* Pittsburgh, Pa.: Association of Theological Schools in the United States and Canada, 1997.

Berry, W. *A Continuous Harmony: Essays Cultural and Agricultural.* Orlando: Harcourt Brace, 1975.

Brueggemann, W. *The Prophetic Imagination.* Minneapolis, Minn.: Augsburg Fortress, 1978.

Chaucer, G. *Canterbury Tales* (A. C. Cawley, ed.). New York: Knopf, 1958.

De Pree, M. *Leadership Is an Art.* New York: Doubleday, 1989.

Frye, N. "The Dialectic of Belief and Vision." *Shenandoah,* 1989, *39*(3), pp. 52–53.

Giamatti, A. B. *A Free and Ordered Space: The Real World of the University.* New York: Norton, 1988.

Greenleaf, R. K. *The Seminary as an Institution: The Work of the Trustee.* Indianapolis, Ind.: Lilly Endowment, 1980.

Greenleaf, R. K. *The Power of Servant-Leadership* (L. C. Spears, ed.). San Francisco: Berrett-Koehler, 1998.

Hall, J. D. *The Steward: A Biblical Symbol Come of Age.* Grand Rapids, Mich.: Eerdmans, 1990.

MacIntyre, A. *After Virtue: A Study in Moral Theory.* (2nd ed.) Notre Dame, Ind.: Notre Dame University Press, 1997.

McCarter, N. D. *The President as Educator: A Study of the Seminary Presidency.* Atlanta: Scholars Press, 1996.

Niebuhr, H. R. *The Purpose of the Church and Its Ministry: Reflections on the Aims of Theological Education.* New York: HarperCollins, 1956.

Oakeshott, M. *Voice of Liberal Learning: Michael Oakeshott on Education* (T. Fuller, ed.). New Haven, Conn.: Yale University Press, 1989.

Remsen, N. "Golden Gate Bound German Visits Bangor by Mistake." *Bangor Daily News,* Oct. 20, 1977, pp. 1–2.

Shriver, D. W., Jr. "Prophetic Inquiry." *Religion in Life,* 1971, 40(4), 519–523.

Underwood, K. (ed.). *The Church, the University, and Social Policy.* 2 vols. Middletown, Conn.: Wesleyan University Press, 1969.

Wehrli, E. S. *Gifted by Their Spirit: Leadership Roles in the New Testament.* Cleveland, Ohio: Pilgrim Press, 1992.

2

THE DUTIES AND RESPONSIBILITIES OF BOARDS OF RELIGIOUS ORGANIZATIONS

Thomas P. Holland

RELIGIOUS ORGANIZATIONS come in many shapes and forms, but they all share a common distinction from secular businesses in that they do not have stockholders. Rather, they are owned and governed by those who participate in them and those who lead them. Such ownership rights have long been recognized in law as well as in common practice. The federal government exempts religious organizations from taxation, and state laws usually defer to denominational policies or ecclesiastical law in matters of internal dispute. Most of the responsibility for these policies, regulations, accountability, and practices rests on the shoulders of the persons who serve on the governing boards of these organizations.

These boards have grown in their duties and responsibilities over the entire history of the existence of boards, especially in the last fifty years. Increasing attention has been focused on their performance as recognition has grown that board leadership (or lack thereof) is vital to the quality of organizations and their programs or services. Governance has become a central concern for those who care deeply about the performance of religious organizations, especially as the media have publicized weaknesses in financial practices, misbehavior of leaders, and other problems that have undermined public confidence. Nothing can do more to build confidence in a religious organization than the actions taken by its governing board to assure everyone that the board's members understand their responsibilities as stewards of the gifts and resources entrusted to them, and that they are committed to ensuring the organization's accountability for its use of these gifts and resources to advance the mission of the organization.

The board is responsible for ensuring that the organization it governs stays clearly focused on the organization's mission. It has the duty to conserve the assets of the organization and to ensure that they are used to carry out that mission faithfully, in accordance with civil law as well as canon or ecclesiastical law. The board serves as a steward or fiduciary whose basic duty is to act for the good of others. These foundational principles of governance were developed first in religious organizations and then borrowed and adapted by other types of nonprofit organizations.

Boards of religious organizations seek to understand and apply principles of faithful stewardship. A list of their duties would include the following:

• *Drawing on the history and traditions of the organization's religious identification, the board interprets and sustains the mission of the organization, ensuring that every component is consistent with the mission and focusing on accomplishing it.* The board formulates policies that guide the organization and uses those policies to address issues or problems that arise in carrying out the organization's programs. For example, a local congregation may be approached by a political group wishing to make use of its meeting rooms or sanctuary for meetings. Such a request should be evaluated by the board in the context of the congregation's mission and purposes. The board of a religiously sponsored health care facility must decide whether accepting a grant from a drug company to carry out experimental research on patients is consistent with the organization's traditions and beliefs.

• *The board represents the interests of the sponsors and members whose resources allow the organization to pursue its mission, while balancing those interests with the needs and concerns of those receiving the services.* In a local congregation, the donors or sponsors may be the same participants as those receiving the services, while in a religious school or seminary, tuition often makes up only a part of the cost of education, with the remainder being covered by donations from outsiders who care about the school, support from congregations or the denomination, endowment income, foundation grants, and other external sources. The board reports back to those sponsors or donors regarding how it has used their contributions. Such steps of accountability are vital to sustaining the trust and continued support of sponsors, members, and other participants.

• *The board guides, supports, and evaluates the chief executive or professional officer,* whether that person is a minister or rabbi, the president of a hospital, the dean or president of a seminary, the headmaster of a school, or the director of a social service agency. In some religious organizations, the bishop or other judicatory office appoints and removes priests of local congregations, while in others these processes involve a collaborative effort between the judicatory office and the board of the congregation. In still other religious organizations, the board is directly responsible for selecting and dismissing the executives or ministers. Yet in whatever way the ultimate decisions of hiring and removing are made, local boards are always responsible for providing the chief professional officer with clear guidance and advice regarding the programs and services of the organization, for setting specific goals and expectations, for helping to raise funds, and for providing evaluative feedback on staff performance.

• *The board translates faith, organizational mission, traditions, beliefs, and values into policies and rules that guide the chief professional officer (whether executive, priest, or minister) and senior staff in their activities.* The board identifies the latitude that staff have for making operational decisions and then monitors their performance for adherence to those limits. For example, the board may specify that the dean of a seminary may offer faculty raises on a percentage basis or up to a certain total amount for salary raises for all faculty combined; or the board of a congregation may approve its minister's request to hire an additional staff person to expand religious education programs for children and decide how much of the budget can be spent for such purposes.

• *The board works with the chief professional officer to develop long-range plans, goals, and objectives for the organization, and then monitors progress toward those goals.* For example, the board of a religiously sponsored school may set as a long-range goal the extension of its programs from grades 1 to 6 to include grades 7 to 12 over the next ten years. It would then work with the headmaster and teachers to plan the steps for achieving that goal, participate in obtaining the resources needed to carry out the plan, and track progress toward interim targets along the way. Should an unexpected barrier arise, the board would join in efforts to identify appropriate solutions or revisions to the plan.

• *The board is responsible for ensuring that the organization has the financial resources needed to carry out its mission and goals.* In many congregations, the board leads the congregation's annual stewardship campaigns and then works to match the coming year's budget with anticipated contributions from members. The board may initiate a capital campaign to increase donations to support specific expansions of programs or services. A seminary board may solicit contributions from wealthy friends and previous donors to increase scholarships for needy students or to build a new building.

• *The board is responsible for making sure that all its decisions and actions meet the requirements of ethics and law, including both civil and religious law.* The board should deal openly and directly with potential conflicts of interest among its members. For example, it should excuse from the meeting a member of the board who owns a private construction company when the group is considering bids from that and several other companies for construction of a new wing for religious education classes. The board of a hospital sponsored by a religious group that opposes abortion must decide how hospital policy and physicians' practices will relate to church law on the matter.

• *The board ensures that the organization uses all of its resources, including people and money, as efficiently and effectively as possible.* The annual budget is a statement of how the board translates its shared faith, beliefs, and commitments into priorities for action in the coming year. Many boards periodically ask the chief professional officer—whether pastor, dean, president, headmaster, or CEO—for reports on how well staff are performing their duties, how well they are controlling expenses, and how well programs are meeting their objectives. Although such steps of accountability are familiar to many boards, they are less likely to ask the same evaluative questions of themselves, such as, How well are we using our time and energy to add value to this organization? Demonstrating accountability for use of time and resources applies to the board as well as to the staff of the organization. It shows everyone that the board takes its responsibilities for accountability just as seriously as it expects others to take theirs.

Board members should periodically ask themselves probing questions about every component of the organization, including the board itself, such as the following:

If we were starting out today, would we carry out our work this way?

Do our decisions and actions demonstrate our faith and match our mission?

What do the intended beneficiaries of our actions think of our performance?

Do the coming years require something different from us?

What should we do to prepare ourselves and this organization to be successful in the future?

As does any list of board duties, this list shows that boards of religious organizations have many complex and challenging responsibilities. To enable them to carry out these functions, most boards typically establish several subgroups or committees to which they delegate specific tasks. For example, there may be a committee on staff and personnel, another on buildings and grounds, one for financial planning and accounting, and another for programs and services. These work groups develop specific plans and recommendations for the full board to consider at its regular plenary meetings. Typically, the full board hears the reports and recommendations of each group, discusses and makes decisions about which steps to authorize, and then charges staff and volunteer groups with implementation.

In addition to creating ongoing or standing committees, some boards also create special ancillary groups to serve specific functions. For example, a hospital board may appoint a special committee to examine and report on a proposed specialty medical service program, with outside medical experts joining board members on the committee and contributing their expertise to its inquiries. A seminary board may create an honorary status of trustee emeritus or authorize the establishment of an alumni association whose members may be convened annually to recognize their contributions to the institution. A congregation's board may appoint an ad hoc committee to screen candidates for its pastorate.

Boards may bring in persons with specialized expertise to assist committees or even the whole board in understanding a complex issue and identifying alternative actions. To plan fundraising, for example, boards of many large religious organizations bring in outside consultants or invite people onto committees who may not be on the board but are recognized as having influence or contacts that will be needed in approaching potential donors. Through its campaign committee or some other structure, the board can link with these individuals and draw on their expertise or contacts to advance its overall plan for the organization. Questions of civil law, accounting, or architecture may indicate a need to bring in experts from those professions to aid the board in reaching conclusions on a complex matter.

Characteristics of Effective Boards

The basic duties and responsibilities of governing boards of religious organizations are the foundation of such boards, the essential tasks they are expected to fulfill. In addition to carrying out these tasks, strong, effective boards have several distinguishing characteristics that can serve as external norms against which other boards can compare their own experiences. Recent studies of boards of religious organizations as well as other nonprofits have identified several features that differentiate the most effective ones from the rest (Chait, Holland, and Taylor, 1993, 1996). Such positive examples can stimulate aspirations to improve.

The Contextual Dimension

Effective boards understand and intentionally act within the context of the beliefs, traditions, values, and norms of the organization they govern. They make explicit use of the organization's distinctive mission, values, and faith tradition in their deliberations and decisions. They are careful to act in ways that embody or exemplify the organization's core values and commitments. Orientation of newcomers to the board includes explicit attention to the organization's beliefs, values, and traditions—the features that distinguish the organization from others that might seem like it. These commitments are reinforced for everyone by repeated attention to them in meetings, reports, and plans. Board members are aware that their actions and decisions are statements grounded in and proceeding from their shared faith.

Most members of the boards of religious organizations are able to articulate some version of the mission and purpose of the organization, though some give more thoughtful, complete, and even passionate descriptions than others. For example, several members of one church board said that their purpose was to provide worship and religious education for people who belong to their denomination or who want to belong to it. Members of some other boards, however, described unresolved conflicts in the way they viewed their church's mission; a seminary board member, for example, said, "We are stuck on the question of whether we are here to educate primarily clergy or laity." The response of a member of another (more effective) board illustrates the difference: "We are a congregation that is spiritually alive, radically inclusive, and justice oriented." The board member went on to cite examples of activities in each of these areas.

Differences between strong and ordinary boards with regard to the contextual dimension show up in the quality of board members' responses to questions about how the organization's mission, faith, and purpose have guided specific recent decisions of the board. Typical responses treated board actions as having been understood in a business or political context. For example, "We just had to add another class for that age group if we wanted those families to keep coming back" or "We chose this minister because we were sure most people in the congregation would like him." These remarks offer only vague explanations of any linkage between the board members' faith and their actions. Compare such responses with those of members of another board, this one governing a small private religious school: "Our board has been concerned about diversity among the students and teachers, because our faith commits us to including all people, regardless of background. So we started by going to work on the composition of our board itself. We felt we first had to walk the talk. Then we invited our faculty to develop an action plan in this area. All these steps prepared us to attract and retain a more diverse student body."

Although virtually all board members will attest to the importance of their organization's religious faith and mission, the most effective members are able to articulate how those contextual foundations have provided explicit guidance in specific board decisions in ways that clearly distinguish their group from others. Mission statements most often seem to be abstract sets of high ideals, somewhat removed from the real work of the board. For this reason, we believe, most boards of religious organizations need to take time to develop their capacities to think and speak theologically about their work, as David Hester discusses in Chapter Four of this volume.

The Strategic Dimension

Effective boards participate in envisioning future directions for the organization and in shaping strategies to reach key goals. They cultivate and concentrate on processes that serve to sharpen organizational priorities. They then organize themselves and structure their meetings and committees to keep focused on these priorities. They anticipate potential problems and act before issues become crises.

These boards monitor their use of time and intentionally structure their agenda to stay concentrated on their top priorities. They keep themselves focused on strategic issues by asking their professional staff to present regular reports on organizational goals and progress toward them, by restricting their attention in meetings to the year's priorities, and by formulating committee charges around each major goal. Reports are presented to the board in the context of some critical step toward a major goal, rather than just "for your information." Reports and key questions needing full board attention are distributed well in advance of meetings, allowing members time for thought and preparation. Information coming to the board is selected to be directly relevant to priorities, is presented in accessible graphic forms, and includes comparisons over time and with other similar organizations, as Lawrence Butler describes in Chapter Ten of this volume.

Many members of boards of religious organizations agree that strategic planning is important, but only a few are actually engaged in the process. In an effort to position themselves for strength in coming years, effective boards go well beyond saluting strategic planning and recreate their entire structure and functions based on rigorous and thoughtful goals. Rather than merely expecting others to add value to the organization, effective boards set the example by formulating clear, time-specific goals and performance criteria for themselves, announcing those goals and criteria to the organization, addressing them consistently, and monitoring them carefully. Such boards provide opportunities for evaluating their work in progress and make changes and adjustments in the original plans as events move forward. Their examples suggest steps that others may consider in planning for the future of their organization, which Richard Chait develops more fully in Chapter Nine of this volume.

Articulating clear goals and steps to address them strengthens the board's *accountability*. Such goals and steps enable the board to ensure that meeting time and attention are kept focused on shared targets, and they create means for members to monitor their own progress toward their own goals and regularly examine their own contributions to the well-being of the organization. Boards that take these steps lead by example and increase the value they add to their organization.

Instead of meetings filled with numerous lengthy reports with preformulated conclusions and recommendations scripted by the organization's administration, effective boards are engaged in discovering and exploring the most important issues and questions themselves. They draw from many external and internal sources (including their own creative imaginations) to identify the most important issues for the institution's future and to explore alternative approaches to dealing with them. They set clear goals and priorities for the board and for each of its committees and they specify steps that will need to be taken to achieve those goals.

These boards are continually experimenting with creating whatever structures and arrangements they need to achieve their strategic priorities. Instead of organizing themselves into committees that parallel traditional administrative divisions, innovative boards create ad hoc work groups that take on specific responsibilities for each of the board's priorities. These groups then explore and critically examine those areas and identify actions and alternatives. They bring plans and options to the board with sufficient information for the board to come to thoughtful conclusions. When the ad hoc group's work is finished, it dissolves. In effect, the board's strategy, not the administration's divisions, guides the board's structure and activities.

Instead of spending their time in meetings filled with reports from every committee, boards should base their time together on the goals for the meeting, which in turn are based on the most important issues facing the group. By basing their structures, meeting formats, time, and resources clearly on strategic priorities, boards can multiply opportunities for critical reflection and maximize the effectiveness of their efforts on behalf of their institutions.

The purpose of all these efforts is to enable members to draw more clearly and consistently on their rich array of skills and resources to strengthen their decisions and their leadership roles. Boards that have undertaken such activities demonstrate that investing effort in improving their performance helps them to become more effective in their governance roles and add greater value to their organizations.

The Analytical Dimension

Effective boards recognize and examine the complexities of the issues before them, accepting ambiguity and uncertainty as healthy components of creative discussions. They do not hesitate to analyze all aspects of multifaceted issues, brainstorming to identify many possible perspectives on them, considering the downsides as well as advantages of each alternative, exploring trade-offs, encouraging differences of opinion, and thinking outside the box of familiar assumptions.

These boards seek to increase the diversity among their membership so that many frames of reference and personal experiences will be brought to the table. They seek the views of many diverse constituents on issues and make sure that the full range of opinions and viewpoints is heard and considered in the analysis of those issues. They are not afraid of probing and rigorous debate among participants. Their faith does not entail superficial niceness or polite deferral to popular opinion or quick recommendations. Rather, it is serious enough to demand the very best thinking and most rigorous analysis possible.

Strengthening a board's critical, analytical, and reflective skills is crucial to improving its performance. Assumptions about saving face or avoiding embarrassment are inhibiting and need to be addressed directly to create an atmosphere that supports critical thinking and rigorous analysis of issues. Participants must learn to recognize all questions as valuable and any assumptions as merely possible ones among many other ways of seeing situations facing the board.

There is much to be done to help most boards use critical analysis skills effectively in their governance responsibilities. Trusting interpersonal relationships are essential to providing a safe group environment in which difficult questions and unfamiliar responses may be explored. Of course there is the danger that a sense of safety may also allow a group to rest content in old and familiar patterns while the outside environment changes and leaves them in the past.

Boards do not add much value to their organizations by listening passively to reports, asking polite questions, or offering minor suggestions in response to committee or administrative recommendations. Instead of depending on the staff to bring them the important issues and to formulate answers for their approval, effective boards expect to be active in discovering the important issues and in examining them along with the staff and other members of the organization. They use multiple information sources to explore and analyze influences bearing on the organization and to identify and critique alternative directions for its future. They take time to brainstorm and to search widely for creative alternative perspectives on issues they face before evaluating the advantages and disadvantages of each possibility.

Certainly the minister, executive, or other paid professional leader is a key actor in the governance of the organization. He or she should be expected to present a vision for the future, along with key recommendations for action, and to have extensive influence in the analysis of and conclusions about important issues. Indeed, this capacity should be an important ingredient in the board's evaluation of senior staff. The board, however, should expand and deepen these processes of discovery, reflection, and analysis. Increasing its skills in doing so should be a goal of any board. Periodic assessment of its performance in this area should be included in the board's responsibilities.

There are many ways that a board can expand its skills of critical analysis. It can take the initiative to create its own windows or perspectives on the organization as well as on the wider field of the whole community. It can purposively expand its own diversity by bringing in members whose backgrounds differ from those of others on the board. It can identify and examine important community issues and societal forces and periodically explore their implications for the organization's future. It can help members recognize that values, beliefs, behaviors, and ideologies are culturally transmitted and subject to rethinking and innovation. It can seek input about vital issues from other key constituents both inside and outside the organization. It can identify and monitor trends in key performance indicators and then brainstorm about alternative scenarios for the future. It can engage in theological reflection on the major issues faced by the organization. It can define the key questions underlying major issues instead of assuming that preformulated recommendations are the best choices.

Intentional opportunities to practice the use of such methods as brainstorming, Delphi and nominal group techniques, as well as other approaches to generating a wide variety of views on any issue should be provided. Boards should be encouraged to exercise greater initiative in raising probing questions and in seeking information and viewpoints that challenge their familiar assumptions about the organization and its future. In these ways, boards can substantially increase the value they add to their organization. Among the many resources that could be used in such efforts is Peter Senge's *The Fifth Discipline: The Art and Practice of the Learning Organization* (1990), especially Chapter Twelve, which examines the specific skills of organizational learning through rigorous and nondefensive analysis of complex issues.

The Political Dimension

Effective boards accept as a primary responsibility the need to develop and maintain healthy relationships among the constituencies of their organization. They understand that many other stakeholders have legitimate claims on the governance process, so they consult often and communicate regularly with them. Because constituents' interests will vary, effective boards protect the integrity of the governance process and seek to minimize win-lose conclusions by finding creative solutions that are acceptable to many.

These boards develop multiple channels of communication by inviting staff and other constituents to sit on board committees; inviting leaders from other, similar organizations to address the board on shared concerns; distributing profiles of board members widely to encourage contacts with them; and seeking others' viewpoints. They work closely with the staff in these efforts, so everyone is kept informed of others' perspectives. Such steps nurture communication channels, broaden participants' understanding of issues, strengthen their responsiveness to others' concerns, and support greater accountability. The vital board functions of building bridges and sustaining positive communications among all of the organization's multiple constituencies are discussed more extensively by Christa Klein in Chapter Seven of this volume.

Strong communication channels work both ways—from the board to others and from others back to the board. Such channels open the board to the range of views held by others, and they keep others informed about what the board is doing. This openness invites other constituencies to respond and let board members know what they think of the board's work, and is thus a vital component of accountable governance.

Although all board members want to do a good job, there are few means for measuring their performance and few penalties for poor governance. Board members as a group are legally responsible for the organization, but they are virtually unaccountable as individuals or as a group. The board is committed to the ideals of the organization, but there are few ways to identify whether any member has done anything to help realize those ideals. Most members can avoid or minimize personal accountability or embarrassment, so they may really have little at stake. It is widely assumed that the chief professional officer, not the board, is ultimately responsible for decisions.

Many underestimate the importance of the board as an essential resource for the organization, which may contribute to the ambiguity about accountability. Popular opinion seems to be that great individual leaders build great organizations, and few people recognize that a strong, effective board is key to a successful organization. The linkages between board performance and organizational performance seem vague and difficult to specify. The perception of a loosely connected cause-effect relationship tempers motivation and dilutes incentive to act. It also enables boards to evade responsibility for decisions by placing all such responsibility on the staff.

There are many possible avenues both for strengthening two-way communications between boards and their constituencies and for increasing the sense of accountability among board members. One approach would be to communicate the board's decisions, plans, and goals openly and widely, and then invite inquiries from constituents about the board's progress in achieving its goals. Boards should expect members to communicate directly and frequently with many constituencies, to solicit and listen to their concerns, and to seek their views of the organization and of the board's leadership. To strengthen their credibility, boards should apply similar expectations of responsiveness and accountability to themselves as they apply to others, remembering that examples are more powerful than admonitions.

The Educational Dimension

Effective boards take the steps necessary to ensure that their members are familiar with all aspects of the organization, its staff, and its services, and with the board's own roles, responsibilities, and performance. They intentionally create opportunities for board education and development, rather than just relying on observation and osmosis to teach members how to serve well. They regularly seek information and feedback about their own performance from others inside and outside the organization. Members often take time to step back from their tasks and reflect on how well they are working together. They periodically assess the group's strengths and limitations, learn from successes and mistakes, and apply those lessons to improving future efforts.

Effective boards strengthen their effectiveness through educational programs focusing on key issues they are facing, through group discussions of underlying dimensions of key issues confronting the organization, by seeking to understand how their faith traditions apply to them, and by inviting others to discuss how they see those issues as well as the board's responses to them. They set aside time at each meeting to learn more about some important matter or to discuss a common reading about governance or some major issue facing the organization. They ask members and senior staff to report briefly on the best ideas they have encountered in recent readings or meetings. They interact with counterparts on other boards, seeking ideas about how those boards approach common problems. They rotate committee assignments so that members learn about the organization from many perspectives. They create mechanisms for regular feedback at the end of meetings and more comprehensive feedback at the end of each year. At periodic retreats they discuss the lessons to be learned from the previous year's experiences and how those lessons can be taken forward into the coming year so the board will become more effective.

Unfortunately, most boards seldom attend to their own education. Some hold retreats occasionally, but members have difficulty identifying any specific changes in board practices that have resulted from those experiences. Descriptions of retreats seldom include much group reflection or discussion of past board problems or successes in order to identify what the board might learn from them or what it might do differently as a result. The press of business as usual, the alleged importance of some long-winded speaker, or perhaps fear of embarrassment or excessive value on politeness appear to preclude taking the time for such valuable self-assessment, learning, and change. Boards that do report such discussions tend to describe them as guarded exchanges that involve assigning blame for some mistake to an individual rather than reflectively examining what the board could learn from the experience about its own performance. Rarely do boards find such sessions sufficiently valuable to invest much time or money in them.

Although the evaluation of board performance is acknowledged by some board members to be an important component of education, most boards have only very informal means, if any at all, for carrying out such evaluations. Few report any systematic steps for obtaining or using feedback about the board's performance, either from members themselves or from outsiders. Those boards that do conduct and make use of such assessments are notably stronger in their overall performance. From their experiences come many of the examples and lessons included in this volume.

Education continues to be seen by many board members as different or distinct from the way they typically deal with business. This distinction continues a separation between critical reflection and "doing the board's work," thus constraining further growth. Primary reliance on retreats may contribute unintentionally to this distinction by virtue of the sharp break of such retreats from typical meetings. Retreats that are developed solely around expert-directed, lecture-dominated, skills-focused workshops are not adequate to address important underlying issues.

Boards should critically examine the popular assumptions and practices that guide typical retreats to strengthen their usefulness as means of learning that is continuous with and integrated into the work of the board. Carefully developed retreats can serve to open participants' awareness of more productive ways of dealing with important issues and pave the way for in-meeting educational efforts. Approaches that use learner-centered and interactive processes in the design of educational experiences are much more likely than traditional retreats to be productive.

Regardless of how they are designed, retreats and conferences call for considerable extra time and expense, both of which are in short supply among board members. For boards to enjoy fully the informative and transformative role of education, opportunities for education cannot be as occasional or as tenuous as exclusive dependence on such external events makes them.

Rather than relying only on the retreat approach to board development, boards should explore ways to incorporate learning into their regular meeting agenda. Some boards convene their members before the regularly scheduled board meeting to discuss an issue of importance and concern to all. Others set aside time for education within the agenda of their regular board meetings. They devote some time to identifying their critical, underlying questions about a key issue that will be raised in future meetings and then delegate tasks for exploring and reporting back on those questions. Some boards take time at the conclusion of meetings to look back over their work together, to reflect on how they have done, and to consider ways to improve future meetings.

Although such steps lack the virtue of the extended time available in a retreat format, they gain the value of proximity to the ongoing work of the board and the practicality of being possible at every meeting. There are many methods for engaging members in learning and many uses of time that can incorporate learning into the continuing work of the board.

Exploring various ways to bridge the gaps between learning and doing and to integrate reflection with work are important challenges warranting a board's purposive attention. Boards need ways to do business that are informed by interactive, critical reflection on their efforts. They can then take responsibility for ongoing, self-directed improvements in their own performance. They can experiment with replacing traditional meeting formats with more thoughtful, creative, and reflective ways of working together. This will require leadership and support for group initiative and risk taking, because many boards hesitate to venture into unfamiliar approaches to doing their work.

Formulating explicit goals for the board itself and then using those goals to reorganize meeting time and attention also contributes to integrating work and reflection. Goals for the board should be based on the goals of the organization and lead to meeting those goals, but they should be sufficiently distinct so as to provide a clear focus for group attention. These goals should guide committee appointments and charges as well as their reports back to the full board. Important next steps for the board would be to

- Develop objective means to monitor their own performance
- Use regular evaluative feedback to examine their own effectiveness
- Identify areas needing improvement and then use those conclusions to plan the next round of educational activities (Holland, 1991)

Another component of board education is to explore better ways to use problems and mistakes as well as successes as opportunities to learn how to improve board performance. Many board members apparently share the popular cultural assumption that mistakes are individual failures that should be overlooked until they become threatening to the organization. At the point of crisis, the appropriate step is to replace the person who committed the error, minimize damage from their action, and move ahead. Using this approach, the board's main role is watchdog—exercising control and oversight and making sure that the staff neither makes nor allows big mistakes. Until the executive clearly commits a major error, the board provides enthusiastic support. This is basically a technical-rational approach to problem solving, in which the "broken part" is fixed or replaced and the system restored to smooth operation.

A more productive approach is for the board to be involved in a process of continuously creating, shaping, and fine-tuning decisions in tandem with the staff as the work of the organization moves ahead. Governance decisions are *group* actions, as should be the processes of learning together by monitoring the consequences of those actions. Inevitably, changes in internal or external circumstances will require boards to revisit some decisions. The board should assume that important decisions will have to be reconsidered routinely, as a normal part of being a dynamic, creative team (Pound, 1994). Midcourse correction processes are central to the board's functioning. Used thoughtfully, problems, dissonances, mistakes, and corrections are vital opportunities for board learning.

The Interpersonal Dimension

Effective boards nurture the development of their members as a working group, a team, attending to its collective well-being and fostering a sense of cohesiveness. They develop among members a sense of inclusiveness and mutual ownership of issues and conclusions, with equal access to information and equal opportunities to participate and influence decisions. Rather than just waiting for "natural" leaders to emerge, effective boards intentionally cultivate leadership skills among members. They set purposive goals for board improvement as well as goals for the organization.

These boards regularly include social time in their agendas—opportunities for members to get to know one another as persons with many other interests. They pair each newcomer with a mentor or coach, making sure that everyone understands the "rules of the game" and finds a useful place on the team. They take time to address leadership issues as part of educational efforts, and they encourage members to take advantage of outside opportunities to strengthen their leadership skills and teamwork. They formulate goals for the group having to do with specific aspects of group performance that will be improved in the coming year.

Most boards are composed of strong and capable individuals who have not integrated their skills into strong teams. They appear to share the popular cultural assumption that a board is but an occasional assembly of capable individuals rather than essentially a group. Members are usually slotted into committee roles according to their perceived individual expertise. The common assumption that the individual is the only unit of social reality undermines attention to learning the crucial skills of effective group interaction. A further common inference is that because every member came aboard because of prior demonstrations of his or her leadership capacities, further study of leadership skills, teamwork, and group processes would be a waste of time.

Boards may be acknowledged as groups, but seldom do their members attend to or explicitly address characteristics of the group. This blind spot limits motivation to take time to build the team, monitor and reflect on the board's performance, learn from its experiences and mistakes, and identify and implement corrective measures. Some women trustees seem to direct attention to this relational dimension more comfortably than some men do, which suggests that boards may be overlooking an important leadership resource to strengthen this area.

The skills of teamwork, of effective group performance, are essential ingredients of successful boards. Members should be encouraged to reflect on group process phenomena as they become experienced in instrumental tasks. A crucial question may be, What are the group processes or patterns that emerge from what we all are doing here as individuals? Exploration of issues related to individual assumptions, preferences, and group processes move those issues from the realm of the unknown or taken-for-granted into matters of group deliberation and intentional choice.

Effective teams learn how to improve their performance by reflecting on their experiences, facing problems and mistakes together, and intentionally using difficult experiences to learn to perform better in the future. An environment in which such self-aware group reflection replaces blaming is vital to the health of groups and organizations. As Senge (1990) reminds us, the best orchestra or sports team will step back from each performance and review how well it did and where changes could be made to improve future work. High-performing groups take time for such practice, for reviewing their performance, and thus learn as a team. Boards can learn from their example. Those that take time to examine and reflect on their performance can identify useful lessons that will guide them into increased effectiveness as leaders of their institutions.

Selecting Members for the Board

A board should be composed of persons who are committed to carrying out the mission of the organization and ensuring that the organization thrives. For some religious organizations, the selection of these persons is a responsibility of the board itself, carried out by a committee on nominations. For other organizations, the selection is done by congregational vote or by judicatory or denominational bodies, by vote in annual meetings or conventions, or through appointment by bishops or other officials. For others, the selection process includes several routes, with some members appointed and others chosen by vote.

Regardless of how members are selected, the goal is to have a cohesive group of dedicated, resourceful, committed members who work together to advance the purposes of the organization. The board members should be able to work well as a group and to exercise strong leadership on behalf of the organization and the constituencies it serves.

Although organizations may set the number of members and terms of office in their bylaws or denominational policy, there are no right numbers for a board to be effective. The board should include as many members as are needed to carry out all of its duties, and few enough to become a cohesive team. A board with too few members is limited in the range of tasks it can carry out; a board with too many members has many complex and time-consuming challenges of communication and work coordination. Many organizations have found somewhere between seven or eight and twenty-six to twenty-eight members to be a workable size. Far more important than numbers is how effectively the group works together. Term limits help to ensure the continuing introduction of new ideas and fresh energy into the board.

Regardless of whether its members are elected by the organization's membership or appointed by outside individuals or groups, the board has a responsibility for recommending appropriate criteria for screening nominees and an interest in suggesting likely candidates for consideration. A good candidate will have some of the following attributes:

- *The candidate will have demonstrated commitment to the organization's mission, to the faith tradition of which it is a part, and to carrying out the work of the board.* Prior experience in a field related to the organization's mission or professional expertise in an area related to the organization's key programs is desirable. For example, a private religious school whose board is planning a capital campaign would do well to have some members with backgrounds in fundraising, while a seminary board that has a goal of increasing diversity in its student body would do well to seek diversity in its board composition.
- *The candidate will have a good reputation as an opinion leader, with esteem or prestige in the congregation or among important constituencies.* Seminary boards may include leaders from other, related institutions or congregations that hire their graduates or accomplished alumni, while hospital boards often include recognized leaders in health care policy or practice from other institutions. Such leaders serve to enhance the board's understanding of the views of those constituencies, but also serve as important channels of communication from the board back to those constituencies.
- *The candidate will be willing to use his or her talents, skills, and time for the organization and be ready to learn how to become a productive team member, not just a lone star.* Without these attributes, any other characteristics are of limited value.

Many boards make the mistake of seeking only stars—persons with outstanding or widely recognized names—without checking to make sure that these individuals are ready to make the time commitment necessary to become useful team contributors. It is demoralizing to any group to have some members touted as really important who seldom show up at meetings or only occasionally drop in to make uninformed pronouncements or to challenge past decisions. If names are important, the board should create some honorary status for them—perhaps calling them the president's advisory panel or the council of regents—and not burden itself with false expectations of work.

A related problem is the new member who has time but little talent for becoming an effective participant in the work of the board as a group. Members who set out on solo tasks, without endorsement from the full board, can be destructive to the organization and to its board. The board acts as a group in examining issues and reaching shared conclusions, and only then does it delegate tasks of implementation to committees or individuals.

Persons from professional or personal backgrounds where solo action is the most important norm often find it difficult to acquire the new skill of group participation and effective teamwork. They become impatient with the sometimes slow and deliberative processes of bringing everyone to shared conclusions—a process that is necessary for effective action on behalf of the whole organization. In seeking new board members, nominating committees should not overlook persons who have demonstrated strong teamwork skills or at least a readiness to learn such skills.

Being a productive member of a group is a skill that is new and uncomfortable for many otherwise very accomplished people. But unless board members invest time in reflecting together on their performance as a group, expanding on strengths and correcting weaknesses, there is little real learning or growth.

Effective boards are composed of members who work intentionally at learning and developing group skills. Cherished traditions and conventional wisdom about the board are discarded for the same reasons that any other organization grows and changes—circumstances change and the times are too turbulent and unpredictable to cling to outdated ways of doing business. Strong boards take time to examine their performance, to learn from their successes as well as their mistakes, and to build skilled teamwork (Senge, 1990).

Conclusions

The boards of religious organizations carry many demanding responsibilities, for which many members are not well prepared. Learning to perform governance duties skillfully is vital to effective leadership, but little time and few resources are available to guide such efforts. Standards and expectations are often ambiguous, preparation is limited, feedback is vague, and accountability for one's performance is ambiguous. Most participants have few means for giving or getting valid information about the quality of their work.

Changing such situations and developing more effective boards can draw on the examples of strong boards. These groups are thoroughly familiar with the organization's mission and see their work as embodying its underlying values and beliefs in specific decisions to guide the organization. They develop explicit goals for the organization and for themselves, understanding that the board is a major resource whose strength contributes to the realization of the organization's goals. They bring diversity and rigorous analytical skills to the issues before them, and they communicate regularly with all constituencies. They take time to educate themselves about the organization, its environment, and their own duties and performance. They build strong, cohesive teams and continue to grow in their leadership skills. They model the behavior they want others to emulate in the organization, they walk the talk, and they lead the way.

If the board demonstrates a commitment to applying its faith to its tasks, holding itself accountable for explicit standards of performance, and assessing its own work critically and making changes on the basis of the findings, then staff members, volunteers, and others are more likely to follow suit. Boards that accept such challenges become more effective in their governance. They demonstrate clearly how to add value to the organization, and they provide grounds for the continued trust of others. The results of such efforts can include measurable successes for the organization as well as increased satisfaction for board members themselves.

REFERENCES

Chait, R. P., Holland, T. P., and Taylor, B. E. *The Effective Board of Trustees.* Phoenix: Oryx Press, 1993.

Chait, R. P., Holland, T. P., and Taylor, B. E. *Improving the Performance of Governing Boards.* Phoenix: Oryx Press, 1996.

Holland, T. P. "Self-Assessment by Nonprofit Boards." *Nonprofit Management and Leadership,* 1991, 2(1), 25–36.

Pound, J. "The Promise of the Governed Corporation." *Harvard Business Review,* 1994, 73(8), 89–98.

Senge, P. *The Fifth Discipline: The Art and Practice of the Learning Organization.* New York: Doubleday, 1990.

3

THE RELIGIOUS MISSION
OF THE BOARD

William L. Sachs

TRYING TO UNDERSTAND the differences between Catholics and Protestants, a friend drew on personal experience. "Growing up Catholic in a small town," she recalled, "religious days were always school holidays. We were expected to observe Ascension Day or All Saints' Day, not just Christmas and Easter. Protestants seemed to have few religious holidays. Yet most of the churches in our town were Protestant. They didn't seem to have the same sort of piety, but they possessed so much social influence. I couldn't understand it. We Catholics had a distinct religious identity. When we were out of school and my Protestant friends were in school, I wondered, what sort of religion is this?"

As I considered how to answer this question, I realized that my friend and I had absorbed different religious perspectives. Growing up Protestant in the late 1950s and 1960s I experienced a close identification between piety and civic loyalty. There were few specifically religious holidays, but there was a pervasive sense that Christian faith was closely aligned with culture. Religious and public life seemed congruent. There were Blue Laws, though they were eroding. There was prayer in public schools, and when we pledged allegiance to the United States, we invoked God. Other religions were visible in our communities, but their public influence was limited by the hegemony of mainstream Protestantism. Intent on uniting faith and culture, these churches saw no breach between sacred and secular America.

44

Historically, a cluster of Protestant churches have been linked under the broad category of "mainline." Presbyterians, Episcopalians, Congregationalists, several Baptist churches, and Methodists were joined by the Disciples of Christ and certain Lutheran churches to form a religious phalanx. These churches share a similar sense of place in American life, an ability to exert public influence, and a similar sense of mission.

These denominations also share a number of characteristic approaches to religious life. Since European people settled North America, the predominant religious form on these shores has been Protestant Christianity. Despite increased religious pluralism in this country and rightful affirmation of it, nearly 85 percent of all Americans now say they are Christians, and three-fourths of those say they are Protestant.

As *Newsweek* reported recently ("Two Thousand Years of Jesus," 1999), Christianity has always been a culture-shaping force. Its organizations and leaders have paid close attention to this task, as the concept of the Protestant ethic attests. All religious organizations face the challenge of living in a nation whose heavily Protestant imprint cannot be denied. That imprint can be seen in the sense of the church's public form and role. The Protestant instinct has been to seek and respond to God through discovery of the inherently sacred nature of seemingly secular organizations and to transform their forms and roles.

Institutional governance has played a large role in this intention. To Christian eyes, not only religious institutions but also organizations devoted to secular concerns possess sacred dimensions. Efforts to create a Christian culture require absorption into everyday life by utilizing its style of organization. Churches have pursued this goal because of a religious outlook in which board life plays an important role. Church leaders have presumed that religious organizations must cultivate ways to link religious purpose with civic form and social convention.

Pivotal to the life of modern organizations, the board bears the challenge of articulating institutional purposes and values in light of their sacred nature. Social reliance on institutions led by boards that possess a deeply religious dimension is a legacy of this outlook. The assumptions that a group must be organized in bureaucratic form and that it must rely on a board that embodies its sacred intent have become common to all American religious movements. To understand the religious mission of the board therefore requires appreciation of the religious contours of American life.

But understanding the board's religious mission today also entails analysis of an important shift. As I describe in this chapter, the effort to infuse the secular form of the board with religious vision is an historical intention that continues today, though the nature of the task has changed.

Evidence of this decisive shift occurred within the span of one generation. When I graduated from a public high school in the 1960s, a local Methodist minister led an elaborate baccalaureate service at which attendance was expected. The senior class, gowned and seated as a group, heard a stirring call to live in ways that blended piety and public responsibility. Directed by the board of education and endorsed by local churches, the baccalaureate was part of the annual observances that expressed Christianity's public role. For decades, the importance and influence of this public ceremony was undisputed.

But a few years ago in the town where I now live, public concern about the baccalaureate surfaced. A notable percentage of the town's residents do not belong to any religious group. Some belong to non-Christian religions; many are Catholic. When an evangelical minister lapsed into proselytism during his baccalaureate message, some people walked out. The local education board and the boards of the town's larger churches reached a new view: the baccalaureate was abolished. Future graduation events with religious themes would be held by churches for their members. Local evangelicals decried the change, while other clergy welcomed it as a way for the churches to focus on their true task and not be confused with civic occasions. Mainline religion's historical sense of public task had shifted in this community, as it had in many others.

The once vivid images of Protestant faith shaping American culture now seem ancient. In recent years, the idea of a religious mainstream has become more memory than reality. There are conflicts over faith and morality within all churches, along with a marked advance of religious pluralism and renewal initiatives within and outside historical denominations. Yet conflict and disarray have signaled an emerging new synthesis of religion and life. Even as historical structures have faltered, a general search for authentic personal and collective spirituality has appeared. Although mainline religion's habitual way of linking faith and culture cannot be sustained, a new sensibility is evident. The effort to unite religion and life has begun a new phase. A different approach to board life is evident.

My friend's question about the nature of Protestantism suggests this chapter's outline. As we trace Protestantism's reliance on board life, we will sense that one of religion's notable achievements has been its ability to subsume varied religious traditions into a common social form and sense of public mission. Although Catholics and Jews were present in colonial America and pluralism became an inescapable reality, the preponderance of early emigrants were religious heirs of the Protestant Reformation. At first they tried to recreate their inherited sense of religious establishment, and eventually an American evangelical religious estab-

lishment arose. Evangelicals drew on the Reformation themes of the sa-
credness of secular tasks and the shared roles of clergy and laity. During
the early national years, the emerging churches also utilized the evangelical view of history to shape their sense of public mission. Their leaders
helped to shape the ethos of the American social environment. The emphasis on board life in this linkage between religion and society has been
profound.

Religious organizations and the American social establishment forged
a common intention to blend faith and life, a commitment that added
great religious significance to secular tasks. In business, education, politics, and philanthropy, leaders of religious organizations left an indelible
mark. Even now its influence can be felt, though the imprint has faded.

To speak of the religious mission of the board at the end of the twentieth century is to speak in terms that not only reflect historical ideals but
also are new. To understand this sensibility, we must trace a major shift in
religious life over the past generation, then explore how religion and board
life now intersect. Clearly a new religious ideal of board life is emerging.

What this religious ideal means, in contrast with what it once meant, is
the focus of this chapter. Philosopher Louis Dupre (1998) has noted that
religion is a socially integrative force. In this light, the focus of this chapter
is the shift from an older reliance on board work as a means of integrating
faith and life to a new sense of how boards must embody such integration.

Americans have long emphasized personal conviction, affect, and grassroots public response. We value freedom of association so we can explore
shared avenues of belief and action. Always individualistic, American religion also prizes shared religious and moral commitment. In the early nineteenth century, this search gave rise to influential forms of mission. As it
did so, the role of board oversight became pivotal.

Historical Roots of Board Practices

The necessity for board oversight of religious life and the form it took
were products of America's historical social circumstances. With independence from Britain and the dismantling of colonial society, religious
groups were compelled to devise their own means of governance. More
than a way to perpetuate inherited institutional forms, religious life focused on the question of mission. In part this was a practical consideration. In the new United States, all religious groups would have to attract
and sustain the loyalties of their followers; loyalty could not be presumed.
Also, in part, governance of religious institutions required amassing and
managing human and material resources. In the wake of the American

revolution, religious bodies were forced to devise their own organizational forms at the national, regional, and local levels. The rise of denominational structures and congregational life as they are now known began soon after the nation's independence was achieved.

Necessitated by circumstance, effective organization of religious bodies also arose from a sense of mission. Not surprisingly, the new denominational structures instinctively followed the contours of the new American political structures. Among Episcopalians, for instance, a system for electing bishops was devised (rather than having them appointed by the Crown, as was the case in Britain). Conventions of laity and clergy in each diocese would elect a bishop when there was an opening. Nationally, Episcopalians adopted a bicameral form for their triennial convention. One house was reserved for bishops while the other consisted of equal numbers of clergy and lay delegates elected by their diocesan conventions.

Other governance structures developed as denominations created boards charged with oversight of programs between their national conventions. During the nineteenth century, denominations, mirroring American organizational trends generally, became increasingly complex institutions. The number of boards within denominational life, and the specificity of their tasks, rapidly multiplied.

At the congregational level, an increasing sense of organization requiring reliance on governing boards also became apparent. Both formerly established churches and dissenting ones shared the task of local organization for self-government. The scope of this task was magnified by America's westward expansion. As the territory of the United States enlarged, religious groups shared in the rush to expand public life. Typically the products of denominational mission programs, these congregations grew apace with new settlements. As at the national level, local congregations had to provide oversight of their common life. They required programs designed to attract and hold followers. They had to raise funds, especially for building programs, then manage such resources. These tasks enlarged the board's role. Laypeople, often elected from within congregations' membership, assumed significant authority and posed complex new questions of how clergy and laity might define and perform their respective roles.

In the American religious environment, the question of how to define authority became, and remains, one of the most intricate governance issues. Yet the need for boards was clear in the early national period. Boards offered the means of translating the ideals of a particular religious tradition into effective structures and programs. Not only did board life create a kind of religious public forum (albeit often only for a select number of the locality's male leaders), but boards elevated a sense of shared hope and destiny. They embodied the American ideals of local initiative and self-government.

The impact of American independence on religious life went beyond the need for reorganization and self-government. In a society where affiliation had become a matter of voluntary, personal loyalty, religious groups now had to define clearly their sense of mission. Seemingly a recipe for competition among the various religious traditions, this circumstance instead encouraged the appearance of broad forms of cooperation among America's historical religious groups. Methodists, Presbyterians, Congregationalists, and Episcopalians forged a set of shared convictions, common styles, and overlapping programs. In this way, these denominations, later joined by the Disciples of Christ and certain Lutheran groups, forged their sense of being America's religious leaders. Their cooperation relied on the creation of boards and elaborate committee structures that stood outside denominational channels but joined laity and clergy from varied confessions in common causes and social reforms, such as Sunday schools and antislavery and temperance programs. Board life became intimately linked to the search for broad forms of shared religious mission.

In their characteristic style of organizing such groups, religious leaders developed regional boards, ladies' auxiliaries, and committees specifically designed to publicize their cause and elicit financial support. At the pinnacle of some of these national movements stood a central board charged with coordinating the work of addressing the issue or promoting the cause that gave the movement its identity.

Like the denominations facing American religious voluntarism, the reform societies that grew out of evangelical awakenings discovered that the reality of voluntary support increased the requirement for a board to direct it. The linkage between board life and religious mission thus received an indelible imprint. Above all, it became the style of organization that has been characteristic of virtually all religious institutions. In their quest to influence American society, these organizations structured their efforts by emulating the bureaucratic revolution that was transforming American life.

The Rise of Organizational Efficiency

These shifts in the organization of religious life were not just unthinking reflections of secular currents. From the outset, the denominational and ecumenical initiatives that gave rise to many American religious organizations hoped to balance the creative absorption of American life with critical distance from it. Secular forms of organization could thus be adapted by religiously inspired reformers to express moral critiques and promote important social changes.

This religious conviction, and not merely institutional or cultural bravado, encouraged many religious leaders to move toward what has been called "the mystique of organizational efficiency." It was not enough that the religious organizations had become large institutions. Their sense of mission now required that they function in efficient ways. This meant that they had to be organized so that their goals would be clear and their procedures would be directly related to attaining those goals. In an era of troubling social change, religious leaders concluded that their organizations could encourage order simply by how they functioned.

Efficiency in religious organizations included such ideas as specialization and delegation of tasks, interlocking structure, and work coordination. The mission intention of programs had to be linked to promotional and fundraising efforts and reflected in budget design as well as in staff assignments. It was during this era that church structures at the national and local levels turned to an annual "every member canvass" to link support with program intentions. Heretofore churches had raised funds mainly by occasional, special campaigns, or by the old system of pew rents. Now fundraising was related directly to mission. This tie was a sign of the quest for efficiency and helped to formalize the role of church boards. Shailer Matthews, dean of the University of Chicago Divinity School, noted in 1912 that the work of the churches would fall short without "the grace of committees."

To be sure, the efficiency mystique included close attention to organizational goals. Christians held to their confessional loyalties and invested energy simply in building up denominational structures. But their leaders were intricately involved in sharing a reliance on organizational forms and continued to collaborate on mutual concerns, especially social issues. Indeed the new emphasis on efficiency challenged the fragmentation of American Christianity into many denominations. Leaders looked for efficiency through increased emphasis on the role of boards. Now board members had to possess specialized financial, managerial, and analytic tools. Boards were expected to analyze complex problems and devise creative responses.

The era of organizational efficiency emphasized the expansion of goods and services that religious organizations provided. Coordinating structures grew and centralized oversight became more important. During this period many denominations created departments of social relations. Such departments required trained staff and complex divisions of labor. In search of efficiency, professional staff amassed large amounts of data from elaborately devised studies. As they presented findings, boards were confronted with the need to assess situations and devise responses, to supervise personnel and allocate resources. If the board was not efficient, how could its ideals permeate the organization and advance its mission?

Emergence of a New Organizational Paradigm

In recent years, a new set of organizational ideals has been emerging. The perspective is based on recognition of cultural changes that have disrupted the old assumptions and practices of religious organizations. But reference to a paradigm entails more than damage assessment. It signals a shift in the presuppositions of institutional life. Over the past generation, new ideals have begun to define how organizations operate. This shift is unfinished, and conflicts over form and function are ongoing. But it is clear that historical institutions are being remade, not just dismantled. This distinction is crucial for understanding the contemporary religious mission of boards.

In his epochal book *The Structure of Scientific Revolutions,* Thomas Kuhn developed the concept of paradigm and suggested that a major shift had begun. (See also Ray and Rinzler, 1991, for a discussion of Kuhn's work and the rise of a new paradigm.) Simply put, a paradigm is the set of governing assumptions that underlie basic scientific conclusions. When new realities challenge old conclusions, even in theoretical realms, the social consequences are significant. New social norms have begun to arise amid old ones.

Drawing on Kuhn's view, we can summarize the realities that are remaking institutional life. To date there has been extensive discussion of how and to what end all organizations should be restructured. The results of this discussion are beginning to be applied to religious organizations and their boards.

The difference between the old and the new organization can be described by contrasting ideals and assumptions, particularly about power and authority (as Thomas Savage discusses further in Chapter Six). In the old paradigm, institutions were expected to become efficient through centralized forms. For-profit and nonprofit groups alike operated according to rational norms and measured pursuit of their goals by quantitative criteria. Adherence to institutional goals was assured by authority vested in hierarchical structures. Success under the old paradigm would result if effective central control was exercised.

The new paradigm adheres to completely different standards. In this perspective, an organization must disperse authority and level hierarchy.

Teamwork is valued and work is successful when performance entails a deep sense of community among those who perform the work. The new paradigm encourages authenticity, alignment, and cooperation rather than efficiency or control. Qualitative measures now must outweigh quantitative ones. Rather than a linear sense of direction, there is reliance on developing a shared vision. Rather than reliance on management, there is cultivation of shared leadership.

The energetic discussion of leadership helps to clarify the dimensions of this paradigm shift. Noted authors such as James Kouzes and Barry Posner (1987) argue that leadership is a shared process that entails clarification and expression of a vision. Rather than reinforce institutional order and stability, leaders enable others to act in ways that draw people together into common purpose. Continuing this theme, Ronald Heifetz (1994) links leadership to the attainment of adaptive change and cites shared values as its greatest resource. Similarly, Lee Bolman and Terrence Deal (1995) believe that leadership requires cultivation of personal and shared sources of meaning. Leadership as an expression of the new paradigm requires attention to shared values, meanings, and purposes.

Often the old and new sets of ideals overlap, and many boards struggle with the transition. But the contrast between the two paradigms is instructive for our purpose. The very concept of large religious organizational systems and the way in which they function arose within older organizational ideals and older hierarchical assumptions about linking religion to life. Despite the changes in institutional realities, most religious organizations clung to their historical sense of form and role. But that ideal has become untenable and even the most conservative organizations are now experiencing demands for change.

Part of the change is concerned with the conflicts and losses that have plagued many denominations. Since the 1960s, bitter disputes have erupted over theology, morality, and social witness. Changes in worship and ministry have encouraged some adherents and dismayed others. The result for the traditionally dominant denominations has been a generation of membership losses, necessary cuts in staff as a result of reduced giving, and a sense that the historically public witness of these denominations is being eclipsed. Both evangelicals and Roman Catholics are conveying an enhanced sense of civic role and a new kind of public religious presence. As Protestant churches debate among themselves about identity and mission, public religious initiative has shifted away from them. The historical mainline churches have been displaced and many now struggle for survival.

If we are speaking simply of the historical legacy of centralized, bureaucratic institutions, their concerns about survival are justified. The former hegemony of mainline religion has been erased. Diverse, broad religious groups, some of which are new, some of which are stronger than others and newly assertive, have assured the triumph of pluralism in American life. All religious groups, however, show signs of religious life's emerging shape. Suspicion of remote authority and hierarchy has produced a local emphasis that has given new prominence to congregational life.

The new paradigm values community. In religious life, this means fresh attention to the activities and beliefs that sustain congregations. Over a decade ago, James Hopewell (1984) awakened this interest when he probed patterns of life in congregations. His work prompted a flurry of studies of both the structures and dynamics of local religious community. In the old approach, religion's center lay in the work of centralized committees and programs. Now religion's center lies in the local, voluntary activities that sustain religious organizations. The purpose and form of wider religious structures are problematic, but the genius of local religious life is clearly appreciated.

The new paradigm implies a new view of the congregation. In earlier years, the emphasis was on adopting organizational strategies for the sake of a religious mission. Now, Stanley Hauerwas (1986) argues, the church's principal task is to be authentically itself. Its identity centers on the story of salvation entrusted to it; its work features telling that story and developing a common life devoted to it. Belief does not require elaborate, formal structures, he argues. Rather, it originates in a community willing to explore the practical implications of the Gospel. The church does not place its hope of transforming the world before the necessary task of shaping itself according to biblical truth. More than being effective or efficient, the church must be authentic and faithful.

Similar influences are shaping all religious groups. An important sign of the emerging pattern is the changing role of the laity. In the old paradigm, centralized religious organizations were led by specialists. At the parish level, this meant that clergy performed the pastoral, teaching, and administrative roles for which they had been carefully trained and groomed. To varying degrees, laity performed ancillary administrative roles such as fundraising. Now, images of partnership, teamwork, and servanthood have taken hold. Religious leadership has become a shared rather than an individual activity. Emphasis on specialization has diminished; leadership has become a process that seeks to elicit a shared spirituality. Leaders encourage a sense of belonging and empowerment. The focus is on group process and its goal is shared spirituality.

The expansion of roles accorded to laity vividly depicts this new sense of religious organizations. In worship, for instance, many congregations now regularly involve laypersons in reading lessons, offering prayers, and administering Holy Communion. Frequently, laypersons are trained in pastoral skills and visit members of the congregation in hospitals and homes. Far from displacing the clergy, this trend expands the range of ministries offered by congregations and reinforces the clergy's role of teaching and empowering their lay members.

But more than an expansion of lay roles is afoot. A key area is the work of the boards of all religious organizations. Governing boards played a pivotal role in the emergence of Protestant denominations. Now the historical assumptions of these boards are under scrutiny. The emerging view of congregations and all religious organizations is being shaped by new ideals of board life. Ironically these ideals reflect the appeal of religious themes to secular organizations. Robert Greenleaf's (1977) ideal of servant leadership has encouraged an image of board members as trustees. From this perspective the concept of holding an institution in trust is taken literally. Greenleaf called for trustees to consider who they serve and to what end. He believed that the work of boards requires empowering people and cultivating long-term vision. Rather than be preoccupied with immediate issues, boards must balance problem solving with development of a sense of shared future. The key to this vision lies in the board's pursuit of a sense of purpose that is shared throughout the institution. Increasingly, even in secular circles, spirituality looms as an organization's greatest resource (Briskin, 1996; Fassel, 1990).

The effects of these revised ideals on religious organizations have been significant. Among Roman Catholics there has been widespread interest in developing parish councils. At times tensions may arise between a council and the parish priest, but with an increasing shortage of priests the council must assume greater responsibility for directing parish life. In addition to overseeing finances and properties, the council may address questions of worship, education, and spiritual growth.

A similar emphasis on shared values and purposes is being experienced in all religious bodies. Although the historical facts of American religious pluralism and voluntarism entail attention to institutional management and fundraising, another historical aspect of governance now receives increasingly vigorous emphasis. The ideal of trusteeship is recrafting the concept of mission.

The renewed contours of boards can be seen in a variety of ways. In the past, boards of religious organizations focused on analytical, managerial, and regulatory roles. The current emphasis on vision requires turning to means of spiritual discernment. Boards must devise ways to build community by assessing and including varieties of moral and religious outlooks. Even more, boards must consider ways to integrate spiritual insights into the activities of congregations and other religious groups. The core of board work and religious mission requires attention to the conditions that evoke and reinforce a shared sense of purpose.

In part this shift in emphasis reflects the flux in traditional forms of religious expression and commitment. But new institutional priorities have also surfaced. Board members must do more than make revisions to the institution; they must also consider participants' questions about why their organizations even exist. The pursuit of spiritual purpose represents the hope of aligning institutional function and intention. The old ambition of transforming American life now seems shortsighted. Instead, mission today requires a search for ways of integrating spiritual commitment into every aspect of organizational function.

If the churches are genuinely to be churches, the current consensus dictates, they must model practical forms of this ideal. The onus of this demand falls on their boards. It is among the designated leaders that an authentic spiritual basis must be found and encouraged throughout the organization. Rather than seeking to transform society, many religious organizations and their boards now concentrate on transforming themselves.

One appealing model for doing such work in congregations has been offered by Charles Olsen (1995). (David Hester offers another in Chapter Four of the present volume.) Olsen outlines how a church board can remake itself into a community of spiritual leaders. He identifies the spiritual practices he encourages church boards to adopt. In his approach, patterns of telling personal and congregational stories encourage the building of shared history. The disciplines of biblical and theological reflection should become pivotal exercises during board meetings. Finally, Olsen wants to shift the idea of the board's work away from decision making and toward discernment. He maintains that such a step is crucial if the old criteria of rationality and efficiency are to be replaced by authenticity and community.

The integration of spirituality into decision making rarely occurs easily and seamlessly, however. Friction results from more than the resistance of board members to modifying their strictly rational approach. Out of necessity, board members must engage issues of financial and property management, personnel and planning. To date there is no clear model for a truly spiritual means of addressing such governance duties, although Hester's chapter provides a possible framework. He and Olsen have taken valuable steps by suggesting some of the necessary ingredients for religiously centered governance. They also illustrate the importance of a sense of common bond among board members. But what a genuine spirituality of board life looks like and how it might be achieved remains a vital challenge for boards of all religious organizations. Fresh attention to the religious mission of the board is emerging, but the details of its new form and practice are not yet clearly in focus.

Part of the problem lies in the contemporary concept of spirituality. By its nature, spirituality resists clear definition. The product of an affective, pluralistic society, American spirituality is inherently subjective, eclectic, and changing. Whereas *religion* is currently a word of dubious appeal, spirituality suggests individual freedom to seek and combine various religious sources into a personally satisfying mix. The casual mix of various traditional practices and beliefs lacks any clear rationale, and easily becomes unfaithful to that which it seeks to emulate. Thus the relation of spirituality to institutional governance is also vague, but when authentic spirituality becomes a criterion of organizational life, when interpersonal relations weigh heavily, the result can be life-giving.

How can boards of religious organizations find an authentic spirituality? Spirituality seems to speak of the intended manner of our connection to one another. Can such depth of commonality appear in wider institutional forms? Can historical institutions be transformed in light of such a spirituality? How might a turn to a profoundly spiritual base reorient and renew the mission of a religious tradition? In what way can spirituality provide a means for boards in all religious groups, and in philanthropic groups generally, to relate more creatively to the world? In fact, how might a spiritual approach allow religious organizations to find a means of refashioning their identity as they renew their mission? The extent of these unanswered questions reveals both the power and the uncertainty of the present moment. The true test of the current spiritual explorations among boards might be the extent to which these challenges can be engaged at the same time as other tasks. In seeking to ground the board's mission, spirituality must now find an adequate moral and religious foundation.

Thus the religious mission of the board has clearly turned the corner toward pursuit of a new set of ideals. But if the ideals stand in clear relief, what practices will emerge to secure them? The next phase of board life should make the practices of board life and board leadership more explicit. In any event, an historical hope of American life remains intact even as its form changes.

REFERENCES

Bolman, L. G., and Deal, T. E. *Leading with Soul*. San Francisco: Jossey-Bass, 1995.

Briskin, A. *The Stirring of Soul in the Workplace.* San Francisco: Jossey-Bass, 1996.

Dupre, L. Comments made during concluding lecture prior to retirement from the Department of Religious Studies, Yale University, May 1998.

Fassel, D. *Working Ourselves to Death.* New York: HarperCollins, 1990.

Greenleaf, R. *Servant Leadership.* New York: Paulist Press, 1977.

Hauerwas, S. *A Community of Character.* South Bend, Ind.: University of Notre Dame Press, 1986.

Heifetz, R. A. *Leadership Without Easy Answers.* Cambridge, Mass.: Belknap Press, 1994.

Hopewell, J. *Congregation.* Minneapolis: Augsburg Fortress, 1984.

Kouzes, J. M., and Posner, B. Z. *The Leadership Challenge.* San Francisco: Jossey-Bass, 1987.

Kuhn, T. S. *The Structure of Scientific Revolutions.* Chicago: University of Chicago Press, 1962.

Mathews, S. *Scientific Management in the Churches.* Chicago: University of Chicago Press, 1912.

Olsen, C. M. *Transforming Church Boards into Communities of Spiritual Leaders.* Washington, D.C.: Alban Institute, 1995.

Ray, M., and Rinzler, A. *The New Paradigm in Business.* New York: Putnam, 1991.

4

PRACTICING GOVERNANCE
IN THE LIGHT OF FAITH

David C. Hester

LET'S BEGIN WITH A STORY, one familiar to anyone connected with governing boards of religious institutions. The setting for the story happens to be a seminary board of trustees, but the experience it relates and the issues it raises also have significant implications for those who serve on congregational governing boards.

Eleanor Freiburg (a pseudonym) left the spring meeting of the board of trustees reeling with questions. She had come to the seminary board of trustees just a year ago, so this was her third meeting. Everything seemed very different from her experience serving on other boards of directors, at the bank and at the community college. Yet many things were the same: they dealt with issues of fundraising, budget, institutional policies, and maintenance and improvement of facilities. Members of the seminary board also asked the administration questions about effectiveness and productivity, even though the organization's "product" was not so easily measured as it is in industry or business.

The difference she felt had to do with the nature of the seminary as a religious institution, which seemed to give the business of the board a different context than that of boards in business and industry. The seminary's board was accountable, for example, not to a group of shareholders but to a religious body and, ultimately, to the religious commitments and values of that body. Eleanor's membership on the other boards was an honor and, arguably, a civic responsibility. But Eleanor was inclined to describe her role on the seminary board as a "calling," something that fulfilled a sense of religious commitment deep inside her. The rituals and symbols that accompanied the seminary board meetings reinforced her sense of the religious significance of what she was doing. Neither the board at the bank nor the board at the college began meetings with prayer, took time to worship together, or installed new members. She had been installed on the seminary's board in a religious liturgy surrounded by stained glass and symbols of the religious community of which the institution and she were apart. The mission statement of the seminary spoke of "preparing students for service in the religious community, guided by the historical traditions of that community"—not exactly the purpose of either the bank or the college.

Finally, as a member of the other boards on which she sat, she felt she had some expertise to offer—in the one case drawing on her experience as a successful businesswoman and in the other on her experience as a student and active alumna. At the seminary, she was a fish out of water. She had, she felt, no theological expertise to draw on, only her beliefs and those of her faith community as she understood them. In fact, she had a hard time imagining what seminary life was like, both in and out of the classroom. At the board meetings, she felt she could raise questions or enter discussion about business issues. But she felt—and other members seemed to as well—dependent for guidance on the president, dean, or faculty members, or on other members of the board who had formal theological education.

What was most on Eleanor's mind as she headed for the parking lot was the discussion the board had begun about the implications of the dramatic drop in enrollment the previous fall. Most entering classes numbered in the sixties or seventies. But this year's class was far smaller. What's more, the projection for future classes indicated that this year's experience would likely become the rule rather than the exception. At the same time, it was clear that the school's facilities were going to need major maintenance attention, given their age. Also, the number of faculty needed to be increased if the curriculum of the school was going to keep pace with opportunities afforded students in other seminaries. All these forecasts would require more money, just as the constituency counted on for financial resources was shrinking.

This was Eleanor's first taste of crisis, or challenge, as more optimistic board members put it. She could see the complexity and interrelated character of the issues, but how, she wondered, would the board be able to sort them out and make good decisions about what to do about them. She recalled her experiences serving on the congregation's governing board and asked herself, almost aloud, "What difference do faith and the purposes served by the church or the seminary really make in the way we govern these institutions?"

The Significance of Context

Although this case is fictitious, it is not unusual when governing boards of religious institutions practice trusteeship. The question the case raises is this: How do governing boards of religious institutions make decisions about the routine and critical issues they must confront in ways that reflect their distinctive character as religious institutions? To put the matter differently, what difference does it make when governing boards are deciding what to do that the context in which they serve is theological?

First, a word about the word *theological* in this context. It is not intended to be restrictive to the Christian tradition, though I am aware that other major religious traditions do not ordinarily refer to their belief systems as theology. To be inclusive at this point would require multiplying expressions in a way that would hinder comprehension rather than help it, in my judgment. But to be forthcoming, as practical theological reflection requires me to be at this point, I am a Christian theologian and educator. Nevertheless, I intend the word *theology* to mean nothing sectarian, and I hope, for our purposes, that it may serve to include any system of religious values and beliefs shared by a community of faith and informed by its particular shared memory or traditions, standards of behavior, and mutual vision of an ultimate purpose or future. By *theological thinking* or *theological reflection* I mean the individual and communal work of reflecting on important issues in light of the particular community's beliefs.

The assumption here, of course, is that the distinctive religious context of governing boards does make a difference. Two good reasons justify this assumption. First, all effective governance is contextual. That is, to be effective, governance must attend to the particularities and peculiarities of the institutional cultural context. Social experience tells us how truly distinctive any particular board and community served by the board are, whether the institution is a seminary or a congregation. Members talk about the identity of an institution in terms of its "character," meaning that it is a place of good reputation; or they speak of a particular way of doing things, an institutional ethos ("the way it's done around here"), to which new members must be introduced and according to which they must learn how to act in order to participate fully in governance. Members also talk about the mission or purpose of the institution, the commitments and values that the institution and, in turn, the board serve. All of these elements and more—including the history and tradition of the institution, past efforts at problem solving, and social location—constitute the governing board's context and are inextricably bound to decision making if the board is to be effective.

A second assumption at work here is that effective governing boards of religious institutions must pay particular attention to the religious or theological aspect of their identity and their work. Too obvious to mention? The results of a recent survey of sixteen theological schools suggest that the theological identity of the institution most often plays a very modest role, if any at all, in the practice of trusteeship (Holland and Hester, 1995). Although trustees affirmed that the institution they served had a mission statement that they considered important, they could not say how the mission statement made any difference in the process the board used to arrive at decisions nor in the decisions themselves.

Experience and anecdotal evidence have convinced me that what appears to be true for seminary boards is, surprisingly, also true for local congregational governing boards. Virtually every Protestant congregation has a mission or purpose statement, often recorded on the back of the weekly bulletin but sometimes buried in the official documents of the church. Where such mission statements are not explicit, they are most surely implicit in the structures and program of the congregation. Yet governing boards seldom bring these statements of faith to bear in the process of decision making, which renders the congregation's board meeting indistinguishable—except for opening and closing prayer—from any other voluntary organization's business meeting.

On the basis of research carried out with college boards, Chait, Holland, and Taylor (1991, p. 12) concluded that "the actions of effective boards are guided by institutional mission, tradition, and history." A thorough knowledge and working understanding of the mission of the institution is characteristic of such boards, to the extent that "trustees on the most effective boards *routinely* invoked the college's mission and traditions as a touchstone and litmus test for decisions that ranged from physical plant to faculty appointments to curriculum revisions" (p. 14, italics in original). What makes governing boards of religious institutions particularly unique in this regard is the theological or religious commitments and values embodied in their mission statements.

The religious character of the institution and its mission statement means that, to put it bluntly, trustees must be able to think theologically, to *practice* theology, if they are to make decisions as a board that are conscientiously informed by the community's beliefs. Yet this is precisely the Achilles heel of many board members who serve religious institutions. Like

Eleanor, the fictional trustee, trustees who may be comfortable thinking about their decisions in light of a college's stated purpose and values find it far more difficult to reflect on problems posed to the board in light of the community's shared beliefs.

The reasons for this discomfort are several. First, although trustees who govern religious institutions ordinarily belong in some way to the larger religious body or to the community the institution serves, shared beliefs that identify the core traditions of the larger community are often more implicit than explicit. (For a discussion of the role of beliefs and traditions in congregational theologies and identity formation, see Ammerman, Carroll, Dudley, and McKinney, 1999, especially pp. 23–38 and 78–102.) Mission statements make certain aspects of these beliefs explicit. Board members, however, participate in a culture, both inside and outside religious institutions, that treats the discussion of faith and religious beliefs as a private matter. My father's injunction to his children is apropos: "You don't talk about religion or politics in public." The beliefs explicitly espoused in the mission statement may be treated as though they were personal beliefs and, therefore, inappropriate for public discussion—even when "public" means in a board meeting.

Second, the professionalization of theology, relegating it to the expertise of religious leaders and faculty, has left laity uneasy about expressing their own religious wisdom, particularly in the presence of professional "experts." Boards of religious institutions often consist of both laity and those with theological degrees. The promise for theological reflection that such a mix offers unfortunately seems seldom to be realized. Some of the lay trustees in the study done by Holland and Hester (1995) expressed a sense of being intimidated: the popular wisdom seemed to be that only ordained religious leaders spoke with authority on matters relating to the religious dimension of community life. It is, of course, not unusual for some trustees to have knowledge or experience in one area or another of life that interfaces with the board's work. Yet what is remarkable in the case of trustees engaged in governance of religious institutions is the degree to which lay trustees discount their own valid and valuable religious experience and knowledge.

It is possible to point to a still more encompassing problem that contributes to the muting of theological reflection in the course of practicing trusteeship. The difficulty that trustees experience with theological reflection is pervasive in communities of faith at large. Members of congregations and religious bodies do not know how to think theologically or reflect critically on what they or their community believes. Nor do they know how to engage these beliefs in the decision making required in everyday life. It is not something that churches, for example, have been accustomed to teaching believers. On the contrary, to many churches it has seemed more important to know the official or traditional institutional point of view. Nevertheless, it may properly be lamented that current evidence suggests that there is scarce knowledge among believers of what their particular community of faith holds to be sacred and true, what its significant traditions may be, and what symbols and rituals that are central to the practice of their faith mean (Hoge, Johnson, and Luidens, 1994).

The ability of believers to think critically about what they and their community of faith believe, to reflect on the significance and meaning of those beliefs, and to be able to use those beliefs in the complex process of problem solving that is intrinsic to contemporary life is crucial to a mature spiritual life. If this habit of faith is outside the experience of congregation members generally, it is no wonder that it also appears elusive to those charged with governance. How to reflect critically on governance issues in light of the beliefs expressed in the institution's mission statement is a skill that has not been taught. This chapter now turns toward that goal.

Governance as a Practice of Faith

My thesis here is that *practicing governance in a religious institution is a calling, an expression of the human vocation to live faithfully in the image of God, to serve God by responding with care in the matters of daily living to God's universal love for all creation.* Governance is, then, a practice of faith, or if you prefer, a practice of theology. That religious governance is a calling is a fact of faith confirmed intuitively by people like Eleanor Freiburg. Moreover, other trustees interviewed have said that's how they understand what they are doing *as trustees* (Holland, Hester, and others, 1995). What is crucial about this perspective is that it places governance within a larger, sacred, vocational context, the goal of which is service to God and God's design for the goodness of the whole Earth community (see Rasmussen, 1996, for a full discussion of the concept of Earth community). The question I asked earlier can now be restated: How can the practice of governance be taught and learned in ways that are appropriate to understanding it as a sacred calling, in which the purpose served is, first and last, God's purpose?

We can get some help in answering this question by first thinking about how people typically talk about "practice" and then contrasting that with what practicing governance as a sacred calling might mean (see Dykstra,

1991). Practice, in our culture, is connected intimately with being a professional. A professional *practices* some profession. The image that immediately comes to my mind is of a physician, one who *practices medicine*. Another example is a person who is learning to be a teacher; the last step in the process of professional education is *practice teaching*, followed by certification that qualifies the person to practice his or her profession in a school system. Finally, we say that lawyers *practice law*, meaning that they are qualified, licensed experts who, as professionals, may be trusted to represent their clients in matters of jurisprudence. What all these activities have in common is that they are considered the work of highly trained experts who do something for and to those who require their skills, often called *clients*. These experts are expected to apply their professional knowledge to provide solutions for problems or needs posed to them by their clients. Professionals have, it is supposed, theoretical knowledge and the know-how to apply that knowledge to specific situations or needs.

If we apply this understanding of practice to religious governance, the fault lines become apparent immediately. What this understanding calls for is precisely what board members as a whole are uncomfortable claiming—namely, expertise. Effective governance is a practice shared by the whole board and, in an extended sense, by the whole community being governed. (See Warford's Chapter One in this volume for an excellent discussion of collaborative governance.) But this is precisely what practice that would require the application of theoretical knowledge and skills by a specialist is not. Indeed, the application of theory to practice is not at all what governance leaders do in performing their responsibilities. This perception of how to solve problems and come to decisions belongs to a mode of thinking that may be called *technical-rational thinking* (Shön, 1983, pp. 21–76), a method associated with scientific reasoning that has been the preeminent approach to problem solving in Western culture for at least the last hundred years. It assumes that reason and knowledge serve practical ends by providing the means to the solution of problems. Solutions are provided by technical application of theoretical or rational principles. Technical-rational thinking assumes that the ends of practical knowledge are external to the practices themselves. The practitioner applies her professional skills to provide "goods" for the client that are external to the practices themselves; hence, an objective point of view is assumed to be requisite for the technical-rational problem solver.

Clearly, a technical-rational approach to practice is neither appropriate nor adequate for understanding what it means to practice religious governance as sacred calling. Practicing trustees and congregational leaders are not professionals—nor should they be. Problem solving, of course, is one thing boards do; but I want to suggest that problem solving at its best does not rely on means-ends thinking, or on theory-to-practice reasoning. Board problem solving, moreover, does not strive for or pretend to be objective. On the contrary, trustees, faculty, students, and other constituents are all deeply invested.

If we refocus on the role of the governing board member as practicing governance as sacred calling in the light of the institution's beliefs and values, it becomes clear that the practical reasoning needed has several special qualities that set it apart from technical-rational thinking. First, the work of governance is a communal effort, rather than the effort of an expert or specialist. Governance is responsibility shared by a number of members of any community who contribute to its practice (MacIntyre, 1984, pp. 187–195). For example, in a seminary, the board shares governance with the president, principal, or dean; with faculty; with students; and with various constituents who have a vested interest in the welfare of the institution. Similarly, in a congregation governance may be the chief responsibility of a ruling council, but it is shared with congregational members, with ordained leadership, and with other district or regional bodies concerned for the welfare of the congregation.

Moreover, this communal participation in governance extends through time, which is a second feature of practical reasoning. The practice of governance in a particular institution shares in the history of that institution's governance practice. To put it differently, the practice of governance has a history connected to the practice of governance generally and to the practice of governance within the tradition of the community being served. To understand how governance is practiced in a particular place requires telling stories of how it has been practiced in the past and how it came to be the way it is now. The board is obligated to continue this tradition, to hand on the story. Because the board faces different issues in a time that is different from that of the earlier practitioners of governance, the tradition it receives will inevitably be changed in the retelling. Practical reasoning's concern with the history and tradition of institutional practice and with its storied character is quite different from the objective, scientific, disinterested mode of technical–rational thinking.

Third, unlike technical–rational thinking, practical reasoning is concerned with goods that are *internal* to the practice of governance, rather than being concerned with *external ends*. This means that the chief goal of being a board member is to fulfill the calling and duty to serve on the board. Other satisfaction that may come with the practice of governance—such as the esteem of other members of the congregation or of colleagues, the successful completion of a capital campaign, or the increase of the institution's endowment—are external goods incidental to the internal goods attendant to practicing governance. Boards raise money and balance budgets, as Eleanor in the earlier example recognized from her experience. Otherwise institutions would not survive, nor would the practices so closely related to them. But in the view of practical reasoning, these are not the true goods of practicing governance. The goods internal to the practice of religious governance are expressed in the institution's mission statement. These might include "preparing men and women for ministry," in the case of a seminary, or "being the body of Christ in the world," in the case of a Protestant congregation, or "serving the needs of the poor and hungry and underprivileged," in the case of a social agency. Practicing governance is essentially about being good governors, as measured by the standards of excellence implicit in the practice itself and expressed in the mission or purpose statement. Included in these standards is the ability to reflect critically on what those who govern do in light of the traditional beliefs and values of the institution, and the ability to make decisions that continue the communal story, reshaping it to address both present and future circumstances.

Focus on Mission

Practicing good governance, then, requires having a clear and explicit understanding of the board's mission or purpose, which is set within the frame of the identity, character, and stated purpose of the religious community the board serves. Critical, constructive, theological reflection depends on such an understanding. The board's search for practical wisdom begins here. The mission statement is intended to set forth the reason for the institution's life together; it means to capture in purposeful terms what is characteristic and essential to the identity of the community whose statement it is. This is a heavy burden to place on a statement necessarily limited in length and formed by a need to say succinctly both what the institution is about and what values and vision guide it. It is no wonder that mission statements are given to generalities and abstraction. Their often inclusive and picturesque language comes closer to poetry than to assertion. The poetic tone of such statements is not bad. On the contrary, language is symbolic, and poetic style can empower symbols that represent the work and character of the institution. Moreover, poetic language invites imagination; it readily spills over into vision and hope, which are essential to constructive theological reflection in governance. However, the strength of the mission statement may also be its weakness. Language of purpose and character that is not easily contained demands interpretation if it is to serve as a guide to practice.

Trustees consequently need to engage one another in thorough discussion of the mission and values of the institution expressed in its statement, in order to develop a meaningful and working interpretation of that statement. Though they belong to a shared tradition, board members nonetheless are likely to express their beliefs in a variety of ways. Vital traditions allow for such diversity, whether in a congregation, a seminary, or another body serving God's good intentions for humankind and all creation. The point here is that although board members may differ in how they individually express their beliefs, these differences should not preclude them from being able to work together to understand and interpret a mission statement that expresses beliefs they hold in common; on the contrary, such differences promise to make the discussion richer and an interpretation more nuanced. Those who govern in religious institutions bring to their practice a wealth of religious experience and deep faith commitments. The aim of theological discussion as a board is to deepen the practical wisdom and enrich the ways of expressing faith that are already present, while providing one another with the support and encouragement necessary to change minds and venture ideas.

Discussion of corporate mission and values requires a setting, opportunity, and leadership that invite open exploration and expression and that do not rush members to reach normative conclusions. A mini-retreat might provide a desirable sort of setting and opportunity away from the boardroom and agendas. The guidance of a trusted and qualified leader is very important, and such leadership should come, preferably, from the board or from the community the board serves. The president of a seminary, for example, needs to play a prominent teaching role with the board, just as the priest, pastor, or rabbi must with a congregation, facilitating reflection about beliefs implicit and explicit in the statement of purpose, toward a goal of mutual understanding and a sense of shared values and purpose. A facilitator might, for example, highlight significant phrases or values in the statement and organize the members to discuss them either in small groups or, if the board is small, all together. Seeing how the strands weave together to form a whole might serve as a way of uniting the parts. As a closing movement, participants could be asked to name characteristics of the community that hallmark it as their own, relating these identifying marks to their shared tradition and its values.

Exhibit 4.1 suggests a format for a nine-hour retreat devoted to discerning the theological meanings of a seminary or congregation's mission statement, without the expense of travel or the cost of securing outside expertise. A retreat model such as this would be good opportunity for equipping a board to center its problem-solving tasks within the frame of

Exhibit 4.1. A Nine-Hour Mini-Retreat for Mission Reflection.

1. Use the congregation or seminary's mission statement for board conversation to identify shared beliefs; ask questions about what it says about who God is, what God is doing in the world, and how we are related to God's purpose; read between the lines. (2 hours)

2. Identify and present an issue currently facing the board, calling for decision; for the retreat, choose a short-term, straightforward issue—for example, deciding on a process for evaluation of performance review. (1 hour)

3. Break the board into small groups of 6–8 people each for conversation drawing on theological meanings in the mission statement, participants' experiences, and knowledge available in the group; arrive at several alternative approaches to solving the problem. (1.5 hours)

4. Have groups present proposals to the full board, explaining how they reached their conclusions and what problems they foresee with each; have the board choose one proposal for further development based on theological insights from the mission statement and participants' experiences. (up to 2 hours)

5. Have small groups reconvene or reconfigure to consider the board's proposal as if it were a new problem, with each group having the task of providing a theologically informed, practical solution to the problem. (1.5 hours)

6. Have the board choose one of the solutions proposed for implementation. (.5 hour)

7. Engage in critical reflection on the process; discuss what has been learned about the board's work of theological reflection in action. (.5 hour)

Note: *If time is a problem, the workshop could be divided into three sessions: (1) step 1, (2) steps 2–4, (3) steps 5–7.*

the institution's mission statement by providing language drawn from the community's traditions for use in practical reasoning. In addition, the framework of the retreat provides a model for doing theological reflection. The board learns in the process a repeatable skill that will be helpful to its practice of governance.

Reading Skills for Practicing Governance

If we pull back for a wide-angle view of what is going on in the process outlined here for interpreting the mission statement, a more generally applicable method and model comes into view. The mission statement provides a vision of shared beliefs and values and as such plays a pivotal role in any process of interpreting, or reading, situations that come before the board requiring decision and action. It expresses in its vision and values the "goods internal," as described earlier, to the practice of governance for a particular board. It provides the guide for normative behavior of the board and, more broadly, of those who belong to the institution. Finally, it establishes the grounds for evaluating the activity of the board, for defining what excellence in board practice in the institution means.

Rather than thinking of governance practice as problem solving, it may be more helpful, as well as more accurate, to think of it as *interpreting situations that call for corporate response in light of the institution's mission or purpose and values in order to act in "good faith," in continuity with the institution's tradition, yet extending the tradition to meet present circumstances.* Theological reflection as a skill necessary for practicing governance, then, would involve a model and method of interpretation.

Situations that a board must interpret come to it routinely in complex forms (on interpreting situations, see Farley, 1987). Recall the story with which this chapter opened. The board in this case must come to understand the *meaning* of falling enrollment and aging physical facilities, and the need for innovation and expansion to meet changing educational needs, all of which are part of the situation it presently faces. A congregational board might have to face losing significant leadership, deciding whether to support a particular social service project in the community, or determining how to participate in ecumenical worship involving other denominations and religious traditions. Life circumstances addressed by religious governance are usually multilayered in a similar fashion. To put it differently, changing situations pose systemic, interrelated problems to which boards must respond at a depth equal to that of the presenting situation.

A Model for Interpretation

A model that has proved useful in other practical theological reflection settings, particularly in preparing students for congregational ministry and with small groups in congregations, is also helpful for a board's interpretive work. This model (detailed in Table 4.1) moves through four phases (see Exhibit 4.2) aimed at exploring in depth the meaning of a situation using the resources of a community's traditions in critical conversation with other resources, such as experience or knowledge from the social sciences or culture. The aim of the phases is to achieve the theologically informed practical wisdom for deciding what to do in keeping with the community's identity, and for planning ways to evaluate the effectiveness of actions taken. The model assumes that the present situation has narrative qualities, that it is a potential part of the growing historical tradition of the community.

Table 4.1. An Interpretation Model of Theological Reflection and Governance.

Presenting Problem:

Naming Situation	Interpreting Meaning	Responding Faithfully	Evaluation and Reflection
Method: Brainstorming, gathering and ordering information, observations, feelings, and opinions	*Method:* Critical reflection through a process of structured conversation on the problem posed	*Method:* Imaginative and creative planning process	*Method:* Critical reflection on practice through interview, observation, and conversation
*Questions for Discernment**	*Conversation Resources*	*Questions for Testing Structures**	

1. Who is involved?	1. The traditions of faith
	  • scripture
	  • theology
	  • history
		1. Is proposed action congruent with and expressive of the institution's mission?	Evaluation planning should be in place before action-response to the posed problem.

2. What's our current practice and how does it relate to our mission statement?	2. The institution's mission statement and planning strategies	2. Does a proposed solution address the need as it is now understood?	

3. What is working and what is not?	3. Interpretive resources from
	  • business and economics
	  • education
	  • governance literature
	  • other human sciences
		3. What changes in the institution's life are required?	

4. Who is affected?	4. Trustee and institutional experience	4. Are there short-term and long-term responses to be made?	Testing for outcomes or effectiveness may be
			  • measurable
			  • narrative
			  • aesthetic

5. What feelings are raised by this issue?		5. Which constituencies are served?	
6. Whose voices need to be heard here?		6. Is a proposed response practical? Can it be done, given • financial limits	
7. What's been my (our) experience with this kind of situation?			
8. What are the questions or concerns of faith visible here on first reading?			

Hoped for Outcomes	Hoped for Outcomes	Hoped for Outcomes
• Clear focus on a problem posed to the board, with an understanding of primary and secondary issues • Getting "on the table" any feelings, opinions, frustrations, and commitments that are likely to affect discussion of the issue • Group-building around a particular issue with importance to the life of the institution • Renewing awareness of present practices and mission vision • Forming a group for practical wisdom	• Full and deep understanding of an issue calling for action • Articulation of what faith requires of a governing board in the present situation (practical wisdom) • Increase in theological reflection skills for trustees	• A plan of action that is reasonable and responsive to the needs of the situation and the mission of the institution • A plan for implementation and accountability

• time constraints
• personnel available

7. Who will carry out the plan of action?

Hoped for Outcomes

• A plan for ongoing evaluation of planned action
• An opportunity for reflection on practice that can lead to future problem-posing and reflection (the practical wisdom circle of action-reflection-action)

*The questions suggested are types from which choices can be made.

Exhibit 4.2. Phases of the Interpretation Model.

1. *Naming:* Take stock of all the complex features of the issue before the board; look for what is there and what is not; listen to all the voices; listen to voices not represented; try to name the heart of the issue in a single sentence, in light of your mission statement.

2. *Interpreting:* Bring all your resources for understanding into honest, mutually correcting conversation with one another, especially attending to the beliefs, vision, and values of your mission statement, in order to understand the meaning of the issue. What's really at stake here? What does it mean to practice governance faithfully in this case?

3. *Responding:* Decide what you will do and how you will implement your decision, in light of your beliefs, vision, and values. Is what you want to do really doable given institutional resources and the time you have to respond to the situation? Does it make sense in light of what you discovered in phases 1 and 2?

4. *Evaluating:* Decide on ways to assess how well you have done. When and how will you know whether and how the situation has been changed by your actions? Also, take time to discuss how you did as a board in the process of interpreting the issue and thinking about it theologically? The new situation now becomes another focus for your reflection and action.

Reading a situation for meaning, therefore, is not unlike reading and interpreting narrative literature—and in the case of religious governance, not unlike reading and interpreting sacred texts.

Three observations need to be made at the outset. First, as part of a practical theological model, the phases move from action to reflection to action to reflection, in contrast to theory-to-practice reasoning. Each of the phases is at any moment both theory laden and action oriented, so separating theory from practice in governance is not in keeping with the reality of the situation. Second, the phases are described as linear, but in truth they are continuously interrelated, with insights in one phase suggesting implications for another. Models are by nature artificial designs intended to shed light on complex realities. Third, because the situation is being read and interpreted in relationship to the tradition of the community being served, that tradition (expressed in the institution's understanding of its mission and shared values) has a predominant voice in the search for understanding of the situation and an appropriate response to it. As we look at the model, we will return to the case with which the chapter began, to imagine how Eleanor and her board might make use of the model.

Phase 1: Naming the Situation

The intention in this phase of the process is to look as carefully and completely as possible at the problem posed. This involves what anthropologist Clifford Geertz has called "thick description" (Geertz, 1973, pp. 3–32). We want to see what lies below the surface of the issue and to recognize various facets of the problem. The difficulty being countered here is our tendency to overlook what we have seen before. Moreover, the point of view from which we see makes a great difference in what we see, and each person comes to an issue with opinions, feelings, and values that shape his or her perspective. Part of the work of description is to identify perspectives among the group that is reading the situation. The "thickness" of description also includes learning the board's history of dealing with situations like this one. This history includes a critical account of how matters have evolved to the way they are. Finally, it includes naming the unheard or unrepresented voices in the process.

Methods suggested for facilitating this phase might include brainstorming or gathering information and opinions in response to specific probing questions. A time line could chart the history of circumstances leading to the present situation. Descriptions of experiences similar to the present situation could be collected and shared by the group. Other interactive methods are easily conceivable. The key here is participation; therefore, methods ought to invite as much involvement by as many people as possible.

The critical outcome to the process of description is to name the problem posed as clearly and succinctly as possible. The statement that emerges from the process will serve as the focus for the phases that follow. It should be shaped with that in mind, and it should connect with the purpose or mission of the institution. Systems theory has helped to distinguish between a *presenting problem* and a *systemic problem*. Similarly, the goal of describing the presenting problem in detail is to understand it systemically, in relationship to the health and well-being of the whole institution.

Let's look at Eleanor's case: How might her board name the situation in which they find themselves? The presenting problem appears to be dropping enrollment, and the implied loss of revenue that goes with it, just as costs seem to be escalating, brought on by the rising maintenance costs attendant to old buildings and the need for a more diverse faculty in order to compete with other schools for students. The tendency might be to name the problem facing the board in a word—money—and the question posed might be, How can we raise more capital to provide for maintenance and hire additional faculty? The negative side of the question is, Why are we losing enrollment and why are the present means of providing money for maintenance not adequate? Each of the facets to the problem might then be given to specialists for evaluation; that is, enrollment issues might be given to the seminary administration, particularly the admissions office; finance issues might be given to the budget and fiance committee of the board; and faculty diversity needs might be handed to the dean and president of the institution, who would eventually report to the academic committee of the board. Recommendations for action could be made by these agents at the next board meeting.

If, however, Eleanor's board listens to the presenting situation at an even deeper level, other dimensions of the issue appear. Beneath the needs for enrollment stabilization, facilities maintenance, and program diversity lies the need for the board to understand the nature and significance of change. The needs they face are really symptomatic of the kind of rapid and often unpredictable change that characterizes contemporary experience—for individuals, families, and organizations. Change (what it means and how to respond to it) is, for Eleanor's board, a theological issue. Regardless of how the conversation within the board is structured, it is essential that the board think about how the tradition within which governance is being practiced understands change—how it happens, where it fits into the framework of institutional beliefs and values, and what would characterize a response that would extend the goods internal to the practice of governance in the particular institution. Perspectives on questions like these in fact provide the context for thinking about the more apparent questions that involve money, enrollment, and program.

Phase 2: Interpreting

In this phase, the process of theological reflection moves from analysis to critical conversation between two significant conversation partners. Resources for understanding and alternative meanings are suggested by various perspectives. Sources for interpreting include, preeminently, the religious tradition of the community, including the identifying documents and belief statements of the local community and of the larger, more inclusive tradition and community of which it is a part. Cultural resources, such as the human sciences and philosophy, also offer ways of understanding contemporary reality. Members of a board are often skilled in many of these areas, such as economics, education, politics, business, and social services. The intention of this phase is to bring these alternative ways of understanding contemporary circumstances into critical and reflective conversation with one another in order, finally, to be able to say what the situation means; that is, to answer the question, How in the light of our tradition, values, and purpose can we make sense of the situation we are facing?

Interpretation as critical conversation is an idea explored thoroughly by theologian David Tracy (1987). What is important here is Tracy's insistence that genuine conversation involves argument, because such conversation must involve persons who are willing to change yet willing to argue for a different point of view and to argue about the convincing quality of another's position. For participants in such conversation in the model being discussed here, genuine, risk-taking engagement with one another in pursuit of practical wisdom means that constructive conflict is appropriate and useful to the work of interpretation. This will be difficult for some boards, which seem to avoid conflict, fearing its destructive possibilities and preferring instead a general sense of harmony and "getting along." It is important, nonetheless, to urge the board members toward honest and open conversation with one another. The outcome intended in this phase is a response to the question implicit in the problem-posing situation: What does the situation require of us to respond to the ongoing, present activity of God in and for the world?

What resources does Eleanor's board have to bring into conversation in search of practical wisdom for their situation? First, they have a mission statement that, it is hoped, members of the board have explored for meaning and made their own through a process of focused discussion and through ongoing introduction of new members to it. Regular corporate reflection on this statement is in fact a good way of incorporating new members into the life and traditions of the board, as well as renewing commitments for long-time board members. Second, the history and tradition of the institution and its practices is a critical resource for the board's search for meaning. Some history here is oral, dependent on the recollection of senior board members, faculty, and staff. Other institutional history is documented, and it is incumbent upon the president, clerk, or another officer to make this history available to board members. Of particular concern in this case is knowledge of how those practicing governance on behalf of the institution previously have thought about and responded to issues like those presently facing the board. Minutes of meetings, as well as memories, can contribute much here. Finally, Eleanor's board would do well to seek the expert knowledge of its own members as well as that of other experts regarding facets of the issue under discussion. In this case, such experts might include people able to interpret statistics, people with economic and investment insight, someone (perhaps the dean) who is alert to the trends and characteristics of current theological education, and someone (perhaps the president or a faculty member) who is particularly able to facilitate theological conversation. How the interpretive conversation might be structured will depend on the size of the board and on time constraints, among other factors. A variety of possibilities exist, including dividing the board into small groups, each responsible for some aspect of the total conversation, or asking one particular group to prepare a guide for the conversation for the whole board, including preliminary comments and evocative questions. It is essential, in any case, that the conversation be open and honest, and that it engage as many participants as possible, so that in the end the understanding of the situation that emerges from the discussion is widely shared.

Phase 3: Responding

This phase invites imaginative and constructive planning, both short range and long range, to address the situation as it is now understood. This is the kind of work that boards are often quite good at doing. Wanting to act, to get things done, seems natural to a group gathered for the purpose of institutional governance. The claim of this model of theological reflection, however, is that appropriate response requires the naming and interpreting steps that precede it and from which action may take direction. In groups that have used this model in congregations and seminary classes, the universal tendency is to jump from problem naming to problem solving, leaving reflection and interpretation aside. Action in this case risks abandoning the tradition, purpose, and values that give particular identity to the institution and substituting technical reasoning for practical wisdom. Methods useful to this phase of the interpretation process might solicit alternative responses from participants, dividing those alternatives into categories, such as "things to do immediately" and "things to do in the future," and connecting suggestions to plans and activities already under way. Imaginative scenarios might be constructed, individually or in groups, to respond to the question, "What if we did. . . ?" Finally, any decisions made need to be realistic; imagination and fantasy are not, after all, the same thing. A group should have some realistic chance of accomplishing whatever decisions it makes in response to the problem posed; otherwise, disappointment and frustration are nearly unavoidable.

Eleanor's board might decide, in light of their practical wisdom regarding change and its manifestations in enrollment, aging buildings, and faculty diversification, to create various responses, some immediate and some more long term. The board needs to set priorities here. Some building maintenance, for example, may not wait; other work might be delayed until a long-term plan that is in keeping with the beliefs, visions, and values of the institution can be set forth. The board might choose to authorize those who usually deal with buildings and grounds expenditures to proceed minimally, while appointing a second group to imagine future needs and ways of attending to them. As at some institutions, such means might include, for example, deciding to sell or share facilities. Student enrollment issues might be addressed by another portion of the community—including but not limited to board members.

How the board interprets the value of this change in enrollment will make all the difference in what it does. It might, for example, decide that the school needs to rethink, in the light of its beliefs, vision, and values, the student constituency being served, and how, as a seminary, it wishes to locate itself among other seminaries within its national religious community. The question of faculty diversity will in some sense have to wait until the question of student constituency has been resolved or the board might want to structure ways of dealing with these two matters in concert.

Phase 4: Evaluation and Reflection

Among the appeals that boards frequently make is for some ongoing means of evaluation. That this is needed is widely conceded; how to do it is less clear. Yet board effectiveness studies show that routine self-evaluation in the course of a board's work is essential to effective performance. In the model of practical theological reflection presented here, evaluation is structured into the process. The means that will be used need to be in place before any action in response to a situation is taken. Moreover, the means of evaluation should be appropriate to the kind of action being planned. Some activity may lend itself to measurable outcomes, particularly activity related to behavioral change. Other activity is more fairly evaluated through narrative, descriptions of experiences, and observations of change. In any case, the guiding standard here is more than "what works." The claim is that tradition, with its values and vision, is the guiding standard for excellence in the practice of trusteeship. To the question "Did it work?" must then be added, "Did it work for good?" and in particular, for the good inherent in the tradition of the institution?

Conclusions

Practical theological reflection as an essential practice of religious governance seems to be an obvious need. It is how what is distinctive about religious institutions finds a determining voice in the board's work. Institutions generally have purpose or mission statements intended to guide their actions and to sustain the identity and ethos that are the institution's character. But only religious institutions have statements of purpose and values that locate the life of the institution and its work, as well as the life of the board, in transcendent purpose related to the presence and intention of God, named and understood in various ways by differing traditions and communities.

The intention of this chapter has been to explore the meaning of theological reflection that is at the heart of the practice of religious trusteeship. In the end, a model and method for discerning the practical wisdom needed for good governance has been suggested. It is obviously one among other possibilities, and the reader is invited to experiment with other models that may be found or created. Indeed, the one offered here is open to alteration and variation.

Nevertheless, the invariable element in any process is the centrality of the community's identity. The character of the community is visible in the tradition that connects the community to its past and its future, to its ethos and distinctive ways of living together, and to its shared values. Because these are at the heart of the institution, they must be at the heart of any effort to practice theological reflection in governance.

Finally, to make practical theological reflection central to practicing religious governance suggests rich possibilities for restructuring the board's time together. Because the situations that the board addresses are most often interrelated, discreet, single-task committees may not be the most helpful structure for discerning meaning and responding to problems posed. Time needed for constructive conversation in search of practical wisdom might suggest different approaches to setting agendas. Committee reports, for example, could be sent out before meetings, and the committees might focus on thinking theologically about their work and the specific issues before them. Or committees might lead the board as a whole in a process of theological reflection that is relevant to the committee's responsibility or to the board's work as a whole.

In any case, practical theological reflection as a part of religious governance is clearly not an add-on to other things the board does. Rather, it is essential and central to the board's work, and as such it may, at its best, become habitual in the best sense of the word. That is our challenge for now.

REFERENCES

Ammerman, N., Carroll, J. W., Dudley, C. S., and McKinney, W. *Studying Congregations: A New Handbook*. Nashville: Abingdon Press, 1999.

Chait, R. P., Holland, T. P., and Taylor, B. E. *The Effective Board of Trustees.* Old Tappan, N.J.: Macmillan, 1991.

Dykstra, C. "Reconceiving Practice." In B. Wheeler and E. Farley (eds.), *Shifting Boundaries: Contextual Approaches to the Structure of Theological Education.* Louisville, Ky.: Westminster/John Knox Press, 1991.

Farley, E. "Interpreting Situations: An Inquiry into the Nature of Practical Theology." In L. S. Mudge and J. N. Poling (eds.), *Formation and Reflection: The Promise of Practical Theology.* Minneapolis: Augsburg Fortress, 1987.

Geertz, C. *The Interpretation of Cultures.* New York: Basic Books, 1973.

Hoge, D. R., Johnson, B., and Luidens, D. A. *Vanishing Boundaries: The Religion of Mainline Protestant Baby Boomers.* Louisville, Ky.: Westminster/John Knox Press, 1994.

Holland, T. P., and Hester, D. C. (eds.). *Education and Performance of Seminary Boards.* Report of an Evaluative Study Undertaken on Behalf of the Lilly Endowment, Inc., Indianapolis, Ind. 1995.

MacIntyre, A. *After Virtue.* Notre Dame, Ind.: University of Notre Dame Press, 1984.

Rasmussen, L. *Earth Community, Earth Ethics.* Maryknoll, N.Y.: Orbis, 1996.

Shön, D. A. *The Reflective Practitioner: How Professionals Think in Action.* New York: Basic Books, 1983.

Tracy, D. *Plurality and Ambiguity: Hermeneutics, Religion, and Hope.* San Francisco: Harper San Francisco, 1987.

PART TWO

IMPROVING THE BOARD'S PERFORMANCE

5

DEVELOPING A MORE EFFECTIVE BOARD

Thomas P. Holland

MOST PEOPLE WHO come onto the board of a religious organization bring substantial life experiences plus skills from other roles in their lives, such as business or professional practice. They accept the position with the hope that they will be able to apply their faith to advancing the mission of the organization, that their skills will be used to serve a cause about which they care deeply.

Soon, however, they confront the realities of endless meetings and wandering discussions of ambiguously identified issues only tangentially related to the important matters facing the organization. Grousing in the hallway or parking lot after the meeting is about as far as they go with their discontents. Some people accept the limitations implicit in the group's behavior, while others leave the role disillusioned and disappointed, vowing never to waste their energy in such efforts again. Few see clear avenues or tools with which they might work to make substantial changes in the quality of the work of the board.

Although boards are responsible for the well-being of their organizations, their specific local duties are often ambiguous and usually there are few penalties for poor performance. As a result, members may not hold themselves to the same high standards in their board work as they do in other aspects of their professional lives. Those members who are the most dissatisfied with the board's performance may simply withdraw rather than fight the tide of routine and the struggle for change. Alternatively, they may accommodate to poor performance by the group and accept it as inevitable. Few members can articulate clear expectations or criteria for board performance, and few boards ever take the time to evaluate their own efforts and draw conclusions about how well they are adding value to their organizations. As a result, many boards of religious organizations underperform and many of their members are dissatisfied with the quality or impacts of their efforts.

Why do so many boards underperform? Some assumptions common to many participants contribute to this circumstance (Chait, Holland, and Taylor, 1996). The senior professionals of many organizations (clergy of congregations, headmasters of schools, deans of seminaries, CEOs of hospitals) see themselves as better prepared to make policy decisions than the members of their boards, who often are laypersons or denominational representatives from some distance. A well-informed board can begin to meddle in day-to-day administrative decisions, undermining the work of the executive and sometimes causing more trouble than help. Experiences with and stories about such boards prompt many presidents or senior clergy to limit or carefully script the information going to their board members about the most important problems the organization faces. As a result, board meetings deal mainly with superficial issues or symbolic gestures.

Another popular assumption about the board's capabilities is that many people believe that an effective executive or minister, not the board, is the real key to the success of the organization. At most, the board plays a background, minor supporting role to that individual's leadership. From this perspective, expecting much of the board or investing much in its development would simply be a misapplication of scarce resources. All that is really needed is to have a minimal board in place to find a replacement if the minister or executive were suddenly to depart or die. Otherwise the group serves only as a monitor, overseeing administrative practice and perhaps serving occasionally as a sounding board for an executive idea.

The negative experiences of some persons with past efforts at board development result in reluctance to direct attention and resources to developing a strong and effective board. Oversimplified and unfocused group exercises or touchy-feely discussions have left memories of disappointment with many who have gone through them. Didactic lectures, authoritative prescriptions about appropriate behavior, and abstract readings of ideal practices fare little better in bringing about substantive changes in board meetings or members' satisfaction with their work.

As a result of such assumptions, most boards are teams that rarely, if ever, practice or rehearse their skills. When they do convene, many are teams in which everyone thinks he is the captain. Many members are influential and successful in other aspects of their lives, accustomed to leadership roles and calling all the shots in their professional positions. Having experienced themselves as experts in other domains, they see little need to examine their performance in this group, to learn from their mistakes here, and to practice better governance. Consequently, there are few occasions for building the team's skills. Individuals end up making decisions for the group, resulting in conflict and frustration for everyone else. Being a productive member of a group is a skill that is new and uncomfortable for many otherwise very accomplished people. But unless the group invests time in reflecting together on its performance, expanding on its strengths and correcting its weaknesses, there is little real learning or growth.

Changing the Board's Culture

Moving from familiar, traditional practices to more useful ones is a lengthy and difficult process. Board practices and customs evolve over long periods, and like any human habit they are resistant to change. Understanding the reasons for habitual practices is useful in identifying steps for change toward better performance and greater accountability.

Every organization has a culture—its constellation of norms, expectations, and customs of doing work ("how we do business here"). These patterns have grown over long periods, starting with the initial leaders, who brought their charismatic gifts and talents to bear on creating and establishing centers for serving some specific human need or interest, whether worship, learning, or providing care for the sick or food and shelter for the homeless. These founding leaders drew around them others who shared the vision and the hard work of turning dreams into bricks and mortar, activities and programs. Over time, new people came into the organization and tasks became specialized—administration, staff, sponsors, overseers. All were drawn by the power of the vision embodied in a specific, living organization. The legends and practices of the founders provided templates or models for newcomers to use to understand their roles and move forward in their tasks of leading the organization.

Among these tasks is dealing with a changing environment. Although many people resist change, every organization has to cope repeatedly with new circumstances in the community, with economic and political pressures, with the needs and concerns of members or clients, and with new organizations coming into the area to address specific aspects of human needs. As this happens, the circumstances and resources that challenged the organization's founders pass into history, and people have to go about the difficult work of adapting themselves to sometimes radically changed environments and expectations (Holland, Leslie, and Holzhalb, 1993).

Such challenges face every congregation, judicatory, school, seminary, hospital, and social service agency.

Private businesses that depend on current customer satisfaction are quickly bankrupt if they don't change their efforts in response to new expectations from their customers. Although religious organizations do not seek to make profits, their survival does depend on the interest and involvement of their members. Those few organizations with large endowments have some buffering from community demands, but most religious organizations do not have that luxury. They seek ways to accommodate to changing circumstances while remaining true to their mission and vision. The sustained involvement of its constituencies is vital to the well-being of every religious organization. The tension between mission and market underlies many issues that come before every board.

Some boards appropriately expect their administrators and staff to pay careful attention to the quality of their own efforts, to make sure they are using scarce resources as efficiently as possible, and to find creative ways to adapt to changing needs or expectations from their members or constituents while remaining true to the organization's historical mission. Boards appropriately expect staff to look to the future, anticipate changes, and prepare to meet them in ways that enable the organization to grow and thrive. Some boards have adapted ideas of long-range or strategic planning from private businesses, applying them to analysis of the organization and preparing for its future. Even those boards that have not attempted to make use of such ideas still expect their administrators to anticipate problems before they turn into crises and to get beyond fire fighting on a daily basis. As circumstances change, they cannot retain practices just because they may have served well in the past. Few boards would accept for long the excuse from staff, "But this is the way we've always done it."

The boards of religious organizations, however, are often the last place to find innovations or changes in practices. Trustees are comfortable telling staff, "Keep an eye on the environment and let us know when any opportunities or threats appear, and make sure that every activity is making efficient use of our limited resources." At the same time, the board itself continues comfortable old habits of work whether they result in appreciable differences to the organization or not. Boards that are familiar with evaluating the performance of their minister or executive seldom take time to assess their own performance and hold themselves equally accountable for results. Rather, expectations of the board are left vague, assessment is avoided, and there are few consequences for poor performance by individual members or by the group as a whole. It is the rare board that develops specific expectations for its members, applies clear criteria to examining its own work, seeks and considers objective information about how its decisions affect others, implements changes in practices to strengthen its own performance, and demonstrates how it expects others to add value to the organization.

It is difficult for any of us to change our habits of work. Our group's customs and approaches may have been successful in dealing with problems in the past and they settle into our minds as semiconscious unspoken assumptions. Newcomers to the board watch and learn subliminally from other members that this is the way we behave here (Schein, 1997). It is difficult for a new member to question or challenge a board's comfortable old practices, and it is even more difficult for the senior members of the group to consider that their familiar ways of working might not be the most effective any more. Even where many members of a board are dissatisfied with the group's performance, few speak up in meetings and offer better ideas about how to proceed. More often, as noted earlier, discontented members grouse in the hallway during breaks or in the parking lot after the session. Some assume that harmony in the group is more important than rigorous analysis of recommendations, and their dysfunctional politeness deprives the group of enriching ideas and perspectives. Other members simply do not recognize or use channels for constructive change.

Many members privately describe the work of their boards as trivial, unsubstantial, and only marginally related to the organization's overall success or failure. All of us consider our time to be valuable, and we dislike situations that seem to be wasting our time or talents. Yet the agenda of many boards rarely requires members to provide much meaningful input or expertise. More often, very capable people sit around a table and are expected to ratify the decisions of others—usually a powerful senior leader or executive committee that carefully scripts what comes to the full board and provides recommended solutions that should not be questioned too vigorously.

Many board meetings follow a time-honored ritual of reading and approving minutes, listening to every committee read its report, voting on predigested recommendations, revisiting some matter of leftover business from a past meeting, and referring any new proposal to a standing committee for later consideration. There are few opportunities for members to dig into major issues or to influence important, unresolved matters. Instead, they are deluged with long reports that often include extensive tables and figures that supposedly support the committee chair's conclusions. As Lawrence Butler discusses in Chapter Ten, volumes of data result in little useful information for participants, leaving them with only obscure perspectives on the truly important issues confronting the organization.

Members of many boards are hesitant to acknowledge an ill-timed or ill-informed decision by the board, perhaps fearing criticism or wanting to save face. It is tacitly assumed that mistakes are individual failures that should be overlooked until they become unavoidable. Then the appropriate step is to replace the failing individual, minimize the damage from that person's error, and move ahead. The board's main role is control and oversight, making sure that the minister or executive does not make big mistakes. Until it is evident that the administrator has committed a major error, the board is to provide enthusiastic support. Such assumptions and the practices that follow from them limit the effectiveness of many boards.

Alternative Assumptions

A more productive approach to governance is to look at the board's performance from a new perspective: the board's main functions are to help the executive or minister identify the most important issues facing the organization in the months and years ahead, to work together to formulate creative responses, and then to shape and fine-tune decisions in partnership as the work of the organization goes forward. It is inevitable that changes in internal or external circumstances will indicate that some decisions are not working as well as expected and need to be revisited. Unexpected barriers arise and unforeseen opportunities are found as the best of plans unfolds, making it necessary for the group to reconsider important decisions and make midcourse corrections (Pound, 1994).

As adults, we learn by reflecting on our experiences, facing mistakes, and making intentional use of them as opportunities to learn how to proceed more effectively. Nurturing an environment where such self-aware reflection can take place without jumping to blaming anyone is vital to the health of any group or organization. Boards that examine their own contributions to decisions (their mistakes as well as their successes) take time to reflect on how they have done their work, and boards that examine unanticipated consequences can identify lessons that will guide them into increasing effectiveness.

Effective boards are composed of members who work intentionally at learning and developing group skills. Cherished traditions and conventional wisdom about the board are discarded for the same reason that any other organization grows and changes—circumstances change and the times are too turbulent and unpredictable to cling to outdated ways of doing business. Strong boards take time to examine their performance, to learn from their successes as well as from their mistakes, and to build skilled teamwork (Senge, 1990).

Requisite Conditions for Successful Board Development

Before a board begins to make changes, a number of obstacles are to be anticipated, including the ambiguous expectations that boards have of their members and of their constituencies as well as the ambiguous expectations that organizations have of their boards, the weak accountability of boards, the unclear returns on investments of time in board development, and members' discomfort over giving up familiar patterns and learning new ones. Overcoming these barriers requires the concerted and sustained attention of the board. Several prerequisites must be in place if these efforts are to be successful (Chait, Holland, and Taylor, 1996).

First, board development cannot be imposed on its members or on the organization's staff. For change to take place, the group must be ready for it and accept the importance of improving its work. The board's chairperson, its senior staff leader, and a substantial number of the board's members must be concerned about the group's performance and want to engage in improving it. These leaders must initiate the process with enthusiasm and clear commitment to mutual efforts to bring about changes. Many of the other board members must come to share these concerns, in the context of loyalty to the organization and its mission. Without this foundation, not much change can be made.

A second prerequisite is to recognize that distinguishing board development efforts from the "real" work of the board is a false dichotomy. A board must take steps to develop improved performance as it works on its business items, rather than do the business and then do development. The processes of learning to work together more effectively should be embedded within the instrumental expectations of the board's responsibilities. Learning involves looking at how the board carries out its tasks and identifying ways that enable the group to work better and produce more useful results as it deals with those tasks.

Next, it is easier to change a board's behavior than to change members' attitudes or personalities. Exhortations and prescriptions do not work nearly as well as changes in routines, procedures, or structures for working together. Members begin to think differently and act differently as a result of such practical steps as bringing thoughtful questions to the board, providing relevant and focused information on the issue, dividing members into small groups to brainstorm alternative solutions and formulate recommendations, and encouraging critical and analytical thinking about issues that are before the group, focusing on specific priorities, and agreeing on steps for accountability.

Development activities should be individually tailored to the specific needs and concerns of the board, rather than assuming that "one size fits all." Although a retreat approach is often useful in getting started, ongoing learning activities should be built into the board's regular agenda and ways of doing business, rather than being treated as separate. Such an approach fits well with the instrumental expectation of many members, who tend to see the board's effectiveness primarily as a means to advance the organization's performance, rather than seeing board development as an end in itself.

Finally, board development must be acknowledged as an extensive, long-term process, not a quick fix. To sustain the process, some board members must be "product champions" for the board and its performance, just as there are advocates for balanced budgets or improved buildings and grounds. The pressures of business as usual are strong, and without continuing, internally initiated attention to how well the board is performing, the board will settle back into comfortable ways of working that may not match the needs of the changing organization or environment.

How a Board Can Begin to Examine Its Own Performance

Board members frequently say they learn their roles through osmosis, by watching and listening to others around the table. Because they have little information about alternative approaches to carrying out governance responsibilities, most newcomers are hesitant to question or criticize a group's customary practices, so they come to accept observed behavior as normative. Usually the meeting agenda is quite crowded with many issues that apparently are important to someone and demanding attention, and chairpersons may pride themselves on limiting discussion to a few direct comments about a committee's recommendation before calling for a vote and moving on. It is the rare participant who is willing to risk looking naive by asking basic questions about why particular matters are included on the agenda or why the group approaches dealing with them as it does—especially if the participant is not prepared to offer an obviously better alternative.

Efficiency at the wrong tasks is hardly productive for anyone. To guide the board's attention to the quality of its own performance, it is important for leaders to find times when and ways in which reflective discussions can take place about how the board is carrying out its work as well as about what it is addressing. Rather than just waiting for some courageous member to question a practice, leaders can take advantage of naturally occurring events in the life of the organization to call attention to how well the board performed in that circumstance (Savage, 1994).

For example, a board could pause after the successful completion of a difficult task or a major project to reflect on what specific things led to success, where the group might have worked more effectively, and what lessons could be learned from the experience to take into the future. The departure of a minister or the election of a new chairperson also provides a natural time for a group to consider how it contributed to the successes or problems of the previous incumbent and what it could do to be more helpful to the newcomer. An opportunity to take on a new program or service, or the threat of a new competitor coming into the region, could be used to instigate thoughtful discussion about how the board deals with the challenge of maintaining faithfulness to its mission while responding appropriately to new and changing circumstances.

More problematic events, such as conflicts among board members or between them and staff or another constituent group, challenge the group's problem-solving skills. Although it is difficult to focus on strengthening those skills while also trying to solve the immediate problem, it would be natural to take time later to discuss what the board learned about itself from the experience and what changes it should make to be better prepared to handle or prevent similar situations in the future. Unfortunately, once the pressure of the crisis is over, so often is the concern of some to look at how the board responded. It is very difficult to resist pulling back into the familiar practice of business as usual.

Boards of religious organizations can draw on their shared beliefs about forgiveness and reconciliation when discussing mistakes. Falling short of high expectations is a common human experience, but religious traditions emphasize the importance of acknowledging failure, forgiving ourselves and others, and embarking on new efforts together. When drawn into board reflections, such resources can make governance one more area in which our faith guides relationships.

Even when it is not facing some major problem, a board can periodically ask its executive or minister to talk candidly about the challenges facing the organization in the coming year. Instead of demanding that the leader present solutions to a problem, the board can enter into a more mutual process of thinking together about emerging issues well before they are formulated as problems. What are the implications of changes in attendance or giving or the age composition of our congregation? How should this seminary deal with the changing expectations of our students or of the congregations who hire them? How should this hospital prepare for coming changes in national and state health policies and for competitors in our region?

Reflective discussions of emerging trends or anticipated future challenges involve the group in identifying and shaping the issues that later it will address more formally. Then the board can ask itself what steps it might take to extend its understanding of these issues so as to be prepared when they must be faced. Basically, the board should make sure that it has in place ways to sustain its awareness of and attention to the few most important issues facing the organization, to formulate priorities and stick with them rather than trying to deal with everything that comes along.

Newcomers' questions about board practices, assumptions, or priorities offer additional opportunities for a board to examine itself and consider alternative ways of carrying out its work. Questions of competing priorities often underlie the issues before a board, and revisiting a group's conclusions about how it balances its mission with its opportunities and constraints can open up creative possibilities that may have been overlooked in the past.

Another window of opportunity for a board to direct attention to its own performance is in discussions of how the organization is dealing with accountability for its use of resources. Many boards expect the top administrator to report on how staff are being held accountable, and some go on to specify expectations of the administrator and criteria for assessing that person's performance. Far fewer boards, however, apply the same principles to themselves and have clear evidence of how the board itself is being accountable for its use of time and resources.

Developing means for demonstrating its own accountability is a major way the board can model the behaviors it expects of others in the organization. This process begins with recognizing that the board has the duty to be accountable for its responsibilities just as other members of the organization do. The next step is for the board to engage in candid discussions of how well it has been carrying out this obligation. Rather than seeking to blame anyone for failure, the board's basic concern is to identify practical steps it could take to improve its own performance. Useful questions for group discussion include the following:

- How is this board adding value to the organization, beyond the contributions of staff and administration?

- What specific steps should the board take to improve its performance and increase the value it adds to the organization?

- What criteria or indicators would be appropriate for monitoring and demonstrating the board's improved performance?

- How will we obtain and use such information to make further improvements in our work?

Accountability is a difficult issue for many people in religious organizations these days. It is often seen through memories of unfortunate past experiences in which authority was misused, provoking understandable resentment and fear. Rather than approaching this matter in terms of forced compliance with external rules or avoidance of blame or public embarrassment, it is far more productive to approach accountability as a matter of mutual expectations and shared commitments among members. Conversations about shared goals, mutual promises, and steps the group will take together to attain their goals serve to build a climate of responsibility and commitment to one another. Such commitments guide behavior more powerfully than external rules or threats (Fry, 1995). Intentional examination of the board's commitments and of the ways it will ensure that they are carried out are major ways to strengthen individual and group performance.

Successes, failures, transitions, competing demands, questions about accountability, and ambiguous issues surface in any organization, and all provide natural opportunities for the board to reflect together on how it has contributed to understanding issues and analyzing them creatively, how it performed in the time leading up to an event or decision, how its initiatives and responses (or the lack of them) may have contributed to the situation and its consequences, and how it might change its practices in order to become more effective in handling such matters in the future. Productive learning may be guided by a board taking time to ask itself reflective questions such as the following:

- How did we get into this situation?

- What indicators or clues did we focus on and which did we miss?

- How did we decide what was important for our attention and what was not?

- Which alternatives did we consider and did we miss some?

- What steps should we take to become more aware of the important factors in such situations, less distracted by unimportant ones, and more aware of creative alternative solutions?

- What should we learn from this experience and how should we apply that learning so we will work more effectively together on situations like this in the future?

Turning Criticisms into Opportunities

Another common experience in many boards is to hear grapevine complaints or discontent from some participants about the board's work. Almost every board chairperson has listened to rumblings from members that their time or talents were not being well used or that the wrong issues or people were taking up the board's attention. Complaints about the behavior of other people often come to the chairperson or the executive. Often those voicing such grumbles have no constructive solutions or only superficial quick fixes that don't address the underlying issues of the board's responsibility and performance.

If the leader accepts sole responsibility for trying to solve the problem presented, the problem will remain a matter of personal failure or success. What the leader needs to do instead is transform the issue into a *group* opportunity, to make use of it as an occasion for the group to probe, question, accept, reject, redefine, understand, and deal with the issue together. By taking this step, the leader makes the situation into an opportunity for the group to develop its governance skills. Most of the group's problems are matters of group performance—often involving its failure to specify and enforce norms of behavior with its own members—so solutions must be found at that level and in that arena.

In whatever way they surface, signals of discontent or blaming can be used by the board's leaders as an occasion for the board to look at itself. Rather than trying to solve problems quietly and in private, questions about how well an individual is doing his or her job can be treated as an invitation to the full board to consider together what it expects of *all* its members or its staff and what steps of accountability it will take. Questions about the meeting agenda can be brought to the floor for consideration: Are we making the best use of our limited time together, focusing on the top priority issues, and keeping ourselves on track and undistracted by peripheral issues? What expectations and criteria should we apply to the performance of all our members? How should we monitor and evaluate everyone's performance as well as that of the group as a whole? What changes should we make as a group in order to keep our attention focused and our actions coordinated on our most important issues? How will we deal with efforts to move our attention to other issues? How can we demonstrate accountability for our own actions as a board?

If the board wants to move from individual judgments to shared ownership and action by the group, the individual's concern must be brought to the table for everyone's attention and work. Defining the problem is a group responsibility, as is finding a solution and implementing it. Such steps enable the discontented individual to take some constructive responsibility for his or her complaints, and they allow the group to consider whether it agrees with the individual's formulation of the problem as well as to consider how to work on finding solutions in which all members can share. Us-versus-them polarizations are destructive to any group, and win-win alternatives should be found that allow the group to come together around solutions that meet everyone's needs and interests.

Effective board leaders don't wait for discontent to fester outside of meetings. A good practice is to take some time at the conclusion of every meeting of the full board as well as its committees to ask evaluative questions about how the group did the work it has just completed. Such an invitation to offer evaluative comments to the whole group allows members to voice concerns well before they become serious problems, and they enable others in the group to offer alternative perspectives that may correct misunderstandings underlying another's complaint. The discussion provides everyone with an opportunity to take responsibility for improving the group's work in future sessions and provides support to leaders in efforts to change meeting practices so that everyone feels more productive and satisfied.

Here are some examples of evaluative questions that may be considered by the group at the conclusion of a committee meeting or a session of the full board:

- Have we spent our time on the most important issues facing this organization? If not, why not?
- Have we stuck to our priorities? If not, how should we set priorities among the many things we are facing? Then what should we do in the future to ensure that we stay focused on them?
- What criteria should we use in selecting and ordering our work?
- What specific expectations do we have for ourselves individually and as a group? How can we make sure that everyone understands and acts on them?
- Are the questions before us clear and specific? If not, what should we do to become clear?
- Do we have the right information with which to work? Is it coming at the right time and in the right forms for us to understand and use it?
- Are we all approaching the issues with similar expectations and value judgments? If not, what should we do to clarify our expectations and identify shared values?

- What practical steps should we take so that our next meeting will be more productive and satisfying? Who will do what? How will we deal with unproductive processes or dissatisfying efforts?

By bringing out members' concerns for consideration by the full group, the board begins to build mutual ownership of issues and solutions, allowing everyone to contribute to the formulation of the issue and to join in finding and implementing mutually acceptable solutions. It thus treats problems as issues belonging to the group rather than just blaming individuals. It makes change a group concern and finding successful solutions a group accomplishment. Time spent on building group ownership of behavior and refining the group's work patterns pays off extensively in future effectiveness.

Assessing the Board's Performance

Discussions about improving board performance can be taken an important step further by getting more extensive information from all members and other constituencies regarding their views of the board's work, areas needing attention, and suggestions for change. A broad inquiry allows individuals to find out if their concerns are shared by others. A related function of gathering such information is that it serves to spread responsibility for findings and conclusions across the whole group, thus building ownership of conclusions and consensus for taking steps of change. As one experienced member emphasized, "Any board interested in improving should get going with an evaluation of its strengths and weaknesses. It should ask a whole series of tough questions about what's working well and what isn't. You can't depend on just a few insiders to run things. You're *all* the owners of the organization and all responsible for finding ways that enable you to help it work better."

Many tools and procedures are available for boards to use in such efforts (Holland, 1991; Jackson and Holland, 1998). They may be divided into those that focus on group performance and those that address individual performance. A few approaches link these domains, including self-evaluations, constituency surveys, third-party reviews, internal reviews by an ad hoc or standing committee, reflective discussions of critical incidents, and feedback at the conclusion of meetings. A board may try out several approaches and decide which ones are most productive and relevant to its concerns, or it may decide to formulate its own criteria.

Probably the easiest way to carry out board assessments is to make a regular practice of taking a few minutes at the end of each meeting to hear and discuss participants' views of how well the work went and what steps might be taken in the next session to help things go better. Both what was done and how well it was carried out are important considerations. The board chairperson could invite comment on such matters as the following:

- The relative importance of items on the agenda
- The clarity of linkages between each agenda item and the board's priorities
- The relevance and helpfulness of background materials, reports, or resources provided
- The specificity of the questions put to the group
- The adequacy of opportunities for members' input
- The overuse or underuse of meeting time for participants' inputs
- The clarity of conclusions
- The feasibility of action plans
- The structure or processes of the meeting
- The roles and actions of the leaders
- Suggestions for changes in the next meeting

Some board members may initially be reluctant to express criticisms openly, so soliciting anonymous written comments may be useful. The leader can distribute paper or index cards on which participants can write comments about aspects of the board that need attention. Whether oral or written comments are collected, the leader should summarize the highlights of the feedback and take explicit steps to incorporate suggestions into the format or procedures of subsequent meetings, thus demonstrating that members' concerns are taken seriously.

Feedback from evaluations done at the end of meetings has the advantage of being informal and nonthreatening, coming from fresh experience, and involving all participants in looking for ways to improve the group's performance. Everyone has opportunities to identify concerns, hear how others view the situation, and join in the search for better approaches. The full group comes to own responsibility for improving its performance.

A variety of more formal board evaluation tools are available that address a wide range of governance roles and functions. Many of these have been developed for other types of nonprofit organizations, but they can be easily adapted for use by religious groups. Typically such tools feature a list of specific duties or expectations of the board, and for each aspect of board performance there are questions inviting respondents to rate the board on a scale ranging from "excellent" to "needs improvement" or from "strong" to "weak."

One good example is the workbook *Self-Assessment for Nonprofit Boards* (Sleisinger, 1991), published by the National Center for Nonprofit Boards. The format of this book includes a number of specific questions on such aspects of the board as the following:

- Clarity of its mission and purpose
- Evaluation and support of the executive
- How well the board monitors organizational programs and services
- Its performance in raising funds and managing financial resources
- Involvement in strategic planning
- Orientations for new members
- Relationships between board and staff
- Public relations and communication with constituencies
- Board operations

Board self-assessment tools such as this are readily available and easily adaptable to local needs and circumstances. A board can use them to generate ideas in designing its own self-assessment process, drawing on existing questions and adding items based on its own goals and its expectations of members. This process should begin with a full discussion of the major tasks and duties the board expects of its members, the goals and purposes the group wants to fulfill for the organization, and important aspects of how it wants to go about doing its work.

This list of expectations provides the basis for formulating a series of questions that compose the evaluation form. For example, one question might be, How well has the board's time been used to work on the most important issues facing the organization? Another might be, How well have your talents and interests been used in the work of this board? After each question, respondents can mark their assessment on a scale ranging from high to low or strong to weak. Space may be left for individual comments and suggestions.

On the boards of some religious organizations, a committee has been asked to take responsibility for distributing and collecting board assessment questionnaires every year or two. This committee may also meet with members to discuss their assessments and then to work out individual learning plans so that each participant grows in effectiveness as a contributor to the team. The committee summarizes the major themes from all respondents in a report to the full board and recommends specific steps to help the board as a whole with problematic areas. For example, if several members express concern over understanding the organization's financial statements, an educational session on that topic for the full board might be needed. Issues that concern only one or two individuals may be addressed in a variety of ways, such as the following:

- Rotating committee assignments
- Serving as an understudy for another board role
- Attending a conference or workshop on a specific issue
- Reading books or articles on an area of concern
- Talking with members of other boards to identify alternative approaches to an issue

Another approach to board assessment makes use of outside experts or consultants who collect and analyze information on the board. These persons may be suggested by a denominational office, judicatory leader, accrediting body, another board, or other respected source. They are selected for their broad experience and knowledge about governance of similar organizations. Their function is somewhat like that of a financial auditor in that they check into a range of areas or aspects of the board's performance, drawing on several sources of information. They may interview board members, senior staff, the participants ("consumers") in the organization, and others. They may review meeting minutes and records, observe board and committee meetings, and talk with other local leaders.

The findings and conclusions of the outside evaluator are pulled together into a written report that identifies strengths and weaknesses and sets forth recommended steps for action to improve the board's performance. These recommendations may draw on the experiences and approaches of other boards in similar situations and from "best practices" across many organizations. The consultant may also meet with the full board to provide an oral presentation of findings and conclusions, followed by discussion of next steps for work on improving the board's performance.

There are several advantages of making use of an outside evaluator. This person is less likely to overlook problems that some board members may be reluctant to face and more likely to raise difficult questions than insiders may dare. Members may consider it safer to disclose their concerns to a neutral outsider, and such a person can more easily separate an issue from an individual source, thus avoiding personalizing differences. The outside expert can bring a wealth of experience from many organizations and knowledge of governance practices that are wider than the experiences of many individual board members. Disadvantages of this approach include the expense, as well as the possibility that the board might not own the conclusions if it has not done the work of evaluation itself.

Retreats as Means to Work on Board Performance

A great many boards have found that periodic retreats are powerful tools for stimulating and extending board growth. Typically a one- or two-day special meeting held off-site, away from wherever the group usually meets, a retreat allows a group to devote extended time to working on a major issue, such as developing or updating its strategic plan, gaining a better understanding of the external environment, clarifying its mission, solving some problem, or many other purposes.

A board development retreat is an investment in the future of the board and the organization it governs. It provides an opportunity to step back from routine business agendas for an in-depth look at the future and the board's role in it. A retreat can be a major boost to the board's efforts to make more effective and efficient use of the time it gives to the organization.

Boards have found that their retreats have served a number of important purposes:

- Strengthening performance through a review of governance processes and the board's roles and responsibilities
- Assessing the board's contributions to the organization and identifying ways it can add greater value
- Establishing priorities for the board and identifying strategies and actions to achieve them
- Enhancing collegiality and working relationships among board members and between board and staff
- Determining next steps in board development and in the implementation of overall action plans

There are numerous resources a board may use in planning and conducting a retreat (Savage, 1994; Holland, 1997). Many denominational organizations have staff, materials, and other resources for conducting board retreats. The National Center for Nonprofit Boards in Washington, D.C., publishes useful resource materials on board development and maintains lists of consultants and facilitators in many regions of the country.

A retreat can generate a great deal of enthusiasm among participants. However, a board can lose momentum when it returns to its regular meeting schedule and revert to familiar patterns. Likewise, turnover in membership will introduce newcomers who are unacquainted with the board's efforts to change behavior and improve performance. Agenda items that are scheduled almost automatically demand attention, and promises made at a retreat may be forgotten like last year's New Year's resolutions. Therefore, it is essential to have explicit methods for reminding everyone of the agreements and changes identified at the retreat, and regular evidence of how those resolutions are being implemented. The underlying goal is to build habits of reflection and learning into the group's culture so that newcomers (as well as old-timers) are socialized into effective patterns of behavior.

Ongoing Board Education

No matter how successful a retreat is, the real work is not yet done. Everyone who has participated in a retreat or in other extended time away in order to concentrate on any issue is familiar with the problem of coming back to the "real world" and trying to implement the great resolutions for change in the face of daily pressures and demands. Without rigorous attention, the best of commitments become but fond memories of what might have been, if only there weren't the urgent demands of today. Although retreats offer extended times for identifying and working on changes in the board's performance, they cannot replace the day-to-day hard work of acting on the plans that boards set for themselves. Improvements in board performance depend on sustained attention to how the board is doing its work, as well as to what it is working on. Ongoing board education, application, assessment, reflection, and improvement must be integrated into the group's basic understanding of what it is all about (Taylor, Chait, and Holland, 1996).

Effective boards acknowledge their need for continuous learning, and they take responsibility for expanding their competencies. They identify topics and issues to examine, develop appropriate programs and resources, and encourage all members to participate in ongoing educational sessions. Special speakers, miniseminars, study groups, visits with other boards, attendance at conferences on governance, and rotation among committee assignments are among the ways that these boards encourage ongoing education among their members.

It is especially important to have thorough orientation programs for all incoming members that enable them to get off to a good start by giving them clear expectations about board membership, extensive explanation of the board's roles and responsibilities, and other appropriate information about the organization. Mentoring of each newcomer by a more experienced member is another useful practice that provides both members with a greater awareness of board performance.

A board can enlarge this process of education by assisting every member to develop an individual learning plan that will enable him or her to make greater contributions to the group in the coming year. This process may be as simple as rotating committee assignments or as extensive as sending members to conferences on governance or bringing in speakers on topics that members want to understand better.

A few boards have developed procedures for all their members to set individual performance goals and obtain feedback from one another on their progress. They make use of feedback to coach members in improving their contributions to the group's overall effectiveness. Such sessions are useful in helping members understand others' views of their behavior and in identifying ways in which they may make more helpful contributions to the group in the future. In these ways boards can make use of individual and group goals, as well as monitor and provide feedback to sustain attention on improving performance.

Outside speakers and mentors from other boards are additional resources useful to helping a board learn. Many national and regional denominational offices can recommend knowledgeable leaders to serve in such educational or consultative roles, and some boards also recruit resource persons from other organizations in their area that are similar to their own. Any board can make occasional use of outside consultants, mentors, or evaluators to help the group gain independent perspectives on its performance, to identify issues needing attention, and to learn about useful practices of other boards.

Restructuring Meeting Time and Committee Work

Every board experiences the dilemma of limited time but virtually unlimited issues and demands. One common way of dealing with this problem is to create various committees, each of which is allocated a set of related issues or tasks. Many boards report that the real work of the board actually goes on in these committee meetings, while plenary sessions of the full board serve mainly to ratify the conclusions reached in the committee meetings. One result is that most members find the committee meetings far more satisfying and productive than the full board meetings.

An important aspect of improving performance is restructuring the board's use of committees and meeting time to emphasize its strategic priorities. Careful use of the scarce resource of meeting time is a concern of many members, and many sense that agendas try to pack too many issues into limited meeting time. Meeting agendas should be designed so that they sustain focus on the few most important issues of strategy and policy. Preparation for making changes in the agenda may begin with having a member simply monitor the amount of time the board spends on each issue in a meeting and then rate its relevance to the board's priorities. The board can discuss the feedback, consider the relationship between its priorities and its actual use of time, and decide together on steps for designing and implementing its meeting agendas.

Better use of meeting time can result from setting clear priorities for the board's attention and leaving nonessential items for individual review. Strong boards limit the agenda of meetings to a few top-priority matters rather than trying to cover the waterfront. Routine reports and nonexceptional motions that require board approval can be clustered into a set, a "consent agenda," that will be voted on in one action rather than voted on separately. Any member can request that an item be separated out for discussion, thus protecting the board's ultimate right to examine any issue. However, the practice of clustering allows the board to concentrate most of its attention on the matters of highest priority to the organization and avoid getting bogged down in operational details.

Restructuring how the board organizes and charges its committees is another way to improve performance. Instead of committees that mirror administrative divisions (such as personnel, programs, finances, or property), boards should let form follow function. The board's strategic priorities provide the point of departure from which work group assignments and meeting agendas are derived. Board committees or teams should be constructed to focus members' efforts directly on each of the board's goals, with a team responsible for sustaining movement on each one and then dissolving when its goal is attained.

Rather than using board meeting time to hear routine reports from every committee, the board can structure each meetings to focus on one or two goals or priorities, with discussions led by the subgroups that have carried out the background preparation and clearly formulated the questions needing attention. Leaders should make sure that every report begins with a clear statement of the questions being presented and how the issue is linked with a specific goal or priority of the board.

For changes to outlast individuals and become embedded in the board's culture there must be some "champions" for the group's performance. To build in advocacy for the board's own learning, the group can assign to a few members the tasks of reminding the board of its commitments, monitoring its performance, and periodically recommending actions that will strengthen meeting processes. Strong boards have their committee on nominations or some other ongoing team or subgroup take the responsibility for developing and implementing steps for monitoring board meetings, soliciting participants' assessments and recommendations for improvement, and arranging for periodic board education sessions and retreats on major issues of interest. This team makes use of its findings to coach members in expanding their leadership contributions to the board, to identify skills needed in new members, and to plan regular educational sessions in areas where the board needs improvement.

The group's experience in carrying out these tasks is directly applicable in its consideration and nomination of future members. What members have learned about the group's performance broadens the scope of characteristics they seek in new members. Instead of just looking for stars, they also consider candidates' skills in such important areas as ability to work with the group, linkages to key constituencies, ability to contribute new perspectives to examining issues, and a track record of making positive contributions to group communication and learning.

Building Group Cohesion and Teamwork

Although many board members are more comfortable considering instrumental and structural changes in the board's work, the interactions among members and their group relationships are equally in need of attention. The most effective boards take careful steps to transform their assembly of talented individuals into a well-integrated team.

Developing a strong team is a long, difficult, and risky process. It requires taking critical issues to the group for deliberation and then taking the time necessary to hear the views of each participant, rather than relying on a few leaders to predigest issues and present preformulated conclusions. It requires that the issues taken to the board be truly vital to the future of the organization, not just window dressing. It requires making sure that everyone has equal access to information about the issues and the organization. It requires taking time for members to get to know one another beyond the formal setting of the boardroom.

Strong boards pay careful attention to expanding communications among members, to nurturing and sustaining inclusive relationships, and to building a sense of mutual responsibility for the board's success. They are aware that it may be the silent member who has some important concerns that the board needs to hear. Social events and informal time for conversations are important means to building trusting relationships.

The most effective steps for building group cohesion are ones that closely link instrumental and relational components and allow members to deal with the latter by means of overt attention to the former. As noted earlier, working to formulate goals for the board itself is a good means for building group cohesion while also serving to focus the board's use of time and energy. Goals for the board should be distinct from but lead to the overall goals it has for the organization. Such goals identify what the board will do to maximize its contributions to the attainment of the organization's strategic goals.

Once the board identifies its own goals, they should be kept in the front of everyone's awareness by posting them in conspicuous places and by repeating them in meetings and at the outset of reports. Keeping the board's goals paramount in meetings by means of the agenda and the focus of each report or discussion serves to sharpen awareness about the purpose and direction of each step. It also allows the board to monitor and evaluate its progress toward its goals.

Throughout these steps, an underlying concern is to develop a stronger sense of inclusiveness and cohesiveness among board members as a group. This requires paying careful attention to communications among members and intentionally nurturing and sustaining inclusive relationships. These processes should begin at recruitment and orientation, be carried forward by all leaders, and be reinforced at social times and retreats. Strong boards are careful to schedule social time and informal interaction for their members. They celebrate members' accomplishments, have meals together before or after meetings, take breaks for refreshments, make regular use of name tags, and participate as a group in social events sponsored by the organization.

Roles of the Chairperson and the Executive

The relationship between the board's chairperson (usually a lay volunteer) and the organization's paid executive (whether priest, rabbi, president, dean, or director) is probably the most important link in the performance of the board and the whole organization. Together they set the level of expectations, pace of change, and model of performance. Their thoughtful leadership is essential in creating and sustaining an effective board. While some administrators fear a strong board and follow the cynical advice of "keep them in the dark so they'll leave you alone," most have come to recognize that a strong board can be their best partner in creating a strong organization. Some take the partial step of gathering around them only a small "kitchen cabinet" of trusted board members, while others rely on a strong executive committee of the board. Because either of these halfway approaches signals that some opinions are more important than others, they limit the growth and potential contributions of the full board.

If the board is to add greatest value to the whole organization, the board's chairperson and the top staff person must be committed to leading the effort to learn better ways of working together, taking the initiative in raising members' sights and expectations of themselves, and modeling the behavior they want others to follow. Together they raise questions by which the group can reflect on its performance and assist members in thinking about new approaches to their work. They describe alternative ways of understanding and dealing with common problems, thus raising members' awareness and aspirations and preparing the group for taking steps of change.

By opening up discussion about the board's performance, the leaders demonstrate that it is appropriate to direct attention to the board's own work and to explore ways of improving it together. Rather than avoiding discontentments or treating problems as occasions for blaming someone, effective leaders turn problems into occasions for the group to learn more effective ways of carrying out its work. Discontentments are moved from back channels to the forefront of everyone's attention, and the group is invited to take on responsibility for diagnosing the problem, identifying solutions, and deciding together on better ways to deal with issues. The leaders model the desired behavior of respectful listening and constructive use of feedback to improve the quality of work, thus inviting others to join in similar steps. In so doing, they confirm that everyone should be committed to doing their jobs more effectively, not just avoiding criticisms, blaming others, or settling for business as usual.

Effective leaders expect and tolerate the anxiety that inevitably comes with questioning old assumptions and relinquishing familiar practices for the unknown. Their persistence in seeking improvements, even when solutions may not yet be apparent, encourages critical thinking and experimentation with new approaches to dealing with tasks, and it invites others to try out alternatives without fear of being blamed for mistakes along the way. Reflecting on experiences together, identifying areas to change, and trying out new approaches are difficult but crucial steps in learning for anyone in the organization, including the board. Leaders recognize and celebrate incremental steps toward the goal of improved board performance, thus establishing the board, itself, as a model for others in the organization.

Conclusions

Boards serve as models to others throughout the organization of the behaviors they value. Board members are appropriately seen as the leaders of the organization, and their decisions are subjected to critical scrutiny by all constituencies. Boards appropriately are concerned about the quality, costs, productivity, and innovation of staff; however, many boards are hesitant to apply the same expectations to themselves. Boards that call for accountability of staff have far greater credibility if they "walk the talk" and show by example how continuous quality improvement is done.

Boards cannot be both leaders of change for the organization and followers of the status quo for themselves. If they want staff to identify and implement changes that will reduce costs and increase productivity, the board should demonstrate that it has defined its own productivity, measured it carefully, and made changes that increase the value it adds to the organization. Such efforts will put the board's own actions in line with its policies for the whole organization and demonstrate commitment to those policies for others to observe and follow.

By working intentionally on its own performance, a board is making some fundamental changes in how it uses its time and energy, not just engaging in a temporary quick fix that will solve immediate problems and then go away. Attention to how it is carrying out its work becomes part of the agenda, rather than something separate from and independent of ongoing tasks and responsibilities. These changes in the board's own culture and processes involve reinventing and rejuvenating the leadership core of the organization. They demonstrate a basic commitment and continuing concern with improving the quality of performance, rather than seeing it as something separate or occasional.

Time and intentional work are essential for such changes to become integrated into the board's culture. Boards have found that to ensure that lessons are learned and used they must allow enough time to address their most important concerns and explore alternatives fully. This cannot be accomplished at one meeting; rather, some attention must be devoted on a regular basis to reflection on the group's work performance. The group should build into its expectations that time will be allocated to discuss how it dealt with key agenda items as well as to work on the tasks themselves. Even a few minutes per meeting on such reflections can lead to greater efficiency and effectiveness of the board. It can also ensure that minor irritants do not mushroom into major problems.

In conclusion, effective boards attend to how they work together as well as to what they do. Members take responsibility for initiating discussions of how the group carries out its work and seek ways to improve performance. They take advantage of breaks or turning points in the organization's experience to draw attention to the board's role in leadership and change. They test their perceptions with others and identify shared concerns of the group. They move ahead by means of assessment of group performance to identify specific issues and goals for change. They lay the foundation for ongoing work by means of retreats and careful follow-up. They reinforce and institutionalize changes through in-meeting discussions of feedback on performance and through educational sessions that contribute to strengthening the board's effectiveness.

These efforts bridge the gap between learning and doing, integrating reflection with work. They help the group to develop a culture of active responsibility for making ongoing, self-directed improvements in its own performance. By taking consistent initiative to improve their work together, boards set the example for others and show how to add greater value to the organization.

REFERENCES

Chait, R. P., Holland, T. P., and Taylor, B. E. *Improving the Performance of Governing Boards.* Phoenix: Oryx Press, 1996.

Fry, R. E. "Accountability in Organizational Life: Problem or Opportunity for Nonprofits?" *Nonprofit Management and Leadership,* 1995, 16(2), 181–196.

Holland, T. P. "Self-Assessment by Nonprofit Boards." *Nonprofit Management and Leadership,* 1991, 2(1), 25–36.

Holland, T. P. "Setting the Stage: Planning Board Retreats." *Board Member,* 1997, 6(4), 10–11.

Holland, T. P., Leslie, D., and Holzhalb, C. "Culture and Change in Nonprofit Boards." *Nonprofit Management and Leadership,* 1993, 4(2), 141–155.

Jackson, D. K., and Holland, T. P. "Measuring the Effectiveness of Nonprofit Boards." *Nonprofit and Voluntary Sector Quarterly,* 1998, 27(2), 159–182.

Pound, J. "The Promise of the Governed Corporation." *Harvard Business Review,* 1994, 73(8), 89–98.

Savage, T. J. *Seven Steps to a More Effective Board.* Rockhurst, Ill.: National Press Publications, 1994.

Schein, E. H. *Organizational Culture and Leadership.* San Francisco: Jossey-Bass, 1997.

Senge, P. *The Fifth Discipline: The Art and Practice of the Learning Organization.* New York: Doubleday, 1990.

Sleisinger, L. *Self-Assessment for Nonprofit Boards.* Washington, D.C.: National Center for Nonprofit Boards, 1991.

Taylor, B. E., Chait, R. P., and Holland, T. P. "The New Work of the Nonprofit Board." *Harvard Business Review,* 1996, 75(5), 36–46.

6

BEYOND HIERARCHIES

TRANSFORMING POWER AND LEADERSHIP

Thomas J. Savage

A TWENTY-FIVE-FOOT STEEP HILL in the backyard and a gang of six fairly competitive sisters and brothers were all the ingredients necessary to inspire a long series of King of the Mountain contests when I was growing up just outside of Boston. The goal of the game was to knock everyone else off the top of the hill and be the sole surviving ruler, standing victoriously on the heights. Winter snow or summer heat never stopped our endless fascination with playing for power. I cannot remember the game ever turning too violent, but there were some bruises at times.

Quite a few lessons about power were discovered, too. Because I was one of the smallest and youngest of the kids, victory was a rare and special treat. Sometimes the right shoes gave the advantage as the others slipped down the slope. That big, tall brother could be tripped up by the little guy on occasion. The David and Goliath story became real for me in the backyard. Despite the reversal of power in this biblical image, however, the core message of our play was that one wins by standing gloriously alone on the top of the hill.

It was the core message until one day my younger sister, beloved as the baby, father's favorite, and mercilessly picked on at times by her nearest rivals, suggested to me that two could be stronger than one. And so it was. We shared power at the top.

Our game revealed some trends in the ages-old cultural assumptions about power. Historically, religious organizations have been among the most hierarchical in structure and authoritarian in governance. For many centuries, power was focused in positions arranged in the form of a pyramid of clergy offices, with members of congregations or consumers of health, educational, or social services having little control over decisions made by organizations intended to serve them. The authority of bishops was central to the governance structures of the Episcopal and Roman Catholic denominations. Congregational denominations emphasized the authority of boards of deacons or elders as well as that of the head minister. Power was assumed to belong rightfully to those in higher positions, whose judgment and decisions were to be accepted and followed by those in lower positions, as illustrated in Figure 6.1.

Major changes in cultural assumptions about power emerged during the last half of the twentieth century. Community groups, corporations, and political parties experienced increasing distrust of centralized decision making and growing demands for devolution of choices to those at lower levels in the system. Citizens demanded more local control of political decisions, and workers pressed for a greater voice in job design. Members of religious organizations began challenging the conclusions of bishops and clergy, and those in minority groups pressed for more extensive and equal participation in decisions affecting all aspects of life. Members of mainline denominations expressed their distrust by withholding both monetary and programmatic support of so-called home boards and central offices.

My sister and I certainly did not know it when we were playing King of the Mountain (it was the allegedly sleepy 1950s) but a revolution had begun and we were part of it. Our society's images of power and who can share it have changed significantly in the decades since then. Hierarchical power, in which each higher level of the pyramid of command increases one's authority, has not quite disappeared from organizational life, but it has certainly been diminished by flattened organizations, collaborative leadership, and team structures. Women are still too often not seen as equal partners in many companies and communities, although great strides have been made. Yet when it comes to governance and trusteeship, there still seems to be a lag in moving beyond hierarchies and glass ceilings. Most organizational charts still show the board at the top.

The stories emerging from congregations of hierarchical behavior on the part of pastoral leadership—such as senior ministers, rabbis, or heads of staff—regardless of polity are unfortunately plentiful. Heads of staff can exercise a virtual choke hold on what other members of the staff do programmatically or on what the committees of the church have authority to do. Official lines of authority, those outlined in polity documents, may not be hierarchical at all. But actual exercise of authority in circumstances

Figure 6.1. Overview of the Structure of Organizations.

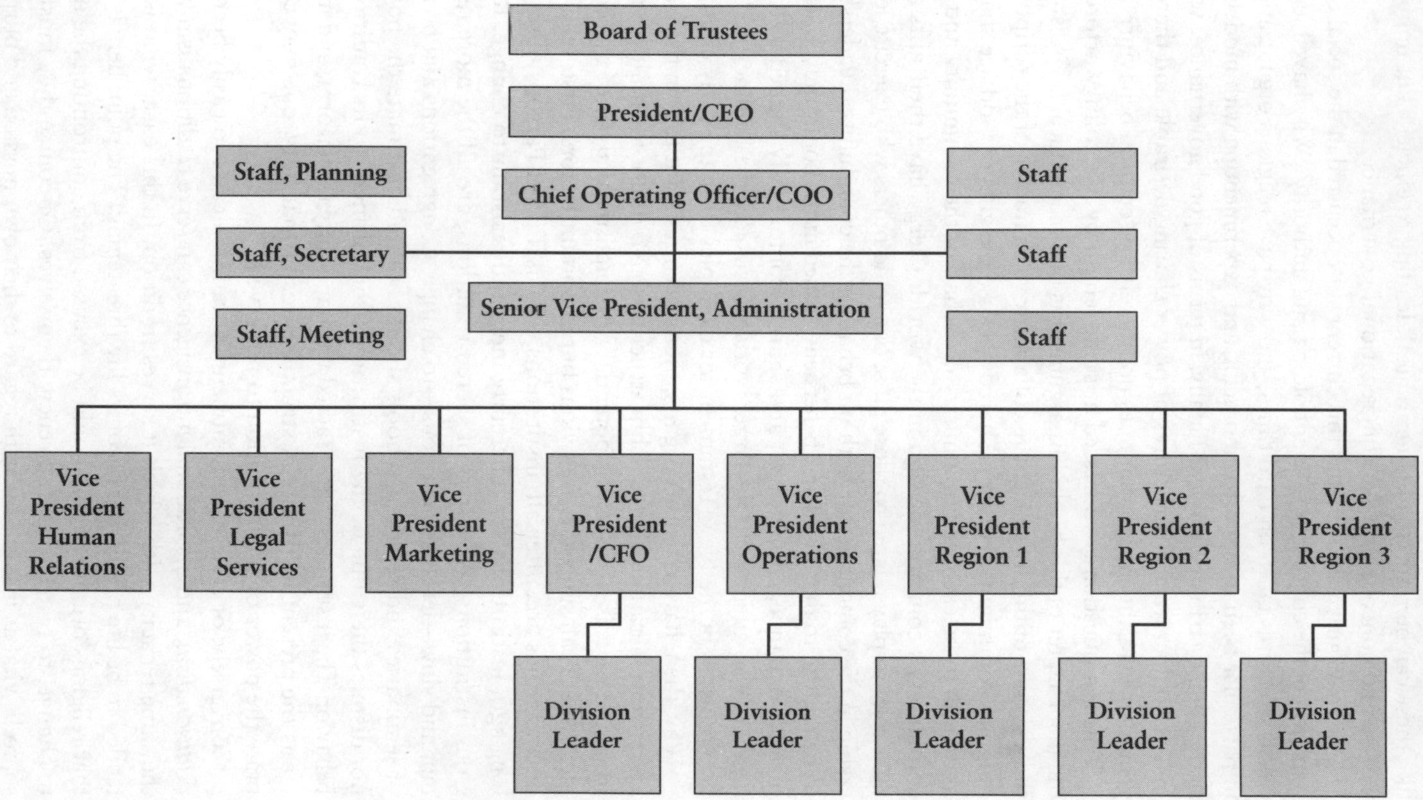

like these can be restrictively hierarchical, leading to efficient but unimaginative and noncollaborative congregational governance.

One may fairly ask, Why has this current shift occurred in the social construction of the concept of power holding and authority? Why have hierarchical structures fallen on hard times, and why have religious organizations in particular been resistant to embracing and experimenting with models of shared and distributed power? Finally, in terms of good governance, what makes nonhierarchical structures of power sharing desirable and thereby genuinely warrant change that does not merely ape cultural behavior?

This last question is addressed at some length by Malcolm Warford in the first chapter of this book. His argument is that hierarchical board structures do not faithfully reflect the collaborative character of the scriptural religious community. Power is shared because the gifts of God are shared and given to be exercised in ministry on behalf of the community and the community's common mission in the world. Clergy have their gifts and their roles to play related to those gifts; but so do others who exercise leadership in the community of faith on behalf of the community. Leadership, to be faithful to the values and beliefs envisioned in the community's scriptures, is dynamic, cooperative, and shared, contextually shaped to local need but also attentive to the larger world's needs (see the Pauline and Pastoral Epistles in the New Testament for examples from the early church).

Why, then, have religious organizations been resistant to join the trend away from hierarchical leadership structures? No doubt for multiple reasons, and there is a dangerous potential for simplistic analysis of this complex issue. I can suggest two obvious but important factors. First, religious organizations are, after all, institutions; and as Talcott Parsons observed long ago, institutions are inherently inert and resistant to change. Religious institutions, as bearers of sacred traditions, are all the more resistant and slow—let us say cautious—to change. Congregations and boards of seminaries and religious schools should not underestimate the power nor dismiss the value of the institution's commitment to its traditional behavior. The institution has a sacred trust and duty to perform, and insofar as the present institutional structures foster that duty, one may celebrate the power of the institution to preserve it.

Conversely, of course, commitment to tradition can too easily become *traditionalism,* and institutional intransigence can serve traditionalism with the same tenacity with which it serves tradition. In this case, what is intended to be life preserving becomes life threatening. The point here is not that religious organizations should be excused from confronting the need to change, to restructure and renew themselves. Of course they must do so, to be vital as institutions with regard to their own mission and purpose and their place in the community at large. But religious institutions, I am suggesting, do have a right and a duty to be cautious about jumping onto cultural bandwagons carrying new and appealing organizational reforms, until these innovations can be weighed in the balance of the institution's religious responsibility.

The second reason I suggest to account for the reluctance of religious organizations to embrace the contemporary shift from hierarchical patterns of institutional control relates to the lasting power of socialization. The contemporary religious community and religious institution has drunk at the bureaucratic well of the modern Western culture as deeply as business and industry in terms of organizational structure. Seminaries, in unguarded moments, speak of "turning out" students; congregations implicitly, if not explicitly, consider their pastor a "chief executive officer" and frequently measure effectiveness in terms of production and increases in membership. Our capitalist culture and economics cut deeply into the way we structure our personal lives and our institutional life, and sociologists would tell us, it's no surprise.

A rather clever television ad for Xerox shows a "head angel" talking with his group of heavenly beings about the present information age. "What happen to the industrial age?" one of them asks. "That was last century," he is told. "Ah, those were the days," the heavenly Xerox band says in unison. "You built it; you sold it." But now things are different; ideas move faster; they are linked by computers from one person to another and built into something that can be reconfigured or deleted in an electronic moment. The times call for a different ordering of power—a networking of power that reflects the networking of information processing. So hierarchical structures have fallen largely because they no longer work in the service-oriented, locally established, and networked world we are in the process of building in the postindustrial and postmodern age.

Changing Assumptions About Power and Leadership

Many religious organizations have yet to come to terms with how this new world order is impinging on their structures. The resistance we see is more a matter of holding on tightly to what is until what may become is born. Dealing constructively with this transition is the pressing, urgent task to which religious leadership is called. Yet surveys of board composition do show the percentage of women and minorities on boards to be growing, and the transformation of cultural assumptions about power and leadership has begun to influence board structure, composition, and practice in many religious organizations. Here are some examples.

Worshipful-Work

Started by Charles M. Olsen, a Presbyterian minister, in 1991, with a four-year grant from the Lilly Endowment, Worshipful-Work is an ecumenical outreach to the governing bodies of judicatories, local congregations, churches, and parishes (Olsen, 1995). Its basic premise is that the governing bodies of religious communities should not simply follow a model based on secular organizations, with their routine, businesslike approach to board agendas. Rather, the practice of the boards of religious bodies should be faith based, their activities should be designed around a worship model rather than a business-meeting model, and ample opportunity should be given to incorporate stories and symbols that are specifically religious and tied to the congregation's specific history. Reactions from the more than ten thousand people on church boards and parish councils that have used Worshipful-Work's ideas have been very positive, with most groups reporting greater satisfaction with a faith-based approach. Leadership is more meaningful and decision making more effective.

For example, a Lutheran pastor from North Dakota used Worshipful-Work–type models by having his parish council stand around the communion table and talk about what happens there, then return to the council table and talk about what happens there. He then asked if there was any connection between the two tables. A rich discussion ensued. Even a few reluctant participants who preferred more businesslike models discovered the power of the faith-based storytelling that motivated council members.

LESSONS FOR GOVERNANCE. Faith-based storytelling can be risky for some, but once begun it has the power to change the nature and practice of the board. Discernment and decision making take time. For the religious organization seeking leadership that is well grounded in a particular faith tradition, discernment and decision making are essential.

Daughters of Charity National Health System

The Daughters of Charity National Health System (DCNHS) is one of the nation's largest nonprofit providers of health care services. Sponsored by a Roman Catholic religious order of women, the Daughters of Charity of St. Vincent de Paul, DCNHS operates more than forty major hospitals and medical centers, plus dozens of affiliated clinics and other medical organizations, with $6 billion in annual revenues and $2 billion in reserve funds. A reorganization begun in late 1997 led to the elimination of a regional organizational structure and the removal of a layer of management so that local health centers would have a more direct link to national management. Encouraging a more team-oriented, integrated system of management nationwide led the CEO to realize that changes in the way governance and sponsorship operated were also required. The traditional hierarchically structured organizational chart would need to be changed. The newly created structure incorporated DCNHS's core values into more team-oriented systems and with multiple local and national stakeholders to produce a powerful new image for the way decision makers are linked together in one integrated system (see Figure 6.2).

LESSONS FOR GOVERNANCE. Design governance to fit the needs of the people or organizations served rather than to fit a preconceived notion of how an organization should be structured. Use signs and symbols that convey the distinctive mission and purpose of the organization, and appeal particularly to the religious motivation, identity, or calling of members.

The Council for Initiatives in Jewish Education

Recognizing the importance of ensuring that Orthodox Jewish beliefs and values permeate every aspect of its member schools nationwide, the Council for Initiatives in Jewish Education invited board leaders from each school to its biannual, week-long workshop for principals, headmasters, and faculty leaders. Formal sessions included topics such as the roles and responsibilities of boards. A rabbi was present at all sessions to point out and reflect on connections between issues of leadership and governance as they are found in biblical, rabbinical, and midrashic traditions.

LESSONS FOR GOVERNANCE. Boards of religious organizations need to be well-educated in the beliefs and practices of their tradition if they are to take responsibility for maintaining organizational mission, identity, and integrity. Rabbis, ministers, priests, and other religious leaders need to help facilitate this learning, be invited to meet with governing bodies if they are not members, and be given formal roles and times to reflect on the religious dimensions of issues that come before a board or council.

National 4-H Council

The National 4-H Council, while not religiously sponsored, is a nonprofit organization experimenting with dramatic changes in board composition designed to match its commitment to an equally dramatic change and renewal of its mission and the way it conducts its business.

Figure 6.2. Organization of the Daughters of Charity National Health System.

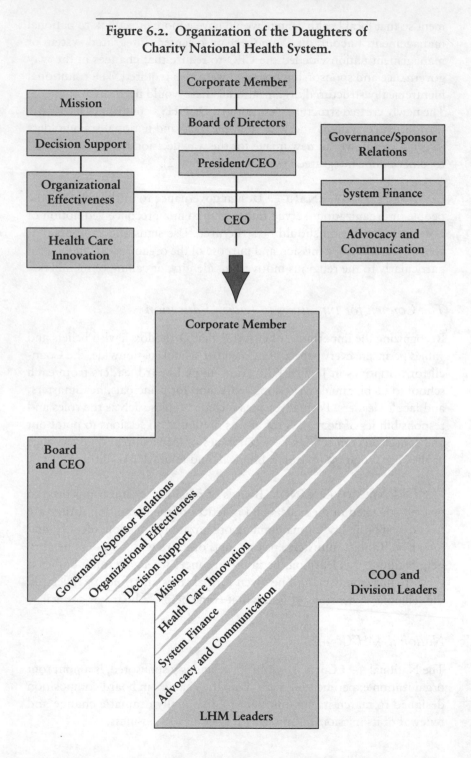

The private partner for the nationwide 4–H programs since 1976, the National 4–H Council helps 4–H reach six million involved young people by working with staff and volunteers across the country. The National 4–H Council had long encouraged youth to be advisors, consultants, and committee and task force members. But such participation did not mean that young people enjoyed real decision-making power in governance. In fact, a 1990 marketing research study of why teens left the organization found them "tired of being in an organization run by adults who thought they knew what was best for kids" (National Assembly of National Voluntary Health and Social Welfare Organizations, 1998).

A change in mission called on the National 4–H Council to be "an uncommon youth development organization fostering innovation and shared learning for youth workers and young leaders." CEO Richard Sauer recognized that "if we really believed what we were saying, we needed to have young people rolling up their sleeves and sitting down at the table with us" (National Assembly of National Voluntary Health and Social Welfare Organizations, 1998). Change did not come easily. There was initial resistance to anything more than token youth representation on the board. But change did come.

Focused now on empowering youth, the National 4–H Council's board of directors recently voted to assign one third of its board positions to young people. Candidates include youth aged twelve to twenty-one, identified nationwide from a pool of 4–H alumni and members and from other youth-driven organizations.

LESSONS FOR GOVERNANCE. Involve the people being served directly in the governance work. If you have a youth organization, empower the youth by enabling them to run the organization. Youth make up a sizable portion of most congregations or parishes. Make sure they represent a significant portion of governance, too.

C.S.A. *Health System*

C.S.A. Health System, sponsored by the Sisters of Charity of St. Augustine, entered into a fifty-fifty partnership with Columbia Healthcare Alliance, a for-profit health corporation. In addition to maintaining its equity position in its four hospitals, C.S.A. now operates four foundations and several ministry-oriented corporations. C.S.A. found its traditional board meeting schedules and agendas no longer effective for managing and governing its complex set of partnership operations and relationships. New formats for board meetings have been invented. Prayer is no longer a perfunctory opening ritual but a reflective and participatory event built into the purpose of the meeting. Routine committee reports have been replaced by focused discussions on key issues and topics. Strategic decisions are fully analyzed and debated. Small groups are used during the board meeting to enable all trustees of the twenty-member board to participate fully in all deliberations. Board satisfaction with meetings has increased and attendance has reached the 100 percent mark for nearly all meetings.

LESSONS FOR GOVERNANCE. Question routine agendas and meeting formats. Take a fresh, creative look at schedules and timetables. Make the structure and practice of the board fit the needs of the organization and the governance tasks that need to be accomplished.

Underlying Dynamics

Underlying these five brief case examples are a variety of powerful and complex forces and social trends.

Demographic changes. Since 1990, the postretirement population has grown significantly, living longer and contributing to society even to advanced ages. The baby boom generation has begun to move into their fifties and has assumed leadership roles. The next generations of those in their twenties and thirties have rediscovered voluntarism and service while living largely suburban lives at a distance from older cities and neighborhoods. Women have assumed almost equal roles in the workplace, while school-age populations have become dramatically diverse, with former minority groups of Latinos, African Americans, and Asians achieving majority status in the most populous states in the West and South. All these changes have had an impact on boards and volunteers, their ideas, beliefs, composition, structure, schedules, time, agenda, culture, and leadership.

Technology, communications, and the role of the media. Here again the dynamics of change have had enormous real and potential impact on the roles and practice of boards. Generational differences in how the world is perceived, in how information is exchanged and communicated, and in language, mobility, and access as virtual networks become stronger and replace place-based relationships, and changes in the role and use of the media have begun to affect board behavior and practice.

Globalization. Local issues and issues from the other side of the globe now exercise competing or complementary demands for attention and crowd the agenda of church-related boards. All organizations today are becoming part of an internationalized world, and even the most locally focused religious organizations confront global dimensions of seemingly local issues.

Changes in the workplace, home, and community. According to Thomas Kocham (1996), the rise of virtual networks, the growth of large Internet enterprises, and the development of networked firms where bureaucracies and hierarchies are replaced by flexible roles, blurred organizational boundaries, and flat, flexible structures are all responses to changes in how we hire and work. More highly educated communities and more mobile, dynamic labor markets are tending to reduce loyalty and long-term commitments to a single employer or organization. Employee, employer, and consumer rights and responsibilities are in flux, and this ambiguity gives rise to disputes and lawsuits. A knowledge-based workforce leads to further inequities in salary, income, and wealth.

The need for effective lateral rather than top-down communication grows amid complex organizations, and a premium is placed on teamwork, problem solving, negotiation, and conflict resolution. Upward mobility in job and community is no longer ensured by conforming to the cultural and social norms of top executive elites. Athletic and entertainment stars model alternative, even if unlikely to be repeated, channels of success. The functionally defined hierarchical organization with focused and limited spans of control has definitely been replaced.

Implications and Recommendations

Following are some of the key lessons to be learned from this brief review of trends in organizational development and renewal.

Respect and renewal. The first lesson is a warning not to initiate trends in business or nonprofit organizations in a superficial way, adopting the latest fads while overlooking the more troublesome aspects. Restructuring, reengineering, and reinvention have become fashionable movements, but many workers and communities know that such efforts can also mean removal of jobs, replacement of workers, retrenchment of services, and reduction of investments. Respect for fundamental rights, responsibilities, and relationships should be the key value in any renewal effort. Learn from other sectors and industries, but do not merely imitate what they do.

New models. Reengineering, as Charles Handy (1997) points out, is a factory-sounding word that suggests that the organization is a factory in need of redesign. Indeed, the assembly-line model was a dominant image of the organization fifty years ago. It seems that some contemporary managers (and consultants) still have the factory model in mind as they seek to refashion work in more productive and efficient ways while they remain as supervisors and controllers at the top. Workers can feel exploited in such a system. Strategic planning and management is also rooted in and based on a particular model, namely the military, with its hierarchies of command, discipline, and rules. This model depends on an enemy and the development of plans and tactics in response to the actual or anticipated moves of such an enemy. Many religious institutions find it very difficult to use this model fully.

Handy suggests an alternate model, the theater, as a guiding image for tomorrow's organization. Here the focus is on producing not things but actions, and it is the audience not the enemy in whom the director wants to create a response. The cast members need to work as a team. They can't be coerced but they need to be convinced. Creativity and imagination are crucial. Money is the means for, not the final point of, production. Theater is a world of individual talents linked together in a common purpose, directed by someone who rarely, if ever, takes the stage. Theater is not a perfect analogy but an eye-opening one for the hierarchically restricted. Many of the elements of theater are also evident in worship. Churches, which ought to be expert in ritual and worship, can apply these same features to leadership and governance.

Use faith-based core values. Faith traditions often excel in articulating and espousing core values that can inspire and motivate renewal and transformation. Some religious organizations have begun to use these values to ground organizational change. For example, several Catholic health systems have begun to decentralize and revive local health ministries and medical centers by using three core Catholic principles: stewardship, subsidiarity, and solidarity. Congregations have engaged in renewal by recognizing and honoring the values that can be made explicit as we tell the stories and faith journeys of members of the community.

The key lesson. Religious leaders should adapt and use the language of their own traditions as they renew their organizations and continue their response to new needs and concerns. Take advantage of newly decentralized, networked information. Not all information needs have to be fulfilled from the top down. Technology today allows many more affinity groups and interest groups to take shape. Encourage and use these more lateral, horizontally rather than hierarchically focused groups.

Conclusion

There is no single right way today to organize a board or develop council, congregational, and organizational leadership. Changes in society are providing solid reasons to transform our notions and images of leadership. It is the job of religious leaders to reflect on their communities' religious values and images in order to identify new models of leadership and governance practice that are well grounded in faith traditions. Two characteristics are likely to be essential to any model created to practice good governance faithfully in religious institutions. First, any model will have to be grounded in love, or more precisely, in an ethic of love that insists that good governance must reflect the generosity of love that redeems and rebuilds and recreates and measures its effectiveness by how well others—namely, those being served—are doing. Second, any model must include a commitment to work for justice, to structure itself, first of all, as a just structure, in terms of how the faith to which the religious community attests understands justice; and it must structure itself to attend to restructuring structures of injustice as they may exist within sight of the religious organization. These two characteristics do not say it all, and they remain at an abstract level, waiting for readers to fill them with local and specific content and meaning. They are not sufficient, to be sure; but they are necessary. Of that we can be sure.

REFERENCES

Handy, C. *Beyond Certainty.* Boston: Harvard Business School Press, 1997.

Kocham, T. A. "The American Corporation as an Employer: Past, Present, and Future Possibilities." In C. Kaysen (ed.), *The American Corporation Today.* New York: Oxford University Press, 1996.

National Assembly of National Voluntary Health and Social Welfare Organizations. *Clients on Board: Profiles of Effective Governance.* Washington, D.C.: National Assembly of National Voluntary Health and Social Welfare Organizations, 1998.

Olsen, C. M. *Transforming Church Boards into Communities of Spiritual Leaders.* Washington, D.C.: Alba Institute, 1995.

7

BOUNDARY SPANNING

BUILDING BRIDGES BETWEEN AN
ORGANIZATION AND ITS ENVIRONMENT

Christa R. Klein

GOVERNING BOARDS are positioned at the boundaries of their organizations. By their composition and purpose, they span the borders because they belong both to the religious organization and to its religious and social environment (Middleton, 1987). As part of the organization, the board bears the responsibility of ensuring the organization's vitality and direction; as part of the environment, the board relies on its members' networks and wisdom to connect the organization to its context and its constituencies. This bridging position makes the board strategic for the two-way exchange of resources and information—essential ingredients for effective performance—across the borders.

Unless this bridging function is fully recognized and actively engaged, boards miss opportunities to strengthen their organizations by sustaining communications and deepening connections. Organizations become impoverished, shortsighted, and insular, without well-developed ties to the outside world. Conversely, without sufficient familiarity with and loyalty to the organization itself, boards cannot act with a clear sense of identity and purpose.

Yet the connections through the board to the social and religious environment may be so complex and laden with multiple commitments or ties of accountability that members of the board and staff and even the public can become cynical about the organization and its prospects for service. When a board becomes captive either to the organization or to particular constituencies in its environment, it has weakened trust and lost its way. Without an orientation that spans the boundaries and includes multiple constituencies, the board is not positioned to mediate interests or mobilize resources. This failing may damage the organization and, further, compromise the community of faith, its members, and even its religious tradition.

Dealing with this dilemma is central to the role of the board member, who must learn to live with dual loyalties, encompassing both the particular organization and the larger faith community or other religious affiliation. Organizations such as church-related social service agencies, colleges, hospitals, theological schools, and congregations all depend on a high measure of shared loyalty; in some cases it is even mandated in the qualifications for board membership.

Tensions are inevitable and none are so significant religiously as those that arise from the competing claims of the organization and the larger religious community for time and attention, fiscal resources, or even interpretations of the religious tradition. Can dual loyalty be maintained without it becoming divided loyalty? How well boards handle their boundary spanning responsibilities depends on how well they keep those loyalties in *dialogue* for the good of the organization and its affiliations, and for the good of those who serve as board members.

This chapter explores the dimensions, threats, and opportunities inherent in the boundary spanning role of the board. It calls for a governance style open to probing the assumptions built into a board's structure and composition. Because boards are not static entities but go through phases in their operation and membership, increased self-awareness helps the board navigate the inevitable changes. Moreover, board members can gain more satisfaction and motivation in their service when they know where they stand and how they are contributing both to the organization and to the larger context to which it belongs.

Dimensions of Boundary Spanning

Although few aspects of governance are more fundamental to a board's structure and processes than boundary spanning, it often gets taken for granted. Such inattention can lead to conflicts as well as to unrealized opportunities to advance the cause of the organization. Hidden organizational resources reside in many cross-boundary relationships, awaiting attention and development.

The design of the governing board is in itself an interpretation of a religious organization's relation to its environment. Through the architecture of governance, passionate founders tried to determine how their new organization should connect to its setting and how it might demonstrate the religious and legal authority undergirding its mission. In effect, they tried to design channels for the flow of authorization, information, advocacy, revenue, services, and other resources. Their successors realize that the vitality of the organization continues to depend on the upkeep and sometimes the replacement of the channels and structures through which these exchanges occur.

The Formal and Functional Dimensions

An organization's bylaws and other constituting documents outline how its board should relate to the organization and to its environment. These documents detail the structure of authority, naming which bodies or positions are responsible for overseeing the stewardship functions and the allocation of institutional resources. Among the most basic elements of boundary spanning are prescriptions about the preferred requirements for board members, the selection or election process, and the length and terms of board service. Requirements for the representation of particular constituencies, for ex officio (by virtue of office) membership, or for multi-organizational election processes guide and define the board's composition and linkages. The board's makeup exhibits and authenticates for the public the organization's legitimacy.

If, for example, a governing board has the authority to legitimate its own composition and actions, then the board is self-perpetuating. If those powers reside in historically related religious bodies or persons with authority over, or relative to, the organization, then the board has a more limited sphere of authority and responsibility for its composition.

Today, the boards of many church-related organizations are hybrids, with some members elected by the board, others elected by constituencies, and others serving by virtue of their office in a related organization. A board's history of reform and adaptation may be exhibited by its various categories of members. The predominant category greatly influences the board's ethos and style of governance.

Whatever the prescriptions are for the board's makeup and responsibilities, its potential must always be measured against its performance. Like the heating, ventilating, and air conditioning system in a new building, a system for governance requires regular monitoring and adjustment to ensure the steady flow of energy, skill, and resources that will keep the organization vital and free to pursue its purposes.

In the recent literature and research about board development, the formal dimension has taken a back seat to the functional dimension (see, for example, Chait, Holland, and Taylor, 1993, 1996). The quality of the board's performance is of course crucial; most religious organizations must work hard to flourish in today's turbulent socioeconomic environment. A board that functions like a team in which every member is capable of stepping up to the plate is a tremendous organizational asset. But an emphasis on performance does not diminish the significance of identities and affiliations represented on the board. The makeup of the board not only interprets the organization's environment, it also structures the work of keeping the organization's connection to that environment vibrant.

The age, gender, racial, and other constituency identities of board members are some of the most obvious linkages across organizational boundaries. Underlying them are the rich mix of members' experiences, accomplishments, and locations in multiple networks of family, friends, coreligionists, and professional and volunteer affiliations. Because such multifaceted identities shape members' performance, they are valued resources for the board.

Thus, the formal and the functional are not so neatly divided, but rather are two aspects of the board's interpretive role. The board brings the organization's environment into its governance work and carries the organization back to its environment. The effectiveness of these processes depends on both formal identity and actual performance. Several aspects of the formal dimension merit closer examination.

Boards of religious organizations come in many shapes and styles, and generalizations about boards drawn from other traditions do not apply to many religious boards, or at most are only partially relevant. Too much of the particularity of any one religious culture is at stake to compress all forms of governance into one general type. For example, some boards can do most of their work in formal sessions at the board table. Other boards do most of their work away from the table in conversation at smaller meetings and with individuals. Either of these ways tells a great deal about how authority and leadership are exercised within particular religious cultures. Who is to say which approach yields the best results for the organization in the long run? Decision making is a matter of cultural style. Sometimes the unspoken is as significant as the spoken at a meeting. Whatever the approach, board members always deserve a thorough orientation, one that clues them into the way this particular board carries out its work and helps them find their own niche and particular contribution to its processes.

SELF-PERPETUATING BOARDS. Among religious organizations, predominantly self-perpetuating forms of governance grow out of specific historical circumstances, such as faith communities with congregational polities, or within nondenominational, ecumenical, or interfaith settings. Sometimes a movement that began nondenominationally, such as a form of religious revivalism or social reform, is organized around founders who assume the role, during the process of incorporation, of the governing board's first directors or trustees.

Self-perpetuating forms of governance offer direct opportunities to guide the organization in defining its publics and to embed it successfully in its environment. These boards establish relationships with their constituencies and others through recruitment and selection of their own members. If the board has a myopic viewpoint, it may feed on the dynamism of the founders' vision without regularly scanning the environment and making changes in response to it. If it takes a broader view, it can create an organization that transcends the limits of the founders, renewing its energy and expanding its resources. This requires continually assessing the impact of the board's work on the organization itself and on the larger faith community of which it is a part.

For example, the Billy Graham Evangelistic Association (incorporated in 1950) always worked through local church councils in the cities where he conducted his preaching crusades. His revivalist style, which netted both new commitment and recommitment among his audiences, aimed to renew faith and reconnect the faithful only incidentally to his own organization but more especially with local congregations. The organization was able to maintain trust over the years because it had a broader goal than to build a private following for Graham himself (Handy, 1976).

Other self-perpetuating boards among evangelical Protestant organizations have exhibited a similar form of leadership. For example, Fuller Theological Seminary and Gordon-Conwell Theological Seminary, both nondenominational schools, have also relied on their boards to read and reinterpret their external settings so that the seminaries' missions could be adapted and applied in changing circumstances and provide leadership for many different congregations, denominations, and parachurch organizations (Marsden, 1987).

APPOINTED BOARDS. In contrast to the membership of self-perpetuating boards, the members of appointed boards are selected by outside bodies. This leads to different responsibilities and opportunities. The effectiveness of such boards necessarily includes tending the channels of communication with their partners in governance to maintain the level of needed resources. With the direction of much of their boundary-spanning work predetermined, these boards must monitor and sustain the system of relationships to make certain it works for the organization, and they must lobby for changes when the system weakens or fails.

An example of one of the more complex governance partnerships emerged among Roman Catholic institutions in the 1960s and 1970s (Fitzgerald, 1984). Educational and health care institutions owned, governed, and managed by religious orders could no longer survive and thrive without the assistance and leadership of laypeople. Two-tiered governance systems evolved, with the *ownership* board, often the leadership of a religious order or community, delegating certain of its governance responsibilities to an *advisory* board. Although the degree of delegated responsibilities varies widely among religious organizations, the ownership board usually has the final say in determining the continued existence of the organization and often in the selection of its executive leadership.

The formal responsibilities of the advisory body may be considerable, but all too often the ambiguities of its role or the seemingly arbitrary intervention of the ownership board generates dissatisfaction among advisory board members. Who has what authority? When such boards have a clear sense of their role and when they have evidence that their advice is respectfully considered and normally honored by the ownership board, then members achieve the loyalty that enables them to make a difference.

EX OFFICIO BOARD MEMBERS. Religious organizations are often the offspring of parent bodies with a vested interest in these new extensions of their mission. That interest has led to the practice of specifying ex officio members to governing boards. For example, the superior of a Catholic religious order or diocese or the superintendent of a Methodist or Nazarene conference of regional churches sits, by virtue of office, on the boards of local religious organizations for health care, social services, or theological education. By statute, this authority figure may even chair the board of the related organization.

Sometimes such a structure of board leadership or membership is required by church law, as for some Roman Catholic, Eastern Orthodox, Episcopal, and other church bodies with hierarchically defined religious authority. Ex officio membership is a means of assuring the wider religious community that the tradition is being honored in each local organization. This assurance is especially important in those organizations designated to teach the religious tradition and prepare leaders for its service.

Required board membership defines the boundary-spanning channels by interlocking the leadership of two or more organizations, often in a hierarchical relationship. This formal dimension always has its informal dynamic, because ex officio members must decide how to allocate their resources, including time, degree of authority, political influence, personality, access to funding, and engagement with the organization's mission.

Ideally, the thoroughly connected ex officio board member enhances the exchange of significant information and resources between the two organizations. When the formal system works, no organization can have better-placed advocates than ex officio members.

But obstacles often emerge, as in any human enterprise. Perhaps the parent organization has so many offshoots that the ex officio leader must juggle numerous meetings that necessarily become constrained in order to accommodate the leader's own calendar. These leaders often have so many formal responsibilities that they find it difficult to be fully engaged in the corporate life of the local board. Their diminished level of engagement is evident when their role becomes perfunctory, or their presiding style may discourage time-consuming discussions at board meetings.

Whether or not they chair the board, ex officio members may be too preoccupied with other issues to recognize the dampening effect on other local board and staff members of their own limited engagement. This can lead to superficial analyses of issues in board meetings and to cynical attitudes of other board members and staff about governance. If such patterns grow, the board has a harder time making productive use of the formal channels through which resources are expected to flow in and out of the organization. Ex officio members do best when they develop a clear self-awareness about their formal role and about how others perceive them. This enables them to maximize their opportunities to encourage the organization and to advocate for it among other related constituencies. Staff members, especially chief executives, do their part by keeping these busy leaders well informed and engaged with a vivid sense of the challenges and opportunities facing the organization.

Changes in the funding of religious organizations often have led to a reconception of ex officio leadership. When externally appointed religious leaders can no longer deliver the needed resources, local members of the board must pick up more of the responsibility for engaging others and convincing them to donate time, talent, and wealth to the organization.

The formal requirements of appointed or ex officio membership on a board may be modified under the pressure of organizational survival. Wise ex officio leaders encourage formal or informal organizational adjustments that allow others to share responsibilities long before they become an issue. Having another board member chair an executive or strategic planning committee brings additional talent to the top while preserving the formal prerogatives of ex officio leadership. Trust and effective communication among all the parties are crucial to this adaptation.

In one theological school created by the joint effort of several religious orders to provide for the education of their own members and those of other religious groups, the several religious superiors serving as ex officio board members came to recognize that the school could no longer afford their predominance on the board. They had neither the time for the work nor access to sufficient resources to ensure the school's vitality. Tipping the formal balance of power to lay leaders by giving them a majority of the seats on the board widened the circle of responsibility for the school while concentrating the focus of the religious leaders on the school's educational mission. In the history of that board, no vote has yet been determined by division along formal lines of authority.

THE REPRESENTATIVE BOARD MEMBER. Many boards of religious organizations feature another kind of board membership: the representative. Representing a geographical region or a particular religious constituency, this board member, unlike the ex officio member, does not link one organization to another through a formal office or leadership position. Rather, the representative is often elected or delegated to board service by the legislative body of a denomination or by an alumni association or other body. Representation is a well-defined custom in American democracy.

The representative principle always brings with it the conundrum of whether the individual representative speaks and votes his or her own conscience or acts on some discernible consensus of a constituency. In times of goodwill, the representation principle provides a largely symbolic way of making certain that the board embodies the interests and purposes of multiple constituencies. Although representatives may be asked to help interpret the views of their sector of the church body, they are usually expected to vote their own minds. In times of religious polarization, representation becomes the formal means by which the parties contend for the control of the organization (Wuthnow, 1988). For example, parties divided over the direction of the Southern Baptist Convention since the 1970s did battle in the election of board members to seek control over colleges, theological schools, mission organizations, and other subsidiaries (Ammerman, 1990; Cothen, 1993).

Whether the times are contentious or not, vague expectations of roles and accountability for the representative members weaken the integrity and performance of the board. Divided loyalty on the part of a board member does neither the organization nor the sponsoring body any good in the long run because the board member is not carrying out the board's two-way bridging function and is no longer effectively interpreting the one party to the other. The work of representative board members is to understand the nature and needs of both the organization and its sponsoring body. But the process of finding such capable board members is not always easy in these governance partnerships.

Too often the explicit boundary-spanning function of the representative board member is limited to such official functions as providing an occasional "state of the organization" report or hosting at an institutional advancement event for the church body's periodic legislative assemblies. Rarely are expectations for giving or getting financial support an explicit part of the arrangement. Sometimes the nominating and election process recognizes a faithful servant of the church without honoring the needs of the organization for skilled and energetic board members.

Limited use of representative board members may have some symbolic value: the high profile of the position in the sponsoring body at the time of election is an opportunity to bring the mission of the organization before the larger system's legislative body. But the potential for board membership is much greater than mere symbolism. Boards and chief executives should work with the nominating process to ensure that candidates who are truly qualified for leadership are on the ballot.

Wise representatives who have ties with broad networks and who bring particular skills to the board can play a crucial interpretative role on the board and help link the organization more closely with its constituencies. In fact, the very process of invigorating the election system to locate quality representatives benefits the whole organization, as has been the experience of some of the social service agencies and theological schools of the Evangelical Lutheran Church in America. The Mennonite Board of Higher Education goes a step further by assisting with the training of representative board members (Stoltzfus, 1992).

In the 1970s, quota systems, both formal and informal, emerged in many religious organizations. Mainline Protestants were among the first to adopt them to bring greater diversity of cultures, networks, and experience to their governing boards by including representation of ordained and lay, male and female, ethnic and racial groups, older and younger members. Although some tokenism remains, many religious organizations have gained greater knowledge of their constituencies by bringing to the board table a mix of talented people more reflective of the religious membership.

Yet some organizations have not openly reckoned with one potential cost of diversifying their board membership. If in the name of inclusiveness members are selected only for their knowledge about and networks in particular constituencies and not also for their capacity to appreciate the larger religious tradition or community, then the board may be sacrificing crucial elements in bridge building. Member selection requires the board to clarify its values and expectations and to seek and educate members explicitly for the work of boundary spanning and sustaining effective communications with multiple constituencies. Religious organizations from traditions honoring the "communion of saints" across time and space have complex sets of values to sort out in discerning the most appropriate representative principle.

The Historical Dimension

The factor of time in governance has strategic importance. The board should not only conduct its current work in a timely and efficient fashion to the benefit of the organization and its members, but it should also pay attention to the organization's history and traditions. When a board recognizes the historical interaction between the organization and its environment over time, its capacity to see and interpret current circumstances is greatly enhanced. Like the long view required of those who invest heavily in equities rather than bonds, a sense of history enhances the board's capacity to make prudent adjustments in its organization's current direction. Without taking the past into account, the lens on the future is bound to be myopic.

History can be full of surprises. The routines of meetings and the staid character of their minutes often mask momentous changes that hold lessons relevant to current challenges facing a board. Consider, for example, the extraordinary influence of federal, state, and local governments in shaping the opportunities and constraints for religious nonprofits over the past several decades. The federal funds made available through the G.I. Bill and work-study programs, legislation supporting college and university campus housing, the building of home and health care facilities for the elderly, and the support of preschool initiatives have all channeled and sometimes co-opted the mission of some religious organizations. The rise of accreditation in all fields throughout the twentieth century has dramatically raised standards and increased costs of conducting most religious missions through nonprofit organizations. Moreover, changes in tax laws and auditing standards have altered patterns of fundraising and accounting.

Easily overlooked because of its pervasive character, the increased professionalization in various church-related vocations has also altered the roles of religious professionals on governing boards. For example, increased specialization, and therefore differences in experience, of clergy and others who staff religious organizations have reduced bonds of understanding and divided the networks in which former understandings used to be forged. Thus, those who hold offices invested with religious authority, such as bishops, executive leaders of divisions in the national offices of religious bodies, and chief executives of religious organizations, have less and less knowledge of one another and their responsibilities. Sociologists describe this phenomenon as *segmentation*. Boards experience the consequences of this phenomenon in the form of blocked, discontinuous, or unconnected channels in their boundary-spanning efforts (Chaves, 1991).

Another example illustrates these changes. Religious philanthropy has been undergoing a steady change from a national to a more regional focus. In the past, substantial funding for many religious organizations was meted out through national or at least regional judicatory coffers. But increasing organizational costs at all levels combined with decreasing contributions at the national level have dramatically reduced allocations for local religious organizations that once were heavily subsidized. As a result, these organizations have had to develop their own offices of institutional advancement and find new sources of funding for themselves. They have necessarily grown more independent of their sponsoring bodies. Consequently, the professional staff in the local organizations and at the national or regional level have less knowledge and appreciation of one another's tasks (Coalter, Mulder, and Weeks, 1992; Mullin and Richey, 1994).

No historical change has affected board life more than this trend. Board membership has been shifting steadily in the second half of this century to include more laypeople and fewer ordained clergy or other traditional authority figures. The need for other forms of expertise, access to wealth and networks of philanthropy, and a greater appreciation of the stake that laypeople have in religious organizations are all part of the shift. At the same time, the importance of local boards to the larger faith communities continues. Only with careful attention can governing boards be present where segmentation can be broken down and mutual understanding can grow as board members deliberate over issues that require knowledge of one another's positions and viewpoints as well as those of their constituencies.

The historical dimension is often maintained through those "tribal storytellers" on staff or on the board who can recount how governance structures and processes have responded to the changing landscape and who have initiated their own adaptations (De Pree, 1990). Stories help the board to recognize how much its role and structure matter in the scope of things. Of course these tales usually include a political dimension. The mediating of competing demands in complicated organizational systems is highly political, even if some church people dislike the word.

The Political Dimension

As boundary spanners, boards are positioned to have an excellent view of the political landscape both within and outside the organization. Boards, especially those with members who are deeply pious in their religious expression, cannot ignore the political configurations underlying power, interests, and resources. Piety can be the foremost expression of power when it shapes what can be spoken and what is consigned, intentionally or unintentionally, to occur without examination or comment. Boards can be of great assistance to the organization's executive leadership in developing a sense of how the religious culture shapes governance and in maintaining the necessary political relationships.

To take advantage of their position, board leaders, chief executives, and staff of any religious organization must be aware of at least three different cultures: that of the board, that of the organization, and that of the primary constituency. Whether at or away from the board table—always a matter of piety and culture—board leaders need to cultivate a deliberative style that is anticipatory, provisional, candid, and purposive. Politics, ever present, can be shaped to the organization's advantage, and board members should cultivate wisdom and skill to guide these important processes.

No dimension of boundary spanning tests individual and institutional integrity more thoroughly than the political. What means should be used to what ends? Which publics should be the primary clients of the organization? Which resources should be pursued and at what cost to the organization? How do we balance divergences between the organization's mission and its market? What level of sacrifice shall be asked of the organization's employees? Is a humane, no less spiritually enriching working environment a priority equal to the service or products provided?

These are all essentially political issues because they involve the balancing of powers, interests, and resources. Ignoring them jeopardizes the board and the organization. An ironic example of the risks may be seen in the rising liability costs of sexual harassment and abuse that were initiated by insurance companies and legislatures demanding more stringent practices by religious organizations. The board should take the initiative in setting even higher standards in its handling of political and moral issues (Middleton, 1987).

The Communal Dimension

None of these dimensions can be fully explored without attending to the communal aspect of boundary spanning. Individual board members may have their private channels to inside or outside constituents, but only the work they do in common creates the fully authorized bridges that can support the wider two-way exchange of information and resources. For that work, both the appearance and the reality of communal effort are essential.

The legal aspects of the board as corporate body are well documented. The only legal authority the board has is corporate, when it is assembled as a group. The symbolic value of group action, beyond the marketing potential, is less well understood. Lists of board members may regularly appear in organizational publications because the prestigious names confer credibility on the organization. But the assembled presence of the board has even more powerful possibilities for its members and for the organization. Where else but on boards do ordained, professional, and lay religious leaders regularly meet to discuss the well-being of organizations that embody religious purposes? Together these board members are shaping the future of religious life in America. The religious nature of their deliberation is often hidden, but it can easily be acknowledged at public events in the organization, including festive dinners, fundraising activities, service events, and worship services. Educational opportunities during board gatherings are imperative. The more seriously the shared work of the board is taken, the more fully board members can commit themselves to it and the greater can be the trust that grows among constituencies.

Opportunities to Strengthen Boundary Spanning

Intentional, conscientious focus on boundary work pays off for any board. It protects the organization from an insular mentality that leaves the organization exposed to unrecognized or unexpected threats. It allows board members the satisfaction of watching their deliberations affect the direction of the organization and the vitality of their religious tradition. Several examples illustrate some concluding principles that boards can explore to be creative on their organization's frontiers.

• *Learning from history helps board members tame their anxieties about current environmental trends and increases their capacity to consider options.* Two examples illustrate this principle. In the first case, a small church-related Protestant college faced multiple issues: decreasing funding from and attenuating ties to denominational constituencies; growing connections with constituencies in the local community, including other denominations; faculty discord; and destabilized leadership. After some preliminary committee work with a consultant, the board, on retreat, engaged in an exercise to review the school's history. Using a long roll of butcher paper on which key events in the organization's and board's history were named, they each "signed in" where they had come to know the organization and filled in from memory their understanding of the history. Events included were national, ecclesiastical, and institutional (Trustee Leadership Development, 1990). A parallel history time-line exercise for congregations is described by Scott Thumma (Thumma, 1998, pp. 209–210).

Because this board included both lay and clergy, town and regional leaders, the shared lore was rich. Members came away with a strengthened sense of time and location. Their school had faced parallel crises before, and in the current situation they recognized both the depth of their own commitments and the height of the stakes. Daunting tasks lay ahead. One publicly unspoken but privately discussed conclusion was that neither they nor the president, who was close to retirement, had been up to the task. The historical overview led them to recognize that they had to position themselves intentionally for new work.

In the second case, contending with the recent past was a less explicit but not less significant task. About a third of the board of this local church-related social service agency had lived through a scandalous episode in the history of the organization: the conviction of the executive director for embezzlement—and that was only the tip of the iceberg. The organization had been on a building spree, courtesy of government funding for homes for the elderly, and had extended its services considerably beyond its means. The board was thrilled with the new executive director and financial officer and with how much progress had been made, but it was somewhat uncertain about how to consolidate the organization's gains and continue to reassure the public.

Most notably, the board worked to reassure the public by demonstrating sound fiscal management, using the rebuilt board as a monitor and exploring institutional partnerships with local congregations and other nearby social services agencies to widen their services in a cost-effective manner. In a fast-paced environment of changing government regulations and health insurance stipulations, they spoke about the past when asked, but emphasized demonstrating good stewardship and recovery of their mission. The board attracted effective new members. History had chastened this group but had also given its members the baseline for a tremendous sense of accomplishment.

- *Constituencies represented on the board can benefit from one another's viewpoints in ways that will improve their own work and educate them for their work in the larger faith community.* It only took an hour. Yet within that time, the three major constituencies represented on the board had spoken to one another about some of their deepest commitments and greatest concerns. Divided into three groups—bishops and diocesan officials, priests, and lay leaders (representing business, education, and the ecumenical church)—trustees of this theological school discussed the assigned topic: what they expected from newly ordained priests today. They were really discussing what they wanted their seminary to accomplish.

After an hour, they returned to the larger group and heard reports from each small group. The bishops told the lay leaders and priests about their need for priests to help the church stay on an even keel and be respected by its publics. The pastors told the lay leaders and bishops how much they wanted associates in their parishes who could carry their own weight and help with the growing burdens of ministry. Lay leaders emphasized to the bishops and priests their craving for excellent preaching, more help in passing on the faith to their children, and greater wisdom about the economic and social realities shaping their own lay vocations.

Each group was deeply informed by the viewpoint of the other two groups. Where else might such a conversation have occurred? Expectations are all too often assumed. This outpouring of opinion would inform the work of the board, the efforts of faculty and administrators, and the reflections of bishops, priests, and lay members of the board. The trustees' dual loyalty to the seminary and to the larger church had been served because high standards had been articulated and affirmed.

• *Reconfiguring governance creates the opportunity to interpret the relationship between an organization and its environment in fresh and powerful ways.* Recent research on theological school boards has revealed that those institutions that were products of mergers had higher standards of performance than those that were not, as indicated on a standardized instrument for self-assessment. A seminary of the Evangelical Lutheran Church in America, a seminary of the United Methodist Church, and seminary of the Presbyterian Church in America each had two or more decades in which to realize the merger of two schools from sister denominations. Each merged institution developed a new form of governance by linking, representing, and negotiating the experience of two previous schools that had different practices and forms of legitimation. Self-consciousness about governance was not avoided but became customary. Board members also had the satisfaction of knowing that the alliances they were forging in their new institutions were contributing to alliances between related denominations that were about to or had recently merged (Klein, 1995).

These boards had to work conscientiously to build new ties, reduce suspicions, and retain multiple cultures and loyalties. The board was the medium and model for much of the change. It provided a deliberative setting in which to negotiate the new partnerships and work out the ramifications. The heritage of intentional, conscientious governance lasted beyond the linking events themselves and is part of the remembered history and culture of the board. The excellence and stability of these schools offers some hope for other organizations within the same or very similar religious traditions that are considering partnerships or mergers. Parishes and congregations, parochial and other private religious schools, and hospital and social service organizations can rely on their boundary-spanning boards to lead the reconfiguration. The effort requires the long view and conscientious effort, which the governing board can model.

Conclusion

Although the examples used in this chapter are drawn from Christian organizations, the governance of all religious organizations, faith communities, or interfaith coalitions provides board members with unique opportunities to exercise their faith and experience on behalf of purposes they value most deeply by guiding the organizations that embody and carry out those values. Both their position and their performance are essential to the work of spanning the organization's boundaries and to sustaining strong, two-way communication with all of its constituencies. Effectiveness in these vital processes is necessary for developing trust in the organization and for gaining the resources necessary for it to carry out its mission. The practice of faith on the ever-changing frontiers of the organization is best experienced by those with passion born of commitment and ingenuity fed by curiosity and wisdom. Religious organizations have the opportunity to participate directly in the reshaping of the nation's landscape at a time when older forms are fading. The leaven provided by people of faith is all the more needed. And that makes governance a calling, a vocation that requires our disciplined and faithful service.

REFERENCES

Ammerman, N. T. *Baptist Battles.* New Brunswick, N.J.: Rutgers University Press, 1990.

Chait, R. P., Holland, T. P., and Taylor, B. E. *The Effective Board of Trustees.* Phoenix: Oryx Press, 1993.

Chait, R. P., Holland, T. P., and Taylor, B. E. *Improving the Performance of Governing Boards.* Phoenix: Oryx Press, 1996.

Chaves, M. "Segmentation in a Religious Labor Market." *Sociological Analysis,* 1991, *52*(2), 143–158.

Coalter, M. J., Mulder, J. M., and Weeks, L. B. *The Organizational Revolution*. Louisville, Ky.: Westminster/John Knox Press, 1992.

Cothen, G. C. *What Happened to the Southern Baptist Convention?* Macon, Ga.: Smyth & Helwys, 1993.

De Pree, M. *Leadership Is an Art*. New York: Dell, 1990.

Fitzgerald, P. A. *The Governance of Jesuit Colleges in the United States, 1920–1970*. Notre Dame, Ind.: University of Notre Dame Press, 1984.

Handy, R. T. *A History of the Churches in the United States and Canada*. New York: Oxford University Press, 1976.

Klein, C. R. "Theological School Governance in Context." Unpublished paper presented at the Consultation on Theological Faculty and Leadership Research, Lilly Endowment, Dec. 1995.

Marsden, G. M. *Reforming Fundamentalism*. Grand Rapids, Mich.: Eerdmans, 1987.

Middleton, M. "Nonprofit Boards of Directors: Beyond the Governance Function." In W. W. Powell (ed.), *The Nonprofit Sector*. New Haven, Conn.: Yale University Press, 1987.

Mullin, R. B., and Richey, R. E. *Reimagining Denominationalism*. New York: Oxford University Press, 1994.

Stoltzfus, V. *Church-Affiliated Higher Education*. Goshen, Ind.: Pinchpenny Press, 1992.

Thumma, S. "Methods for Congregational Study." In N. T. Ammerman, J. W. Carroll, C. S. Dudley, and W. McKinney (eds.), *Studying Congregations*. Nashville, Tenn.: Abingdon Press, 1998.

Trustee Leadership Development. "Trustee Education Manual." Indianapolis, Ind.: Lilly Endowment, 1990.

Wuthnow, R. *The Restructuring of American Religion*. Princeton, N.J.: Princeton University Press, 1988.

8

THE MERGER CHALLENGE

BUILDING A COHESIVE CULTURE

David J. Nygren, Julie Hickman Burg,
Dennis A. Ross

THE MERGER of any two organizations or institutions requires delicate balancing of interests, timing, and a tough stomach to consolidate and integrate effectively. The announcement of an impending merger activates a series of events and consequences that need diligent planning and managing. Without planning at every level in the organization, what happens most often is a degree of chaos and misdirection that results in collective inertia. Conversely, well-planned mergers can lead to achieving the mission and accomplishing strategic and financial goals identified at the outset.

This chapter examines the dynamic processes of mergers. Specifically, opportunities for successful integration are intensified by certain actions of effective leaders, governing bodies, and managers who attend to the cultural dynamics, to process effectiveness issues, and to adaptive challenges that are largely psychological. Because the health care industry at the present time is so stretched by the challenges of integrating effectively, both successful and ineffective health care integration processes will be illustrated. Within the population of hospitals that are undergoing radical affiliations, religiously sponsored organizations have an additional set of challenges. Religious schools, seminaries, social service agencies, and small congregations are also facing the challenges of mergers and integrations. The dynamics of these processes described in this chapter may be relevant to any two organizations intending to partner in some significant fashion, regardless of the sector they represent.

The psychological and human toll of a merger often prevents individual leaders, board members, and even employees from directing the change processes required for an effective integration to occur. There are a variety of reasons for such resistance behavior. At the very least is the question of whose jobs or positions will be affected by the merger. Even board members in a merger are not without this concern for their own positions. Leadership paralysis often sets in because the leader of the new and combined entity is often chosen from within and the two incumbent leaders often vie, however covertly, for the position that truly only one can hold. Efforts to avoid the hard task of appointing a leader should be countered by the board, and action should be directed toward securing effective leadership.

An extreme example of such avoidance behavior occurred when six hospitals merged into a large regional system. Rather than appointing a leader to shape the consolidation, the board authorized moving the CEOs of all the facilities to the corporate office without identifying their respective roles and authority. Needless to say, group pandemonium evolved. Once a new leader from outside the system was appointed, all the other leaders found their way out of the organization entirely. The institutional memory evaporated, the facilities were without direction, and the balance sheet was looking dismal.

The implication, which would appear obvious, is that undermanaged mergers can have significant negative consequences. In this example, the politics of religion, personal relationships, and fear of pushing the process too fast led very smart people to make some very regrettable choices. Why? There is no one clear explanation, but the dynamics we elaborate in this chapter suggest some ways that such seemingly obvious mistakes can be avoided in the future.

Achieving Integration Success

So what groups of tasks are critical to the basic integration of organizations? We have identified four: cultural cohesion, process effectiveness, structural alignment, and a growth strategy. These are depicted in Figure 8.1, which outlines our method of analyzing the merger process. The integration pyramid illustrates the complex tasks of integration. A framework for isolating the key concerns in most mergers, it highlights the essential process, key tasks, and methods necessary for a successful outcome.

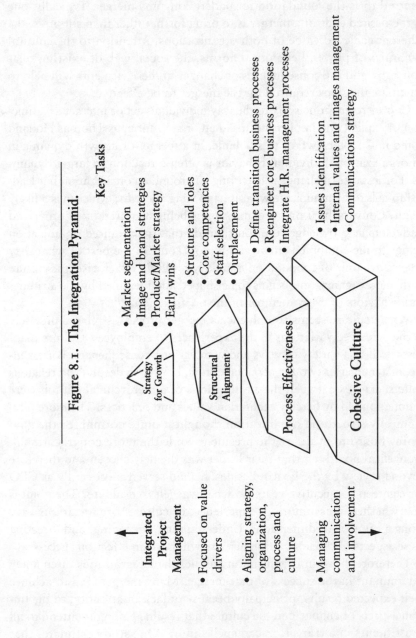

Figure 8.1. The Integration Pyramid.

Key Tasks

Strategy for Growth
- Market segmentation
- Image and brand strategies
- Product/Market strategy
- Early wins

Structural Alignment
- Structure and roles
- Core competencies
- Staff selection
- Outplacement

Process Effectiveness
- Define transition business processes
- Reengineer core business processes
- Integrate H.R. management processes

Cohesive Culture
- Issues identification
- Internal values and images management
- Communications strategy

Integrated Project Management
- Focused on value drivers
- Aligning strategy, organization, process and culture
- Managing communication and involvement

Cohesive Culture

At the base of the integration pyramid is a cohesive culture, which is often referred to as the foundation for undertaking any merger. Typically, one of the desired ends of a merger is to bring forth, rather than suppress, the inherent achieved value of both organizations. Attention to the cultural dynamics of power, behavioral norms, the social web of existing relationships, and the consequences of changes in these elements will help to articulate the steps required for the merger to be effective.

Culture refers principally to the way individuals act or interact as a function of explicit and implicit norms in an organization, as Thomas Holland noted in Chapter Two of this volume. In a merger or growth dynamic in an organization, individual behavior is often a reaction to larger dynamics. For instance, if change is occurring all around an organization but leadership fails to communicate what is happening and why, cynicism is a likely result. Conversely, if one organization is being acquired by another and leadership acknowledges the contribution that the acquired organization brings to the combined entity and honors some of the best of what they offer, a dynamic of cooperation is a likely result. In either case, the culture of the new organization begins to be shaped and identified by the attitudes and behaviors of every member of the organization.

Where culture seems to influence a merger process is related precisely to the perceived variations in the experiences of employees. Culture manifests itself in a variety of ways and with varying consequences. For example, in a merger of two former competitors, both with deeply held religious beliefs, clashes between the assumptions of a hierarchical church were counterpointed by fiercely egalitarian values and practices. The more hierarchically structured organization thought it quite normal for the governing board to evaluate the president while the more congregational, evangelical board felt that their leader was divinely chosen and therefore beyond review by the board. Besides, he had served successfully as CEO for eighteen consecutive years, so what was left to evaluate? The point is that whether in assumption, experience, or culture, organizations vary along a number of dimensions. Understanding, managing, and directing these aspects of the integration activity will have an effect on success.

Therefore, how an organization handles the integration is often a key determinant in the success of that merger. Many mergers fail to achieve their expected results, principally because of lack of attention to the human aspects of change and the culture that results. Failing to attend to all constituents in a transition can spell failure. One study estimates that approximately one-third to one-half of all mergers fail due to "employee problems" (Davy, Kinicki, Kilroy, and Scheck, 1988). Comments such as "things have really changed around here" are as much statements about culture as about morale or structure.

Loyalty and morale erode when an integration is implemented and communicated poorly. Language and leadership action are viewed as symptomatic of the cultural direction to be advanced. The economic consequences of poorly organized and communicated mergers can be staggering. One study estimates that two hours of productivity are lost per day during the early stages of a merger (Wishard, 1985). This loss results from distracting rumors and gossip about the integration and does not include losses in productivity due to dissatisfaction and stress.

Process Effectiveness

Process effectiveness during integration refers to evaluating existing business, customer, and organizational processes to assess their effectiveness. Because both organizations are essentially "unfrozen" as the change process begins, the opportunity to build new systems is evident. Often the frenzy of the merger process and the fear of making necessary changes causes organizations to import from the existing organizations the "best" of either system. Instead, the merger should provide an opportunity for careful reconsideration of business processes, operational restructuring, and job redesign.

Managers on either side of the merger may be fearful of declaring that existing processes need review or change. There is a felt need to defend the systems that are in place in either organization. This is often the case even if these systems have at other times been called archaic, personality driven, or simply poor business process. Who in any organization would prefer to learn new work processes rather than use the ones they already know? Yet with the rapid expansion of technological solutions and the enormous cost of making changes to them, organizations are rightly slow to exchange an existing technology for another one.

What works in one system may not be compatible with the multitude of interfacing systems that link business results. Two hospitals or schools deciding to consolidate human resource information systems, for instance, would be unraveled to think that payroll systems might not work after the conversion. Nevertheless, if one of the drivers for an affiliation or integration is system efficiency—as in cost reduction by eliminating duplication of services—such hard choices must be considered. Mergers present a unique window for change. Because processes are essentially fluid during integration, there will probably not be a more opportune time to insert efficiencies and tighter systems aligned with the strategic intent of the merger.

Structural Alignment

The integration pyramid suggests that another critical dynamic is aligning structures and organizational forms to match the strategic intent and expanded business efficiency goals. *Alignment* refers to the manner in which the newly combined or integrated organization will function. Alignment is required among strategy and leadership, core competencies and capabilities of the workforce, and reporting relationships that are defined as clearly as possible. Structural changes should reflect both cultural and business process redefinition. Cultural dynamics are embedded in organizational design.

Social architecture, as some would call it, refers to the design of work, relationships to support output, and the climate of work that allows individuals to remain committed to the organization. This architecture can easily be disrupted. Dabbling with the organizational chart will have an effect not only on people but also on processes.

Probably no action more explicitly reflects the intention of the board and leadership than the delegation of authority to individual jobs in the new organization. The new organizational chart defines quickly a new set of relationships. Very often even board structures are altered. As roles and relationships change, the new strategy or organization often requires a new set of competencies. In some instances new competencies may be required for individual members, leaders, the board, or staff. It is sometimes true that the core competence of the organization may be altered.

For example, when hospitals form integrated delivery networks and systems, the competency profiles of many key systems and the persons who operate them require change. When organizations in areas with overlapping markets form partnerships, an institutionally focused board makes little business sense if what it is now governing is a market or region. In addition, as the strategic intent changes, all levels of the organization may require new competence to execute operations effectively. Too often, in our experience, boards are least receptive to their obligation to reconsider their competence, their composition, the size of the board, committee structure, and fundamental ways of governing in light of the exigencies of the integration.

Particular challenges emerge in mergers. Depending on the strength of emphasis on operational or programmatic integration, huge effects can be felt. In a merger between a Catholic hospital and a Baptist hospital located one mile apart, leaders decided to merge some premier services into one of the facilities. Although the intention was good from nearly every business and clinical point of view, physicians stopped the integration process entirely. They refused to cooperate, arguing that patients and their medical practices would be affected adversely by the merger. Additionally, the move of premier services from one facility to the other signaled to employees that the larger of the two facilities was actually "taking over."

Even small actions can be exaggerated in importance if not explained. For instance, in the same merger, an executive responsible for organizational mission was located in the Baptist hospital. Because this individual was a Catholic nun, the Baptist partner felt that the Catholics were taking over. Being careful to explain the intention fully, and the desired results, is one way to position the new organization and leadership for success.

Strategy for Growth

The capstone of the integration pyramid points to strategic growth as the driver behind any merger. In health care alone, the number of mergers and consolidations in the 1990s was astonishing. Successful mergers are driven by a strategic intent to grow. Organizations are either growing or in decline (Zangwill, 1993). To mobilize the transition and advance the internal and external perception of growth and positive market positioning, the board and leadership must move rapidly from an internal alignment focus to external competitive positioning.

In one large national hospital system, the consolidation of two regions was so inwardly focused that internal wrangling for independence between the regions didn't stop until market share diminished by 11 percent and deficits exceeded $200 million. By that point, the turnaround plan nearly crippled the entire organization. As this example demonstrates, too much time can easily be spent on internal mechanics rather than attending to the organization's external positioning for growth.

In summary, the integration pyramid is intended to organize some of the logical processes that should be considered during a merger or integration. No matter how clearly delineated the steps in the integration process may appear, they are generally felt to be chaotic and haphazard. To minimize cynicism and keep morale and work flow concentrated positively, several steps can be taken. Table 8.1 outlines a method of describing the work of a transition team whose job is to coordinate and integrate all the activities of integration and to communicate about these activities as often and as clearly as is necessary.

Table 8.1. Transition Priorities, Objectives, and Key Actions During Integration.

Transition Priority Issues	Objectives	Key Actions
Value Preservation	Develop thorough understanding of both cultures Establish new cultural norms Determine what values must be preserved in order to optimize the integration Get commitment to operational values	Conduct interviews and focus groups during early weeks of integration to assess current organizational practices and potential problems Administer organizational questionnaires to assess pre- and postintegration attitudes and pinpoint areas of concern by department Facilitate planning sessions to develop cultural integration goals and strategy
Morale Maintenance	Manage transition effectively Involve employees in decision making Present employees with positive, realistic view of future	Form transition team with approximately equal number of key stakeholders from both organizations Obtain employee perceptions through focus groups and/or interviews Establish communication and strategy
Strategic Capabilities Transfer	Develop policy and criteria for personnel changes Retain star performers	Form special task force charged with personnel changes Reassure key employees of their value and place in the new organization
Demand-to-Resource Equilibration	Align business processes Imagine business synergies where possible	Dedicate alignment responsibility to key personnel Plan and monitor business alignment issues
Strategic/ Goal-Oriented Operating Style	Policy and procedures reinforce desired practices	Establish best-practice or integration task force groups to redesign or reconcile procedures and systems Implement processes to measure accomplishment of integration goals

Processes for Achieving Integration Outcomes

Careful staging and timing of an integration process helps to ensure the achievement of desired outcomes. Toward this end, the integration can be divided into three phases: premerger, merger, and postmerger. Examining the objectives and activities required in each of the three phases will help ensure that integration priorities do not slip through the cracks. Thoughtful planning will also help to reduce constituents' anxiety by clearly communicating integration expectations and action plans.

The Premerger Phase

The *premerger phase* is the time between the intent to integrate and the finalization of the agreement. During this phase, the priority is to articulate the vision, strategy, and objectives for the integration. To define and communicate the vision, two important activities prevail: gaining a solid knowledge of both merger partners and modeling the employee involvement process.

Having a firm understanding of the values, history, culture, and operating practices of both merger partners is the foundation for the integration itself. Though this seems obvious, more than a few mergers proceed with incorrect assumptions about one or both organizations' culture, strategies, or readiness for change. Providing an opportunity for the transition team to perform a high-level strategy and system review will assist in deepening the knowledge base of both partners. The review may include strategic agenda, performance, history, values, culture, customer profile, employee profile, and personnel capabilities, among other things. To accomplish this understanding, one system administered a culture survey to employees of both organizations in order to get a clear picture of each organization's culture. The survey results provided a basis for assessing the similarities and differences among each culture and the organizations' readiness for change.

The culture survey process of gathering employee perspectives leads us to the second activity of the premerger phase, that is, *modeling the employee involvement process*. Employee involvement at all levels is essential to each phase of the integration. It strengthens commitment to the integration and ensures that good ideas and learning are shared. The same organization that asked employees for input through the culture survey process gained input from senior management by interviewing each senior manager individually. They were asked for their perceptions of the key issues, critical success factors, and perceived barriers to the integration.

The information obtained through the interviews gave insight into senior management perspectives, capabilities, and agendas, and into the strategic issues of the integration.

Based on the knowledge acquired from these activities, the outcome of the premerger phase was a specification of the vision, strategy, and objectives of the integration. Included in such specifications should be descriptions of key issues, barriers to change, required performance, and transition project roles, and identification of immediate actions, or "quick wins." Finally, the premerger plan should describe the strategy for ongoing communication and employee involvement.

The Merger Phase

The merger process itself typically encompasses the first six to nine months after the integration agreement is completed. The outcome of the merger phase is to design and implement the merger's "master plan," that is, to identify and implement the work that needs to occur in order to redesign processes and combine the organizations. The master plan describes work to be accomplished across the system by each transition team, including the charges, end results, timing, and deliverables.

One hospital system chose to organize eight transition teams according to cross-functional bodies of work (such as leadership and governance, finance, information technology, human resources, and communications). Liaison members were appointed to ensure alignment and idea sharing across teams. This organization took special care to consider the key enabling processes required for merger success, including communications, training and education, organizational development, and information technology and information systems. Monitoring and feedback mechanisms were created to assess progress toward goal accomplishment and time lines. Throughout this period, employees were involved as members of transition teams and their perceptions were monitored through employee forums.

The Postmerger Phase

The postmerger phase is the period after the transition plan has been implemented. Postmerger requires activities to stabilize the organization and strengthen organizational identity and commitment. Employee involvement in the form of board and leadership development meetings and employee forums assist the organization in continuing to shape and refine the work agenda, build support for strategic direction, manage expectations, and reduce anxiety.

Another critical activity during this phase is the implementation of a *decision support process* to update the organization's strategy routinely. This process assists the organization in continuing to refine and further its strategic direction.

In every phase of the merger, each constituency in the process has a unique set of challenges and concerns. For leadership, governance, sponsors, employees, and in the case of health care mergers, physicians and patients, initial perceptions of the success or failure of the new organization endure. Perceptions of leadership, for example, are formed even before the leader is ready to emerge for public scrutiny.

The president of the merger of two small health care facilities in a rather tight community of 200,000 residents thought it best to fill jobs quickly. He built his team rapidly, with 80 percent of the members coming from one side of the merger. Regardless of the team's competence, their greatest challenge was then to gain credibility. In another, much larger system, the executive insisted on a perfect-balance formula for staffing and selected a tit-for-tat selection process. The unintended result was that competence was overlooked as the chief criteria in selection and key talent was rapidly lost to competitors. How well the integration process is managed is the first criteria for assessing both the board and senior leadership.

Integration of Constituencies

This section highlights "best practices" in managing various constituencies in the merger process. Each stakeholder group has specific concerns and expectations that must be managed. Building individual groups' confidence in the transition process is an additional challenge. Again the focus is on building commitment to the strategic value of the merger, and anything that can be done to keep people informed and involved in the process will help. Following are a few examples of integrating activities by group.

Leadership

Everyone wants to know to whom they will be reporting when a merger is complete. One of the first steps to stabilizing and directing the new combined organization is for the board to determine the mission-critical competencies that will result in the achievement of the organization's strategic vision and direction. A second step is to assess both partners to note the distinctive value and core competence of each organization. Knowing what assets to protect in the uniting process can affect ultimately the new value of the merged enterprise. The third step is to identify areas of mutual agreement and overlap, areas of divergence, and unique areas where no overlaps exist among the operating styles and principles of both organizations. Such identification begins to spell out assumptions that are likely to affect the transaction. The fourth step is to conduct an objective review of the talent pool from both organizations and develop a reasonable approach to retention, severance arrangements, and a new contract process. The fifth step is to refine key leadership and management positions to fit the new organization's strategy, and to select individuals carefully and quickly. The final step is to communicate as clearly as reasonable the scope of change, new appointments, and anything that is likely to have an impact on the willingness of individuals to remain in the new organization.

Governance

Integrating the governance processes for the new organization is tricky. Often in a merger of two relatively strong organizations, retaining valued contributors to a board can be as important as the selection of management. Sharing governance responsibilities is often, but not always, part of the expectation of the merger process. Several steps can be helpful when considering board composition and development. First, define a set of principles or values that will shape the development of a new governance structure. Set the size of and membership criteria for the new board. Determine the individual and group competency requirements required for governing the new organization. Avoid selecting members solely on the basis of tenure within either organization.

Frequently, many newer boards think the bulk of the work is complete once members have been selected. In reality, the real work begins here. Orienting the board to the business, strategic priorities, board expectations, and criteria for evaluation will launch the new organization. Perhaps conduct an initial board retreat to build commitment to the combined mission, values, and strategic imperatives. Consider foundational assumptions about leadership, religious orientation to work, attitudes toward specific populations served, and so on. Build the board's agenda for the next six to twelve months. Review the information needs of the board. Create any needed committees and task forces of the board, and define their charter, tasks, and timetables for reporting back to the full board. Finally, identify the board's relationship with various stakeholders, including both super and subsidiary boards, and define when and how boards will interact.

The work of the new board includes clarifying the agenda process, establishing committee charges, and engaging informally so that members get to know one another even before work is required of them. In large systems with complex governing and advisory groups, respective responsibilities should be clarified to avoid duplicate work or, even worse, conflicts over the same work. An easy way should be found to share with board members the initiatives of the organization by coordinating site visits with board meetings, rotating the location of those meetings among different facilities and sites whenever possible. An annual review of board governance is an important process and a way to advance development of the board. Adjusting board composition every two years to reflect the new strategic agenda of the organization can also be helpful.

Employees

The human side of change needs to be considered carefully. Individuals build a sense of commitment to their employer over a long period. In the best case, employees identify with the organization's mission, developing a sense of belonging and purpose in the organization. As cultures merge, a key challenge is to assure the work force, to the extent possible, that the process is being managed and that their concerns will be taken seriously. Unless the transaction is a fifty-fifty merger (and even this is no guarantee), employees in the perceived "acquired" organization can easily feel undervalued, that their commitment and loyalty are not recognized; consequently, morale generally sinks and turnover can intensify.

In addition, from the point of view of efficiency and productivity, one of the key challenges in the process is to retain top talent and transfer the value and strategic capabilities of the two organizations into the combined entity. Surely it will be the case that some individuals choose to exit or are not offered positions. Alignment of the business processes and the building of organizational synergies within each new business unit is in fact one of the goals of a merger. Equilibration between supply and demand or staffing and work intensity requires a focused process that will have felt consequences, which in turn must also be managed.

Mirvis and Marks (1991) illustrate some of the major issues affecting integration and some of the objectives and actions that leaders can take to limit unintended consequences to the workforce (see also Mirvis and Marks, 1992). The factors most likely to influence employee morale after the integration include, first, how the process is managed by leadership. Employees who feel they are informed about the process, who believe they understand why it happened, and who see top management dealing effectively with new demands are significantly more likely to show higher morale. The second greatest predictor of overall morale in integrations is the extent to which employees identify with the organization. Workers who trust management, identify with company goals and policies, and see working for the organization as something more than a job suffer smaller declines in morale and satisfaction and express less desire to leave the organization. For these people, commitment to an organization is bowed but not broken during an integration.

Organizations with a tradition of effective and caring management, that involve employees in decision making and keep them informed, have significantly more satisfied employees in the postintegration period. Paradoxically, involvement in the integration process, planning and fighting for or creating a new corporate culture, is synergizing; creating esprit de corps among managers is less stressful than not participating in the transition process. People who get along with their managers, supervisors, and coworkers are much less likely to leave and more likely to have higher morale.

Finally, and interestingly, demographic characteristics seem to have little influence on morale or satisfaction. Conversely, those hired around or during a tumultuous integration period almost always rate the organization lower than their tenured or future counterparts. They become a "lost generation."

Professional Staff

The involvement of the professional staff, whether physicians in hospitals or faculty in schools or seminaries, will most likely control the success or failure of the integration. A hospital governing body and management must involve their professional staff early in merger plans and in every aspect of the merger, acquisition, conversion, or affiliation. In clinical or operational affairs, a committee consisting of governance, management, and physicians may help assure clinicians that their concerns will be considered, that methods will be put in place to resolve issues and share information, and that they will have some input into the decision-making process that could affect their patients, work, and livelihood. There should be an ongoing liaison mechanism between the governing body and the professional staff to handle not only mergers, consolidations, acquisitions, and closures, but all issues of concern both to the governing body and to the staff.

In addition to the committee of governance, management, and professional leaders, the staffs from the merging or consolidating organizations should form a joint committee to address and resolve any differences regarding organizational structure, staff bylaws, credentialing processes, continuous quality improvement or utilization review, peer review, and other professional staff functions.

The research of Alexander, Halpern, and Lee (1996) indicates that the attitudes of hospital administration and the governing body toward a hospital merger have a strong impact on the reactions of the affected staffs. When administrators are open about plans, clear about objectives, and inclusive of the opinions of the staff, the staff generally support the merger and work hard to resolve the resultant issues. They are less likely to fear additional changes, because they expect to be consulted and to be kept informed. When secrecy is prevalent and the grapevine is the best source of information, distrust runs high on all sides and continues in the aftermath of the merger.

Operational integration is perhaps the most complex of all processes in a merger. Because such integration is a relatively recent phenomenon, research and best practice are still being developed. What is known, however, is that the closing of programs or departments or the loss of professional staff positions may be the most difficult process of all to manage. Research by the American Medical Association (1996) shows that when medical staffs are not consulted or informed in advance about a consolidation, they react more negatively to the entire merger process. Most systems appear to involve professional staffs in these decisions, and processes seem to run relatively smoothly. The key to working with professional staff such as physicians or faculty, as with most other groups in a merger process, is to involve them if their lives are likely to be affected by the change.

Guidelines

Although there is no simple way to produce all the effects desired in the merger process, there are some rules of thumb to remember.

Communicate. Frequent open and honest communication that conveys a realistic picture of the process and desired future state helps immensely to gain trust. Face-to-face communication forums, special integration newsletters, and employee feedback mechanisms can also be helpful. Preparing special manager briefing materials that help to orient employees builds consistency and some standards for beginning to shape a new culture. Two prominent merging medical research facilities found that a weekly newsletter updating employees on transition events was so successful, they standardized the communiqué as *Transition*. It is in its third year of publication and the transitions have not stopped.

Document a thoroughly planned transition. Employees get anxious under conditions of uncertainty. Clarifying the steps to achieving integration and the employees' role in the process minimizes useless worry. So does paying attention to timing and staging the process carefully. One multiorganizational system put the chronology of key events of the merger on their Intranet so that anyone interested could access it. Predictability reduces anxiety.

Attempt to boost morale. Build on small wins and acknowledge employees who demonstrate the new spirit or culture. Positioning management visibly and fostering high employee involvement in the process also tends to increase satisfaction.

Reduce the workforce by attrition. Only rarely does a dramatic reduction in workforce accomplish more than grief, especially if it is done without fairness. If some reduction is required, there are humane and just ways to support those who leave and those who stay. Ensuring criteria for any downsizing efforts and administering them fairly will have impacts on the organization's life for years afterward. If some job elimination is necessary, reassuring star performers of their value or place in the new organization can affect retention of the core competence required to do business.

Manage the transition. Large mergers or transitions are often best overseen by a team, with at least the leader devoted to the task. Monitoring results throughout the first two years is one way of measuring how strongly the organization is integrating. The Mercer Consulting Group studied forty-three complete and fifty-four pending mergers between 1985 and 1995. They found that strong leadership and postintegration management are key distinguishing factors in any merger strategy. Furthermore, results indicate that integration done for strategic rather than financial purposes has a better chance of success (Mirvis and Marks, 1991).

Conclusion

A notable and experienced board leader says of mergers, "When you've seen a merger, you've seen a merger." Ending this chapter on such a note may contradict the apparent purpose of our dissection of the integration process. Certainly it is true that every merger has its idiosyncrasies. Our observation of mergers allows us to break them into somewhat distinct processes, phases, and ends. If every merger were entirely new, we could predict that few leaders would have the courage to step up to the work and few boards would be willing to risk failure. Ezra Pound says of poetry that "it helps you remember what you never knew you knew." Perhaps not as eloquently, we say of mergers managed well that they are a great deal of common sense and, like poetry, deceptively simple.

REFERENCES

Alexander, J., Halpern, M., and Lee, S. "The Short-Term Effects of Merger on Hospital Operations." *Health Services Research*, 1996, *30*(6), 827–847.

American Medical Association. *Report of the Organized Medical Staff Section Governing Council.* Chicago: American Medical Association, 1996.

Davy, J., Kinicki, A., Kilroy, J., and Scheck, C. "After the Merger: Dealing with People's Uncertainty." *Training & Development Journal*, 1988, *42*(11), 57–61.

Mirvis P., and Marks, M. *Managing the Merger.* Englewood Cliffs, N.J.: Prentice-Hall, 1991.

Mirvis, P., and Marks, M. "The Human Side of Merger Planning: Assessing and Analyzing 'Fit.'" *Human Resource Planning*, 1992, *15*(3), 69–92.

Wishard, B. "Mergers: Human Dimensions." *The Magazine of Bank Administration*, 1985, *61*(6), 74–79.

Zangwill, W. *Lightning Strategies for Innovation.* San Francisco: New Lexington Press, 1993.

9

THE BOARD'S ROLE
IN SHAPING STRATEGY

Richard P. Chait

AT FIRST BLUSH, and even upon reflection, the idea that a board could play a central role in the strategy process probably strikes many people as rather preposterous. Consider for a moment the typical board of a religious organization. It has eighteen to twenty-four members and meets as a whole three or four times a year, usually for less than a day. Many members have no professional background in religious organizations and may have no prior experience in governance of any sort of organization.

Naturally enough, the question arises whether or not a rather large clergy and lay body that meets intermittently can or should participate meaningfully in the shaping of strategy for a complex organization in a highly competitive environment. Doubtful of the board's capacity to be a major player, some writers have questioned whether boards should be involved at all in strategy formulation. Keller (1983), for example, said that perhaps one or two board members might be party to "key strategy sessions," but because many "board members are busy executives themselves, they often prefer to make more rapid yes-no decisions" and to leave the details and deliberations to the executive. Annual board retreat would be a "useful way of informing trustees and involving them in strategy development" (p. 39). Once-a-year exposure to strategy may be as much as anyone should expect.

Reprinted with permission of Peterson's, a division of International Thomson Publishing, from *Strategy & Finance in Higher Education,* © 1992 by Peterson's Guides, Inc.

In examining this issue with respect to hospitals, Andre Delbecq, former dean of the business school at Santa Clara University, and Sandra Gill, president of Performance Management Resources, staked out a still more controversial position. In their 1988 article "Developing Strategic Direction for Governing Boards," based on a study of boards of trustees of hospitals and health care organizations, they concluded that the size, composition, committee structure, and decision-making processes of traditional boards all mitigated against effective governance, given the technical nature of health care, the confusing marketplace, unpredictable regulations, and the need to seize opportunities quickly.

Conditions parallel to these exist in religious organizations, including theological schools and congregations. Board members must deal with complex theological language, relatively abstract goals and objectives, fluctuating membership or enrollment, and the need to act decisively, often within a relatively brief time frame. Delbecq and Gill recommend that instead of depending on an unwieldy, voluntary, representational board, organizations should establish a small strategy board composed of five to seven compensated experts in the field who would function as a "strategic think tank" for the chief executive officer. All members of such a board would offer their best thinking and judgment, and because strategy deals with an unforeseeable future marketing risk, the board would be expected to risk giving implementation authority to the administration without requiring consensus from the board. The agendas of such boards would focus on broad environmental concerns and trends, current and potential markets or constituencies, and other strategic issues. The strategy board would exist primarily to challenge organizational tunnel vision. Its essential function would be to support, counsel, stimulate, and evaluate the strategy that the executive has responsibility to implement. The strategy board would be supplemented by an auxiliary board that would help raise money and foster amicable community relations.

The strategy board these writers propose certainly bears little resemblance to the typical board of most religious organizations. The case for strategy boards maintains that traditional boards are anachronisms at best, predicated on the naive assumption that full-time professionals need the wisdom of part-time amateurs to forge and implement organizational strategy. Conventional boards, the argument continues, actually impede the organization's ability to act strategically because they are too slow to respond to narrow windows of opportunity and too politically cowardly to act decisively.

These arguments cannot be summarily dismissed. Crafting and enacting an organizational strategy does indeed require a considerable, if not detailed, understanding of the enterprise, its history and competitors, and its environment. The process also requires a substantial and sustained commitment of time. Quite understandably, there are scholars and practitioners who believe that boards as traditionally constituted are not equal to the task. In addition, legions of executives and other leaders are repeatedly warning board members not to immerse themselves in the details of administration or day-to-day programming. Understandably, trustees start to wonder where they fit in.

The confusion about the board's role in the strategy process stems in part from a failure to separate into component parts the universe of religious organizations. It is difficult to generalize across the many forms of such organizations, from congregations and small community service agencies to multisite health care systems and international religious denominations. This chapter addresses primarily boards that govern single institutions and also enjoy some measure of autonomy, regardless of their size.

The boards of many religious organizations face formidable barriers along the path to strategy, including the politics of representation or appointment of members, statutory and regulatory limitations on the board's latitude, too few members from the local organization or with a comparable emotional attachment to the site, and disagreement among some trustees about the board's most basic roles. Is the board fundamentally the organization's guardian, the denomination's watchdog, the bishop's emissary, the constituents' representative, or all of the above?

The second source of confusion about the trustees' role, even in independent organizations, arises from a failure to recognize that the board's principal role differs at various stages of the strategy process. These stages include envisioning a future, formulating strategy, implementing strategy, and monitoring progress. The process is never quite as linear as that because not all functional areas of any organization march in lockstep. Some parts move forward while some slip backward and others stand still. Nevertheless, I believe we can profitably examine the board's role in the process stage by stage.

Envisioning a Future

Lately so much emphasis has been placed on the need for a vision that one might reasonably conclude that every executive and board member is supposed to be a prophet. Ordinary leadership is no longer enough; the times demand visionary, transformational leadership. Unfortunately, this burgeoning point of view, epitomized by the writings of James Fisher

(1984), appears to have impelled some leaders to withdraw to a lofty aerie from which they descend a few days later with "The Vision" in hand.

Other students of leadership, such as Robert Birnbaum (1988), take the more realistic approach of counseling leaders to synthesize the prevalent views and ambitions of the organization's constituents into a vision compatible with the prevalent culture and the traditions and beliefs of the religious organization. See where the group is headed, in fact, and then nudge them in that direction.

At this stage of the process, the board is singularly equipped to make a pivotal contribution because the most able trustees are blessed with "temporal double vision," the facility to train one eye on the past and the other on the future simultaneously. Especially on boards where local members constitute a significant fraction of the group, trustees have a sense of the organization's history, lore, and legend. As Lawrence Butler, chairman of The Cheswick Center, once noted, a board of trustees is (or should be) the organization's DNA: it carries the genetic code that transmits the institution's values, beliefs, heritage, and defining characteristics (L. Butler, personal communication). Without being reactionaries, trustees can usefully expose administrators to the bedrock beneath the topsoil they turn when rethinking the organization's mission or reshaping the organization's vision.

While it is mindful of tradition, the effective board also has the ability to foresee alternative futures precisely because it is not intimately immersed in the organization's internal operations and it stays on the periphery of the intricate and arcane rules that guide internal activities. The board, quite simply, is not bound by as many givens nor constrained by as many conventions as the institution is. Just as inexperienced students are often more imaginative and less cynical than seasoned administrators in analyzing case studies, many trustees, I find, are remarkably inventive.

On average, many board members are also more familiar than religious professionals with the environmental trends and political and economic forces that are likely to affect institutional conditions. Trustees are therefore well-situated to play a major role in envisioning an institution's future because they have a rich understanding of its past, a limited but important understanding of its present, and through their service as its unit of analysis, a unique focus on the organization as a whole.

At an anecdotal level, I have observed several boards, working with multiconstituency task forces, contributing significantly to the envisioning process. In a typical format, small groups of trustees conducted a mental tour of their organization circa 2002. At a subsequent plenary session each group reported the most tangible, visible, and palpable signs of change they observed while "walking" around the site. In the main, the board members' vivid and fertile imaginations both stimulated and broadened the discussion about the organization's future course.

Envisioning cannot be the stuff of every board meeting or even every committee meeting. It is an activity probably best undertaken intermittently, ideally on an extended retreat. Formulating strategy, however, is an ongoing effort. What is the board's role at this stage of the process?

Formulating Strategy

As a point of departure, it would be useful to define the concept of strategy. I am partial to a definition offered more than a decade ago by Kenneth Andrews (1980), who was then a professor at the Harvard Business School: Corporate strategy is the pattern of decisions in a company that determines and reveals its objectives, purposes, or goals; produces the principal policies and plans for achieving those goals; and defines the range of business the company is to pursue—preferably in a way that focuses resources to convert distinctive competencies into competitive advantage. In other words, formulating strategy is the process by which any organization wrestles a vision of the future into the realm of reality. It is the act of orchestration, of harnessing the parts in a way that sums to more than the whole.

To take a concrete example, suppose a seminary envisions a future as a genuinely and comprehensively multicultural campus. As Andrews stressed, this organization must develop a pattern of policies, procedures, decisions, and actions that synergistically communicate, advance, and reinforce its chosen course. Just for starters, this requires attention to student and faculty recruitment, the nature and content of the curriculum, student and community life, financial aid policies, housing accommodations, and the ethical dimensions of endowment investment. Clearly the formulation of a comprehensive strategic plan is more than a weekend's worth of work. It requires the ability to link one realm of the organization to another, to tie plans to budgets, to align incentives with priorities, and to match talents to tasks.

Suppose a congregation envisions its mission as providing temporary shelter and food for a growing homeless population in the community. Strategic planning to achieve this goal would require a comprehensive process involving clergy, lay leadership, and members in formulating opportunities for education, discussion, and analysis of available congregational and community resources that may be enlisted, and the development of means to ensure the appropriate location of these activities within the scriptural and liturgical tradition that provides the congregation with significant signs and symbols of its identity and mission.

To state the case baldly, I submit that no board of trustees can readily or easily do this. No governing board can, in effect, spin the whole intricate web that constitutes organizational strategy. This is not appropriate work for the board; this is the work the board makes certain that others get done.

The board is best positioned to ensure that organization leaders think strategically and devise an organizational strategy in the first instance. At a basic level, the board can gauge whether the plan contains the elements of an identifiable, consistent, competitive, and realistic strategy. Lofty but vague plans to be the finest hospital or seminary in the region or to increase utilization rates, enrollments, or congregational membership by 15 percent are aspirations, not strategies—a confusion boards can clarify. The board is also well positioned to evaluate whether the plan makes sense, both literally (Is it understandable?) and conceptually (Is it viable?).

Performing its role in the formulation of organizational strategy, however, the board leads largely by questions and not by answers. Through a line of inquiry common to analyzing any organizational strategy, Kenneth Andrews's (1980) classic book on the subject offers key guidelines that are readily applicable to the boards of religious organizations. The board can constructively challenge the executive and senior staff to articulate the plan clearly, explain their reasoning persuasively, and confront squarely the plan's feasibility, including its downside and its blind spots. In particular, the board should assess whether the plan serves the long-term welfare of the organization as a whole or the short-term indulgences of various constituents.

The board must probe respectfully but persistently. Trustees must not be excessively deferential, though too many are. If one accepts the premise that the board cannot formulate strategy, then its responsibility to evaluate strategy assumes the utmost importance. If ever a board is to add value to the institution, this is the moment.

The same protocol, perhaps with more depth and less breadth, applies to board committees in which senior staff normally present more detailed elements of the strategy for review. In actuality, such committees may be unable to do more than raise questions, regardless of how valuable that service may be. At the committee level, trustees can better assess the trade-offs that proposals inevitably entail. Should we, for example, devote a still greater portion of the operating budget to financial aid in order to attract a more diverse student population? Will the recruitment plan enhance multiculturalism? If so, what will be the reaction from those not included in the special benefits? Or if we as a congregation want to increase membership, shall we adopt church growth methods that have been shown to work, despite methodological conflict with traditional ways of doing evangelism within our denomination? Board committees can proliferate options and explore alternative tactics to achieve the desired vision.

I doubt, however, that a board can formulate a complete strategic plan per se. Indeed, to concede that a complex and interconnected pattern of policies and practices can be forged by laypeople meeting only sporadically would be to trivialize the notion of strategic planning. Earlier I maintained that the board should play a central and active role with respect to vision and mission. By contrast, I think trustees should play an ongoing but essentially reactive role with respect to strategy formulation. Boards are not well designed to conceive, draft, or edit strategic plans. Instead, they should ask questions, examine the data, express concerns, state objections, suggest alternatives, and when necessary, ask the chief officer to return with a better plan.

Implementing Strategy

Obviously I do not regard the board of trustees as a major player in the implementation of strategy. By and large that is the province of the administration and the staff of the organization. The professionals must execute the strategy and manage day-to-day human, financial, and physical resources. I would like, however, to highlight a few notable exceptions—areas where the board collectively or members individually might be engaged in implementation.

Many religious organizations enlist their board members to help raise money. Some denominationally supported organizations may seek board members' influence in the course of appropriations, legislation, and other matters of policy. To the extent that acquisition of resources meets the definition of strategy implementation, board members are hardly backbenchers. Furthermore, at smaller, thinly staffed organizations, trustees are often recruited to provide expertise, for example, on real estate, construction, portfolio management, and legal matters. These activities are all readily apparent examples of boards implementing strategy.

Less obviously, the board itself can be a strategic asset. Boards are apt to examine every facet of the organization except the board itself in terms of real or potential value added to the attainment of the strategy and the overriding vision.

Let's return to the seminary that aspired to be an example of multiculturalism. How can the board, as a board, contribute to that organization's comparative advantage? Of course the board itself must be diverse in its leadership as well as in its membership. A board that has maintained open channels of communication with alumni can be deployed to try to allay the anxieties of the skeptics as the once homogeneous campus becomes more diverse. The board's commitment to the new vision could be symbolically underscored by its funding of special scholarships or through its provision of internships. The board could decide that all new trustees must participate in the same orientations to multiculturalism now required for all new faculty and staff, or the trustees could develop a systematic plan to raise the board's profile, distinct from the seminary's profile, within the African American, Hispanic, and Asian American communities.

I offer this illustration only to suggest that if charity begins at home, maybe strategy does, too. The board of trustees, as an organizational entity, cannot and should not be exempt from the obligation to translate the institutional vision into a strategic game plan for the board as well as for the organization's operating units—quite the opposite, in fact, because the board should lead the way and set the pace. In that spirit, the board of one congregation that had just completed a year-long envisioning process planned to modify the board's committee structure to reinforce the newly declared priorities. Thus the board contemplated committees on, for example, the congregation's relationships with the local community, international outreach, and leadership development for its young people.

With its own house in order, a board can spur the instrumental efforts of other constituencies with a considerably greater degree of moral authority and political legitimacy. Religious organizations sometimes need to be prodded and provoked lest the urgent drive out the important. As if afflicted with lazy-eye syndrome, administrators and staff can gradually, inexorably shift their focus away from, or even sail beyond the periphery of, strategy. Because the refinement and implementation of strategy requires sustained attention, boards must work to counteract this drift and every now and then nudge the administration, or its clerical equivalent, as well as committees, to place the strategic process at the crosshairs and keep it there.

Unfortunately, boards have an uneven record at best on this score. Of the hundreds of board members I and my colleagues have interviewed over the past decade (Chait, Holland, and Taylor, 1993), the majority could not recall the organization's strategic priorities. These findings add credence to Delbecq and Gill's (1988) doubts about the utility of traditional boards. There are, however, some measures that boards can adopt to "keep an eye on the prize," to borrow a phrase from the civil rights movement.

As a first step toward creating agendas that concentrate attention on strategy, the board, in consultation with senior staff, could develop an annual calendar, or "continuous agenda," that explicitly links the work of the board and its committees to the organization's overall strategic priorities. For each item on the agenda at a meeting of the board or one of its committees, the administration should answer, in writing and in advance, the question most trustees have (though too few are brave enough to ever ask): Why are we discussing this? If the answer is not compelling or is concerned with a minor fiduciary responsibility, the board might profitably relegate the issue to a "consent agenda," which includes all routine actions that will be taken unless a member requests that the matter be removed from the consent agenda for board discussion.

For topics too significant to consign to the consent agenda, the appropriate senior officer should regularly provide a précis prior to the meeting that places each agenda item in a larger, more strategic context, along with a set of questions that seem desirable to raise with the board relevant to the matter at hand. This approach would help the administration and the board alike to keep their eye on the target and make decisions in light of organizational strategy. For instance, a proposal before a community outreach and service committee to establish a shelter for homeless persons in the area could be structured to precipitate a discussion about the implications of the congregation's mission in relation to its community and about the range of alternative steps that should be considered in working toward the achievement of strategic goals in this area. The issue could be positioned as a springboard to discuss strategy or as a dead weight to mire trustees in operational details. The board bears ultimate responsibility for the choice, and its effectiveness at this stage of the process rides in no small measure on its ability to place and decide within the broader framework of strategy the issues that come before it.

Boards can adopt numerous other measures to keep the organization focused on strategy, such as prioritizing agenda items, setting time guidelines as a function of each issue's relative importance, and reserving a period at each meeting for the executive to discuss what is uppermost in his or her mind. Whatever approach a board chooses, the principle remains the same—keep focused on the priorities. As a member of one board observed during an interview, "The board has one key job: to preserve the organization's clarity of purpose. There is no board agenda apart from this."

Monitoring Progress

Through constant attention to strategic priorities, the board can materially influence the direction of administrative efforts. But efforts alone are not enough; there should be progress, too. Nevertheless, administrators and board members, as a rule, appear to be more knowledgeable about efforts than about measurable movement in implementing a strategy to achieve a vision.

We do not lack the technology to monitor progress. For example, the Association of Governing Boards has developed extremely informative strategic performance indicators and useful constructs for comparative analyses. Projects by Kent Chabotar (1989) and Gordon Winston (1991) have yielded pertinent financial ratios and practical formats for boards to interpret financial performance. Lawrence Butler sets forth another approach in Chapter Ten of this volume.

Despite these advances, why does it seem that administrators and trustees are more familiar with the aspirations of their strategic plans ("Oh, that's so important, and we covered it on page 18") than with the effects to date ("Gee, I don't know what's happening")? It may be because their boards of trustees do not ask for—no, *demand*—the data. Trustees deliberate at length and ultimately decide major policy questions—such as staff compensation plans, capital outlays, and membership criteria, all represented at the time as essential ingredients of organizational strategy—without ever asking if, when, and how the board will know whether the policy just adopted has in fact produced the desired results.

One can easily imagine that at the seminary committed to multiculturalism that was profiled earlier, the board will learn three years from now whether or not the heterogeneity of the student body and the faculty actually increased or decreased. Data will probably be supplied about the mix of financial aid packages and the dollar volume. But at the onset of this initiative did the board ask for or did the administration offer approaches to calibrating changes in the racial climate, estimating the degree of penetration of multiculturalism into the curriculum, or measuring the morale of faculty members from underrepresented racial and ethnic groups? Progress can, in fact, be charted through periodic surveys, interviews, and reviews of programs, though these may or may not be appropriate in different organizations. In fact, there may be no more critical role for the board in the strategy process than to compel the professionals to identify the most informative and reliable indicators, however imperfect, of organizational performance; the effects of strategies; and the pace of progress toward the enactment of a vision. In fact, the envisioning process itself needs to include envisioning appropriate ways to evaluate movement toward fulfillment of the vision.

Without such strategic, normative, selective, and graphic information, it will be difficult to tell if the organization is gaining or losing ground or whether anything the board or anyone else does actually makes a difference.

Those of us who draw a salary and enjoy academic exercises may be delighted to play in a game where no one keeps score. But for trustees, this could get old in a hurry. In fact, some board members may and do leave the board in favor of another activity where the fruits of their labors are more easily discerned.

But all this begs the most fundamental issue of all. Most members of the boards of religious organizations are selflessly devoted to the betterment of the institutions they serve. Monitoring the strategy process is one of the most pivotal contributions a board can make toward that end. There may be no more effective way for a board to enable the organization it governs to realize its ambitions than by insisting that its leaders keep track of the institution's progress. This is less to hold the administration's feet to the fire, though admittedly this enters into it, than to hold up a mirror to the constituencies and the community. In this way, the board openly demonstrates and models accountability for use of the organization's resources.

Downsizing

If the board vigilantly tracks the rate of progress toward realization of the organization's vision, it should be able to identify performance gaps sooner and explore remedial actions earlier. In concert with the executive, the board could establish some trip wires or similar mechanisms that signal imminent financial difficulties—a task greatly simplified by the handbooks on strategic questions, indicators, and analyses published by the Association of Governing Boards (1985, 1987), *In Trust* (McCarthy and Turner, 1998), and others (Taylor, Meyerson, Moffell, and Park, 1991; Winston, 1991).

The board's role as sentinel assumes increasing importance as more and more religious organizations, battered by a depressed economy and unfavorable demographics, confront the need to downsize because of financial strains. The board must be the strongest voice for fiscal prudence. In reality this means that the board has to place a governor on the motor that drives the expense side because most staff seem genetically disposed to overspend and to budget for miracles on the revenue side. Many boards are too timid in this regard and approve deficit budgets that would not be tolerated in a for-profit environment.

Just as significant, perhaps only the board can prompt the staff to think the unthinkable and to probe explicitly the trade-offs they may be loath to consider and quick to dismiss. For example, is a new facility for our congregation's young people really necessary when there is other unused

THE BOARD'S ROLE IN SHAPING STRATEGY   167

space they might use? Particularly during periods of financial hardship, staff tend to avoid considering difficult trade-offs. For example, as even the wealthiest seminaries examine the viability of need-blind admissions, few have placed on the table a range of policy options that might preserve the principle of access. Such alternatives, which are likely to be unpopular and outlandish from the faculty's point of view, include programmatic "growth by substitution," a higher student-faculty ratio, fewer "boutique" electives, financially self-sufficient service programs, and reconsideration of tuition subsidies for the dependents of faculty and senior administrators. Like the best teachers and researchers, the best boards will challenge conventional thinking with some regularity.

In organizations where administrators are slow to seize the initiative, boards should direct the executive to develop principles, policies, and procedures to govern retrenchment. Should the cuts be selective or across the board? Should the sanctity of tenure be preserved at all costs? Should the decision-making process be consultative and decentralized and thus inevitably protracted, or do some special circumstances warrant "command" decisions? These are questions that trustees should ask and administrators should answer, preferably well before the need for action arises.

The process will not, however, be entirely rational. A strategic approach relies primarily on a reasoned process informed by objective indicators of quality, centrality, and cost. Where can we eliminate weakness? Where can we add strength? How do we optimize the allocation of resources? How do we deal with these things and remain true to our mission?

As a practical matter, however, politics and emotions are both powerful and influential forces, as veterans of reorganizing periods in many religious organizations can attest. No sooner has a logical analysis identified a program or site for reduction or elimination than constituents from many sectors start to organize in opposition. These protests so often reverse or compromise rational, defensible recommendations that one wonders whether boards and senior management should have a publicly available strategy at all. In all too many cases, the "hit list" provides the safest harbor because that status inevitably leads to a review of program quality, which indicates that the area, while not first-rate, is somewhat better than assumed and could in fact be topflight with the infusion of marginal resources. In the meantime, the champions of the program or the site rally the troops to defend the territory. In the wry words of one veteran of such battles, "It may just be easier and more efficient in the long run to starve a program than try to shoot it."

In any case, if a strategy has been devised and approved, the board simply must stand shoulder to shoulder with the administration in the face of a rising tide of protests. It must be unequivocally steadfast when reorganization, authorized by the board and executed by the administration in accordance with criteria endorsed by the board, produces attacks on the organization's leaders. To do otherwise would jeopardize the management as well as the strategy.

Conclusion

I have suggested that boards should fulfill several different yet essential roles in the strategy process. During the envisioning and monitoring phases, the board should be on stage, if not always at its center. By contrast, when strategy is being formulated and implemented, the board should be off in the wings, supporting the cast and facilitating the action. In effect, boards have multiple roles: part playwright, part actor, part impresario, and sometime stagehand. To extend the metaphor a little, if the trustees find themselves with a hit on their hands—a vision that has truly come to life—they should be the first to lead the organization in celebration. In fact, that may be one of the board's most indispensable roles; certainly it is one of the board's most delicious privileges.

REFERENCES

Andrews, K. *The Concept of Corporate Strategy.* (Rev. ed.) Burr Ridge, Ill.: Irwin, 1980.

Association of Governing Boards of Universities and Colleges. *Composition of Governing Boards.* Washington, D.C.: Association of Governing Boards of Universities and Colleges, 1985.

Association of Governing Boards of Universities and Colleges. *Strategic Decision Making: Key Questions and Indicators for Trustees.* Washington, D.C.: Association of Governing Boards of Universities and Colleges, 1987.

Birnbaum, R. *How Colleges Work.* San Francisco: Jossey-Bass, 1988.

Chabotar, K. "Financial Ratio Analysis Comes to Nonprofits." *Journal of Higher Education,* 1989, 60(2), 188–208.

Chait, R., Holland, T., and Taylor, B. *The Effective Board of Trustees.* Phoenix: Oryx Press, 1993.

Delbecq, A., and Gill, S. "Developing Strategic Direction for Governing Boards." *Hospital and Health Services Administration,* 1988, 33(1), 25–35.

Fisher, J. L. *The Power of the Presidency.* New York: American Council on Education/Macmillan, 1984.

Keller, G. *Academic Strategy: The Management Revolution in Higher Education.* Baltimore: Johns Hopkins University Press, 1983.

McCarthy, J. H., and Turner, R. M. "Balance Sheet: Managing a School's Money." *In Trust,* 1998, 9(2), 18–21.

Taylor, B., Meyerson, J., Moffell, L., and Park, D., Jr. *Strategic Analysis: Using Comparative Data to Understand Your Institution.* Washington, D.C.: Association of Governing Boards of Colleges and Universities, 1991.

Winston, G. "Organizing Economic Information for Colleges and Universities: An Alternative to Fund Accounting." Williamstown, Mass.: Williams College Project on the Economics of Higher Education, 1991.

PROVIDING MEANINGFUL INFORMATION FOR GOVERNANCE

Lawrence M. Butler

GOVERNING BOARDS of religious organizations are confronted by complex and often conflicting messages arising from people within the organizations they govern, from denominational representatives, from sponsors and donors, and from society at large. These boards have a particularly compelling need for better ways to make sense of the information they receive. Unfortunately, too many board members are frustrated because the information they routinely receive from administrative staff is inadequately designed to support their governance functions.

Inadequacies of Board Information

Following are some of the information inadequacies that are all too recognizable to board members.

- *Data overload.* Information is often provided in indigestible quantities that require more time and expertise than anyone, particularly busy board members, can apply to it. This may create the illusion of an informed board while in fact leaving the board disoriented and frustrated.
- *Inappropriate levels of detail.* Data can be presented at too fine a level of detail. This can create or reinforce a tendency for the board to micromanage the organization. The opposite extreme can also pose prob-

lems. Use of global trend information unlinked to the institution's mission or strategic situation may provide knowledge, but at the expense of true understanding.

• *Administrative versus governance perspective.* To a greater degree than administration, governance requires consideration of mission and values, organizational liability, fiduciary integrity, long-range environmental trends, opportunities for interorganizational collaboration, and the needs of sponsors and other publics. Information for the board that is merely a subset of the management information system can tend to underplay or totally ignore these governance concerns.

• *Lack of strategic relevance.* Strategic issues are those that affect the long-term viability of the organization, in terms of both mission and financial performance. Information, however interesting, that fails to highlight such issues diffuses the board's proper focus.

• *Individual trustee versus whole board education.* Providing specialized or detailed information to select board members can serve a valid purpose, but it does not expand the whole board's core knowledge base, and only the whole board is empowered to act on behalf of the organization.

• *Unresponsiveness to board members' time constraints.* The special need for boards to use their time efficiently is not served through information flows that are excessive, too detailed, or tangential to governance concerns. The use of nongraphic formats or presentation techniques that make rapid understanding difficult also contributes to the waste of board time.

• *Reliance on the anecdotal and episodic.* In the absence of predetermined and objective performance indicators agreed to by both board and administration, there can be a tendency for hearsay and inconsistently derived "facts" to surface that then require inordinate amounts of time and energy to substantiate or refute.

• *Lack of interpretive context.* Information is valuable only to the extent that it can be put to use for the benefit of the organization. Performance data that are reported without reference to some context—such as predetermined standards of performance (such as budgets) or performance in previous periods or comparable settings—provide insufficient interpretive meaning on which to base any advice or guidance.

As these inadequacies suggest, governing boards have special information requirements that can be both substantively and operationally different from those of management. They have a special responsibility regarding mission and strategy that shapes the kinds of information they need; and as collective entities they have special requirements for processing the information when it is received. What they need, in essence, are *board information systems* (BIS)—the governance equivalent of management information systems. Such systems convey information on key aspects of organizational performance that are mission sensitive and strategic, and they do so in formats and at levels of detail appropriate to the needs of a time-constrained group of board members. The balance of this chapter focuses on three such needs expressed by trustees: the need for more meaningful information, the need for greater mission and strategy support, and the need for enhanced collective understanding.

Infusing Information with Meaning

"We have plenty of information, but what does it all really mean?" "How can our board monitor the organization's operating performance so that it fully understands the facts and their significance without being overwhelmed by details?" This section discusses answers to such common questions and offers a number of ideas for improving the communicative and interpretive power of board information. All of these ideas are derived from actual experience with boards of religious organizations.

DashBoard Reports

One type of information format that has proven to be particularly effective in focusing the board's attention on key issues is what professional board members have come to refer to as *DashBoard Reports*. These reports are presented at each board meeting and often at executive committee meetings as well. They compress a great deal of information into one or two pages and thereby offer a snapshot of how the organization is performing. This enables board members to spot trends and identify problems quickly.

DashBoard Reports serve the same function as the instrument panel on the dashboard of an automobile. They contain several key indicators of organizational performance that provide an overview of the organization's status and overall direction. Instead of showing speed, revolutions per minute, and engine temperature, DashBoard Reports typically display summary information about the organization's finances, its volume of services, and its client population.

As with an automobile dashboard, these reports often contain the equivalent of warning lights that light up only when there is a problem or when certain variables stray outside of predetermined limits. This latter feature enhances a governing board's sense of confidence that it can ignore a great deal of operational information, knowing that it will be alerted if a problem arises that requires attention. The DashBoard Report shown in Figure

10.1 is a good example. Designed to meet the needs of a museum board, it combines graphic displays with numbers and brief narrative comments.

Figures 10.2a through 10.2d are selected pages from a set of DashBoard Reports for a theological school called, hypothetically, Eastern School of Religion. As with all reports presented in DashBoard style, these examples combine a number of related indicators on a single page so that the reader can more readily see connections among the various pieces of information. (Similar indicators are relevant in other religiously sponsored organizations, such as congregations, hospitals, and social service agencies.)

DashBoard Reports appeal to the right as well as left brain through a combination of graphic, numeric, and narrative elements. Boards are not monolithic entities but groups of individuals, each of whom has his or her own style of information acquisition and processing. The goal here is not so much to be sure that each board member receives exactly the same message in the same way as everyone else, but to empower all of them to derive their own meaning from the data and, through the posing of questions and the sharing of perspectives, to emerge with a collective understanding that is richer and more complete than that of any individual.

The report structure diagram in Figure 10.2a serves as a kind of road map showing the interrelationships among the various reports. It also provides a conceptual framework that can orient the user over time. For example, although the several reports that make up this particular set can be viewed as a single package that is produced annually, they need not be presented to the board all at once. Certain reports can be reviewed by different board committees at different points during the year.

Graphic Display

The foregoing examples demonstrate, among other things, that using certain basic graphic display techniques can make otherwise opaque statistical reports not only comprehensible but also dramatic and powerful. Through the use of graphics, large amounts of information can be conveyed in ways that assist the board in understanding key issues and trends.

Boards should consider how the data it now receives in undifferentiated, tabular form might be converted into more powerful graphic displays, such as line charts, bar graphs, pie charts, data maps, and so on. Given the availability of relatively inexpensive graphics software packages, displays that were once time-consuming projects can be produced at the touch of a keyboard or mouse.

Two rather simple techniques require no conversion of data into special graphic formats, yet they reduce the time it takes to focus on key data. These are *highlighting* and *warning light* reports. Certain key figures or

Figure 10.1. Monthly Status Report for
Eastern Art Museum, May 1994.

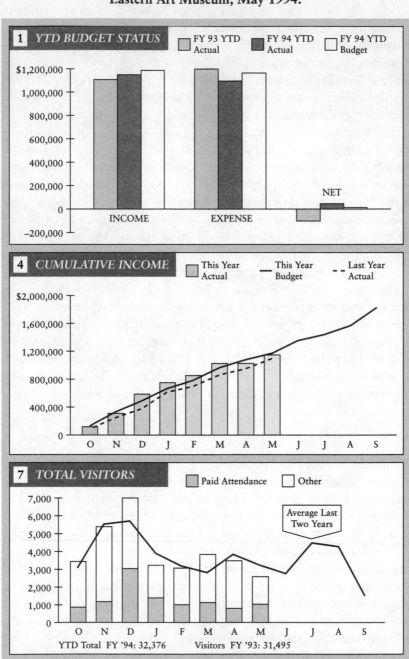

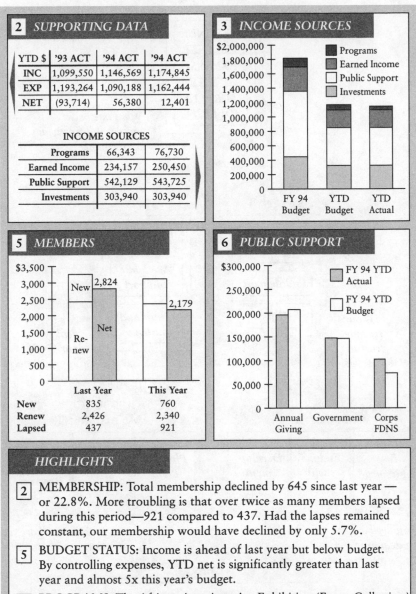

2 SUPPORTING DATA

YTD $	'93 ACT	'94 ACT	'94 ACT
INC	1,099,550	1,146,569	1,174,845
EXP	1,193,264	1,090,188	1,162,444
NET	(93,714)	56,380	12,401

INCOME SOURCES

Programs	66,343	76,730
Earned Income	234,157	250,450
Public Support	542,129	543,725
Investments	303,940	303,940

3 INCOME SOURCES

- Programs
- Earned Income
- Public Support
- Investments

FY 94 Budget / YTD Budget / YTD Actual

5 MEMBERS

New 2,824
Re-new
Net
2,179

	Last Year	This Year
New	835	760
Renew	2,426	2,340
Lapsed	437	921

6 PUBLIC SUPPORT

- FY 94 YTD Actual
- FY 94 YTD Budget

Annual Giving / Government / Corps FDNS

HIGHLIGHTS

2 MEMBERSHIP: Total membership declined by 645 since last year — or 22.8%. More troubling is that over twice as many members lapsed during this period—921 compared to 437. Had the lapses remained constant, our membership would have declined by only 5.7%.

5 BUDGET STATUS: Income is ahead of last year but below budget. By controlling expenses, YTD net is significantly greater than last year and almost 5x this year's budget.

1 PROGRAMS: The African-American Art Exhibition (Evans Collection) was a critical and financial success drawing large numbers of visitors —especially in March—and greatly improving our outreach.

Figure 10.2A. Eastern School of Religion Information Flow.

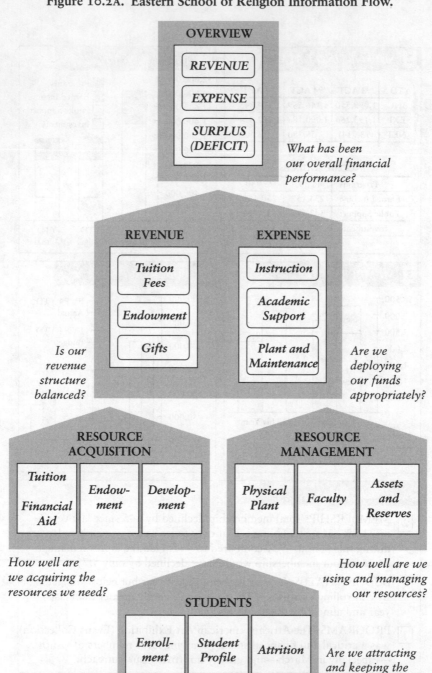

Figure 10.2B. Eastern School of Religion Financial Performance, 1996–1998.

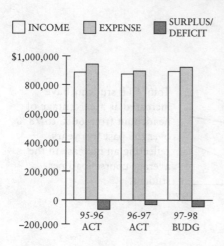

	95-96 ACT	96–97 ACT	97–98 BUDG
INCOME			
Tuition/Fees	171,432	174,607	212,580
Gifts	340,436	320,664	295,000
Endowment	375,000	380,000	384,000
Interest	2,524	(197)	1,000
Total	889,392	875,074	892,580
EXPENSE			
Admin	394,798	403,039	395,354
Academic	378,685	355,609	393,955
Plant	84,939	69,740	70,082
Financial Aid	44,890	40,226	51,000
Net Aux	39,665	28,594	15,570
Total	942,977	897,208	925,961
OP'G SURP/DEF	(53,585)	(22,134)	(33,381)

INCOME

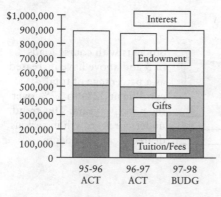

Despite an increase in Tuition and Fee Income (of 21.7%), the operating deficit is projected to increase in FY98 by $11,247.

This is primarily due to an increase in faculty salaries (accounting for an increase in Academic Support of 10.8%) and a decline in Net Auxilliary Income of 45.5%. More commuting students generating less Room and Board Income is expected to account for this decline.

EXPENSE

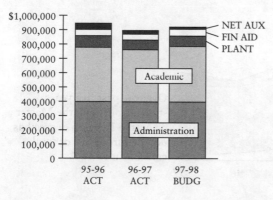

Figure 10.2C. Eastern School of Religion Enrollment Profile, 1993–1997.

TOTAL STUDENTS
FULL-TIME EQUIVALENTS

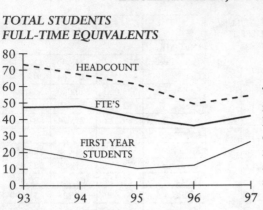

Total FTE students have increased as a percentage of headcount from 66% to 78% over the past five years, reflecting an increase in the average course load per student.

COURSE ENROLLMENT

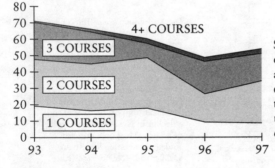

Students with course loads of 3 and above have increased as a percentage of total enrollment 32% to 37% over the past five years. This trend underscores growth in serious, degree-seeking students.

PROGRAMS OF STUDY

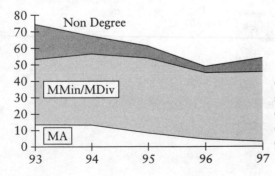

Over the past five years, students pursuing the Master of Arts in Religion degree has declined from 5% of total enrollment to 18%.

Figure 10.2D. Eastern School of Religion Student Profile, FTE Students, 1993–1997.

GENDER

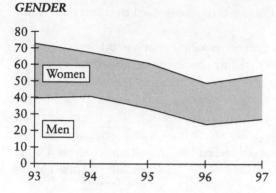

Although women have increased from 45% to 50% of total FTE enrollment since 1993, the gender balance has stabilized over the past two years.

AGE

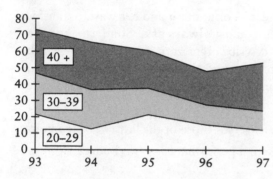

Students 30 and older have fairly consistently accounted for about 70% of total enrollment over the past five years.

MARITAL STATUS

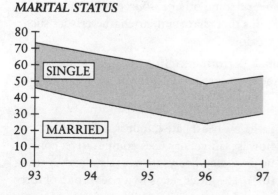

Single students constitute the core of community life at ESR. Their proportion of the student body has increased from 35% in 1993 to 43% in 1997.

data elements in a standard tabular report can be highlighted by a box, a different color, or a halftone overlay, thereby drawing the viewer's eye more quickly to the pertinent information. This is particularly useful in conjunction with financial statements that may need to retain their traditional formats.

Warning light reports work on the principle that a good deal of routine reporting of data can be eliminated by specifying in advance the range of outcomes the board would consider acceptable and the point at which it would want to be alerted to a situation in which performance had begun to deviate in either a positive or negative direction. The board can then receive a warning light report indicating that each of a series of important factors is being monitored, but only when performance has exceeded some threshold will the "light" come on and the actual data be reported along with an explanation of what has happened.

Comparative Context

To derive meaning from raw data—or to put it another way, to transform data into information—boards must always ask, Compared to what? Whenever possible, data that describe organizational operations—whether enrollment, financial performance, student scores, staff salaries, occupations, and so forth—gain in meaning when presented comparatively. Several types of comparison are available:

Trends: This year's results versus those of the last five to ten years

Goals and objectives: Actual performance versus budget or preestablished targets

Market and peers: How the organization is doing in a particular area versus (a) how other organizations that compete for members, students, research dollars, or some other resource are doing; or (b) how other organizations that share similar characteristics such as size or sponsorship are doing.

Norms: The organization's performance (for example, a financial ratio) compared with the norm or standard for other organizations of its type or size.

A DashBoard Report for a religiously affiliated, four-year liberal arts college hypothetically called Midwest University uses comparative, contextual elements in two ways—by providing five-year trend data and by using peer group data (see Figure 10.3). The latter refers to a peer group of forty private, four-year colleges with tuitions over $10,000 from a national survey reported in Taylor, Meyerson, and Massey (1993). Figure 10.4 is a DashBoard Report for Eastern School of Religion in which several financial indicators are compared with those of a peer group of seminaries in the Association of Theological Schools.

Use of the budget for goal comparison is common practice. Virtually all boards are familiar with the traditional actual-to-budget variance reports that display by line the organization's operating performance to date. These reports are typically organized to show the most recent period, year-to-date, and comparisons of these to the same periods in the previous year. Figure 10.5 is an example of a DashBoard version of such a report that conveys the same information in graphic terms. Note that the components of revenue—tuition, fees, and gifts—are displayed on a cumulative monthly basis that readily allows the board to visualize the degree to which these actual revenues are deviating from the projected cumulative budget figures for these same components.

Often the very exercise of setting comparative or normative standards requires the board to think through what it considers to be an appropriate level of good or bad performance. In doing this, the board must look for guidance to its mission, values, and strategic concerns.

The use of what-if simulations is yet another way to enhance data interpretation through comparison—such as comparison of alternative futures. Once a board feels that it has a good grasp of current performance and historical trends, it will often want to gain a better understanding of future outcomes that might result from adopting particular policies or from the combined impact of various factors, best- and worst-case scenarios, and the like.

Figure 10.6 illustrates how easily what-if scenarios can be integrated into a trendline graphic. Here are three projections of the bottom-line financial impact under three different assumptions about enrollment. The value of this kind of display lies principally in conveying an understanding of the sensitivity of the organization's financial viability to changes in a key variable. Extending the current and historical data into the future via simulation creates an "envisioning partnership" with the board in a realm of great importance to trustees—the future.

Telling a Story

The Midwest University report shown in Figure 10.3 is but one of a set of DashBoard Reports derived from an actual college's annual "fact book"— a fifty-page compendium of numerical data densely arrayed in columns and rows. Although the facts were there for the board to see, it was the

Figure 10.3. Midwest University Revenue Report.

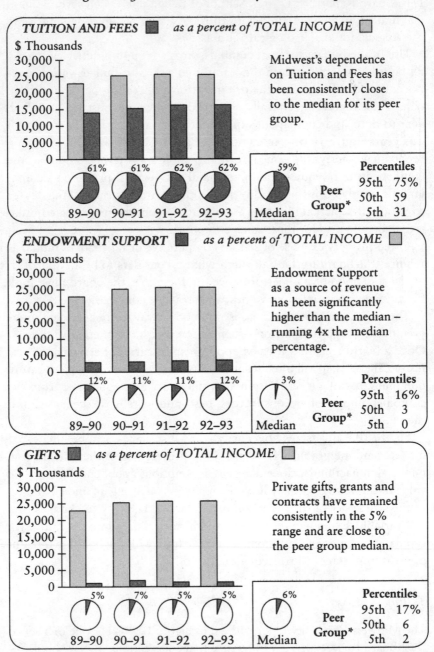

TUITION AND FEES ■ *as a percent of* TOTAL INCOME ▢

Midwest's dependence on Tuition and Fees has been consistently close to the median for its peer group.

ENDOWMENT SUPPORT ■ *as a percent of* TOTAL INCOME ▢

Endowment Support as a source of revenue has been significantly higher than the median – running 4x the median percentage.

GIFTS ■ *as a percent of* TOTAL INCOME ▢

Private gifts, grants and contracts have remained consistently in the 5% range and are close to the peer group median.

•Peer Group = 140 private four-year colleges with tuitions over $10,000 from national survey reported in: Taylor, Meyerson and Massey, *Strategic Indicators for Higher Education: Improving Performance*. Princeton, NJ: Peterson's Guides, 1993.

Figure 10.4. Eastern School of Religion Peer Group Comparisons with Association of Theological Schools.

ATS Peer Group Comparisons
All Data for FY '97

ATS PEER GROUP — STUDENT HEAD COUNT

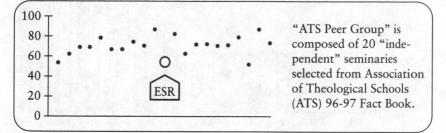

"ATS Peer Group" is composed of 20 "independent" seminaries selected from Association of Theological Schools (ATS) 96-97 Fact Book.

AV. E&G EXPENDITURES

$ Thousands

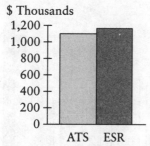

AV. ENDOWMENT

$ Thousands

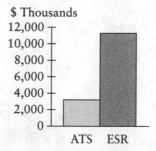

AV. E&G EXPENDITURES PER STUDENT FTE

$ Thousands

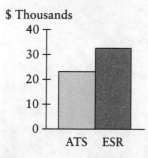

AV. ENDOWMENT PER STUDENT FTE

$ Thousands

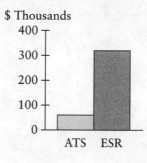

Figure 10.5. Cumulative Monthly Revenues for
Eastern School of Religion.

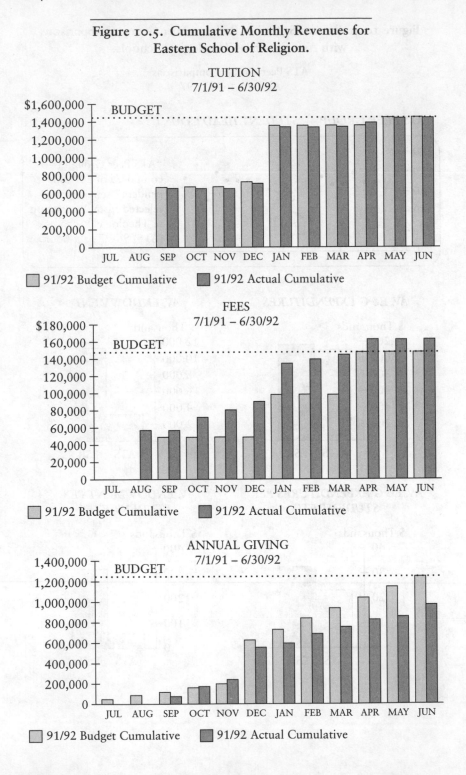

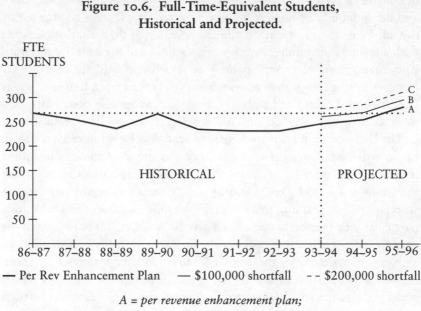

Figure 10.6. Full-Time-Equivalent Students, Historical and Projected.

— Per Rev Enhancement Plan   — $100,000 shortfall   - - $200,000 shortfall

A = per revenue enhancement plan;
B = to offset a $100,000 shortfall in other revenues;
C = to offset a $200,000 shortfall in other revenues.
Each $100,000 = approximately 15 FTE students.

rare board member who ever ventured into this data swamp. Through graphically enhanced formatting of key elements from that book, the board now has a fighting chance to understand what the data are saying.

The original statistical fact book represents one extreme on a continuum of interpretive guidance—that is, raw data unenhanced by any attempt to assist the board in understanding their significance. Moving along this continuum, ever greater amounts of guidance can be offered— from selected indicators alone to indicators plus narrative interpretation to a sequenced set of displays leading to specific conclusions and recommendations. In other words, the other end of the continuum is the *telling of a story.*

The advantage of presentation as story is that it provides the maximum interpretive guidance. The downside of such an approach is that it may not encourage individual board members to do the kind of free roaming through the information that will enable them to develop their own insights and piece together their own stories.

The extent to which a board welcomes or even tolerates staff guidance will be conditioned by the culture of the board in relating to staff and by the degree of confidence developed over time in the accuracy, timeliness, and dependability of the information received. It will also be affected by the nature of the information and the urgency of the situation. Coping with a financial or public relations crisis would call for a straightforward story that quickly gets to the point. Conversely, a consideration of future trends affecting long-range plans might well benefit from multiple points of entry into the data and a presentation that encourages board members to make their own connections and develop their own interpretations.

The Midwest University and Eastern School of Religion reports shown earlier strike a balance between guidance and empowerment by including comments that offer some clarification of the graphic material. Although they draw attention to key points or trends, these comments nevertheless stop short of explaining their strategic significance. On the whole, this particular set of reports is organized around a functional paradigm of the organization. Their value resides to a large extent in the fact that, whatever their content, they appear in the same predictable formats from meeting to meeting. To compensate for the nonlinear nature of this report structure, a summary chart is provided (see Figure 10.7) that reconstructs a story from some of the more salient points noted in the preceding Dash-Boards. Although still a story devoid of editorial comment, it does attempt to show the interrelationships among the factors being discussed.

A step further in the direction of telling a story is a budget presentation made to a seminary board. The material in Figure 10.8 is a subset of the overhead transparencies that were used. Partially altered here to preserve confidentiality, this material combined graphic and numerical data and, perhaps more importantly, followed a very clear narrative flow, propelled forward with brief headline points. Instead of the traditional line-item, columnar budget presentation, what we have here is the telling of a story of strategically significant changes. It guided the board through a logical sequence that maintained the discussion at a level appropriate to the governance perspective.

Past budget discussions had typically bogged down around line item details and tangential issues. This presentation, by contrast, moved along efficiently, identified the major issues, and left plenty of time to discuss them. It was, in fact, the first time in the memory of many of the board members that a budget and its strategic implications had been so well understood.

Finally, DashBoard Reports need not always be quantitative. A useful technique is to create a one-page cover sheet that summarizes in brief narrative paragraphs or keyword commentaries the current status of a major strategic direction or mission-sensitive issue.

Figure 10.7. Midwest University Summary of Major Trends and Indicators, 1990–1993.

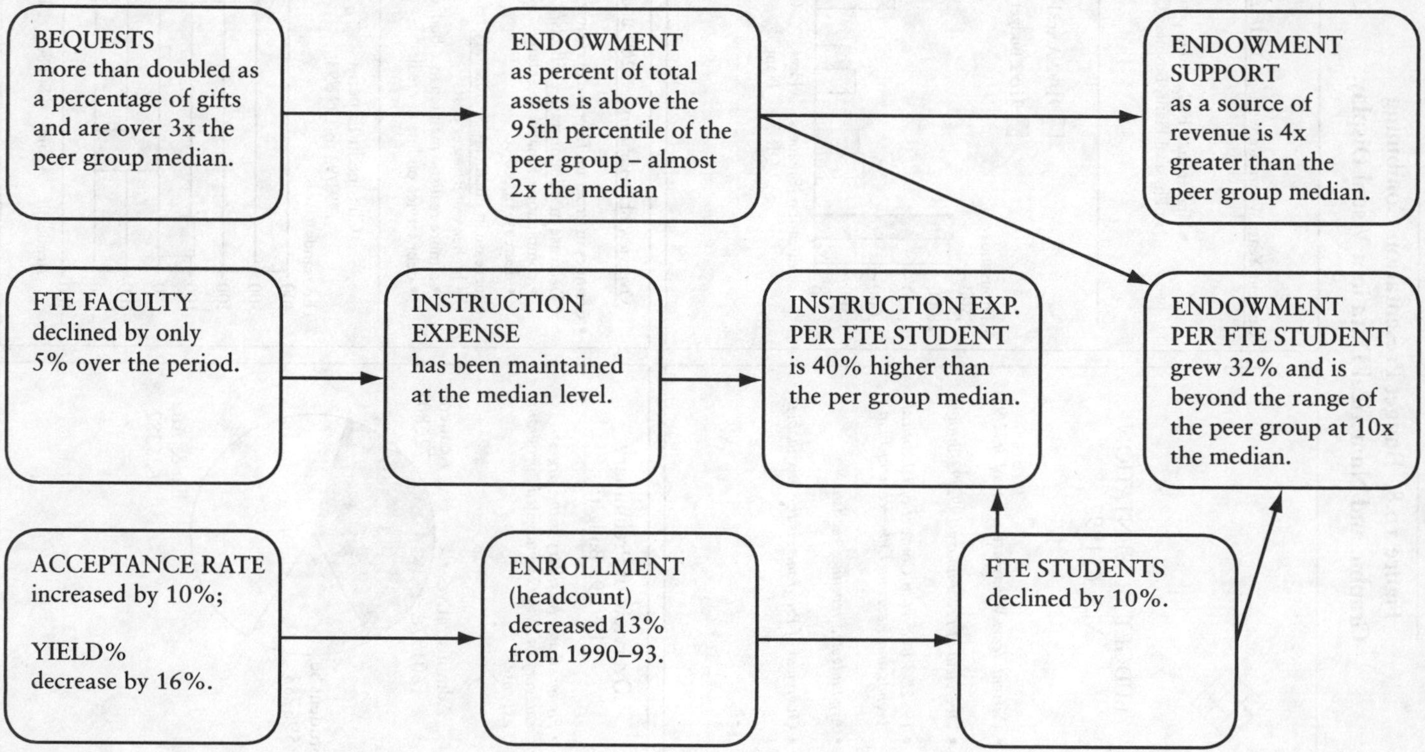

BEQUESTS more than doubled as a percentage of gifts and are over 3x the peer group median.

FTE FACULTY declined by only 5% over the period.

ACCEPTANCE RATE increased by 10%; **YIELD%** decrease by 16%.

ENDOWMENT as percent of total assets is above the 95th percentile of the peer group – almost 2x the median

INSTRUCTION EXPENSE has been maintained at the median level.

ENROLLMENT (headcount) decreased 13% from 1990–93.

ENDOWMENT SUPPORT as a source of revenue is 4x greater than the peer group median.

ENDOWMENT PER FTE STUDENT grew 32% and is beyond the range of the peer group at 10x the median.

INSTRUCTION EXP. PER FTE STUDENT is 40% higher than the per group median.

FTE STUDENTS declined by 10%.

Figure 10.8. Budget Presentation Combining
Graphic and Numerical Data in a Visual Display.

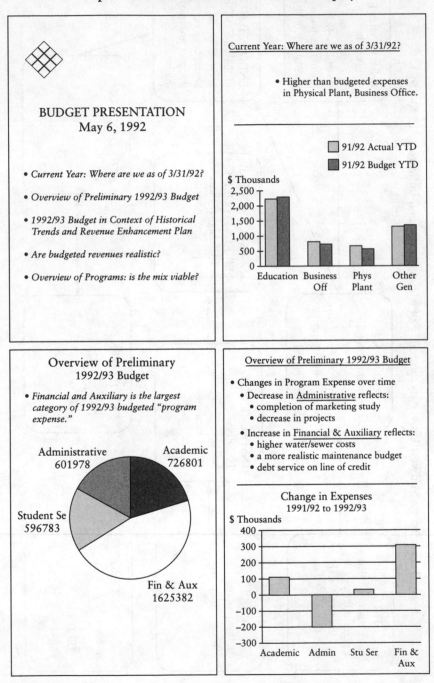

BUDGET PRESENTATION
May 6, 1992

• *Current Year: Where are we as of 3/31/92?*

• *Overview of Preliminary 1992/93 Budget*

• *1992/93 Budget in Context of Historical Trends and Revenue Enhancement Plan*

• *Are budgeted revenues realistic?*

• *Overview of Programs: is the mix viable?*

Current Year: Where are we as of 3/31/92?

• Higher than budgeted expenses in Physical Plant, Business Office.

■ 91/92 Actual YTD
■ 91/92 Budget YTD

$ Thousands

(Education, Business Off, Phys Plant, Other Gen)

Overview of Preliminary
1992/93 Budget

• *Financial and Auxiliary is the largest category of 1992/93 budgeted "program expense."*

Administrative 601978

Academic 726801

Student Se 596783

Fin & Aux 1625382

Overview of Preliminary 1992/93 Budget

• Changes in Program Expense over time
  • Decrease in Administrative reflects:
    • completion of marketing study
    • decrease in projects
  • Increase in Financial & Auxiliary reflects:
    • higher water/sewer costs
    • a more realistic maintenance budget
    • debt service on line of credit

Change in Expenses
1991/92 to 1992/93

$ Thousands

(Academic, Admin, Stu Ser, Fin & Aux)

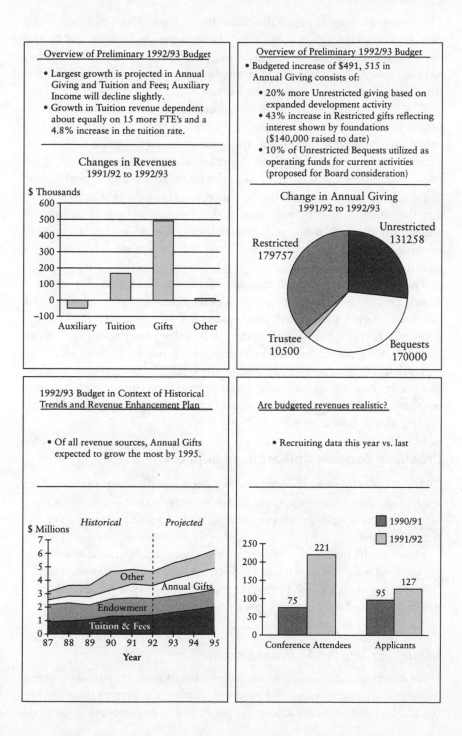

Overview of Preliminary 1992/93 Budget

- Largest growth is projected in Annual Giving and Tuition and Fees; Auxiliary Income will decline slightly.
- Growth in Tuition revenue dependent about equally on 15 more FTE's and a 4.8% increase in the tuition rate.

Changes in Revenues
1991/92 to 1992/93

$ Thousands

Auxiliary   Tuition   Gifts   Other

Overview of Preliminary 1992/93 Budget

- Budgeted increase of $491, 515 in Annual Giving consists of:
  - 20% more Unrestricted giving based on expanded development activity
  - 43% increase in Restricted gifts reflecting interest shown by foundations ($140,000 raised to date)
  - 10% of Unrestricted Bequests utilized as operating funds for current activities (proposed for Board consideration)

Change in Annual Giving
1991/92 to 1992/93

Unrestricted
131258

Restricted
179757

Trustee
10500

Bequests
170000

1992/93 Budget in Context of Historical Trends and Revenue Enhancement Plan

- Of all revenue sources, Annual Gifts expected to grow the most by 1995.

$ Millions

Historical   *Projected*

Other

Annual Gifts

Endowment

Tuition & Fees

87 88 89 90 91 92 93 94 95
Year

Are budgeted revenues realistic?

- Recruiting data this year vs. last

■ 1990/91
□ 1991/92

221

75

95   127

Conference Attendees   Applicants

Committee Reports

The budget-as-story example illustrates how the need for efficiency in the presentation of information at the full board level can be balanced by the need for greater depth of understanding at the committee level. It was, after all, the finance committee that predigested the budget details and distilled the key points to transmit to the full board.

The BIS, in other words, can be structured so that reports to the full board highlight only that subset of indicators needed to reflect global organizational performance of a strategic nature. At the same time, it can provide access to the underlying information base for board committee use or when strategic indicators alert the board to a possible problem or opportunity. Thus, what the full board receives on a routine basis is actually the tip of an information iceberg that extends to board committees and subcommittees. In this way, greater levels of detail are made available to those whose committee responsibilities require a more detailed understanding of particular issues.

These different levels of informational detail can be linked via an agenda-setting process in which the annual calendars of committee meetings and full board meetings are coordinated in such a way that certain topics work their way up the agenda ladder to the full board at preset points during the year. It is not possible, of course, to anticipate a year in advance all of the issues that will need to be addressed by the board, so board meeting agendas can be structured to allow for staff presentations at any time on non-routine but otherwise significant issues that require discussion or decision making by the board.

Providing Mission and Strategy Support

"We don't want to rubber-stamp and we don't want to micromanage. Can we receive information appropriate for governing that keeps us focused on mission and strategy and enables us to add value?" asked a typical board member.

How can the board stay focused on the organization's mission and major strategic issues so that it can guide the organization and yet not duplicate management's role? In fact, the development of a BIS can help to define the boundaries between governance and management in ways that enhance both functions.

Identifying Mission-Relevant Information

Most board members of religious organizations instinctively understand the importance of mission and values in shaping the lives of their institutions. The problem is how, in practical terms, to incorporate values and mission considerations into the operational life of the board and, more specifically, into the reports and other mechanisms that constitute its information system.

To approach this task, it helps to adopt a mission-sensitive framework for thinking about the board's information needs. One possible framework posits four generic categories of information that respond to basic governance questions:

Service mix: In responding to the needs of our publics, are we providing an appropriate mix of services? Are we meeting their needs?

Service quality: Are we providing these services at a level of quality that is acceptable both to our publics and to ourselves?

Resource acquisition: How effectively are we able to acquire the resources—both human and financial—that we need?

Resource management: Are we managing these resources with proper stewardship? Are we efficient in our use of financial resources and fair in our dealings with our people?

Organizational mission and values drive the answers to these questions by defining what is meant by the terms *publics, appropriate, acceptable, effective,* and *proper.* Viewed in this way, a board can make meaningful judgments about any of the information it receives only if it has an explicit understanding of mission. Consider the following examples:

Service mix: A mission that emphasizes a seminary's reason for being as "preparation for ordained ministry" may require careful monitoring of trends that encourage lay ministry and of the impact of those trends on applications and enrollments.

Service quality: A school's mission that stresses the importance of the "highest standards of scholarship" may call for the monitoring and evaluation of the scholarly research output of the faculty and of the perceived value of that research in the academic community.

Resource acquisition: A hospital's mission commitment to "reach out and provide health care to the underprivileged and underserved" may require that the institution pay special attention to fundraising for unreimbursed care and other forms of patient support.

Resource management: A mission highlighting the value of human dignity may point to the need for periodic assessment of the attitudes of participants, visitors, and staff toward the organization and how it treats them.

As these examples suggest, the board's understanding of organizational mission and values creates a set of predispositions that works like a spotlight shining across a vast information landscape, picking out particular issues for special attention and closer scrutiny. The signals the board sends by aiming that spotlight in certain directions rather than others can themselves be powerful forces guiding the institution toward its mission objectives. In this sense, a BIS is as much about the board informing the organization about what it considers fundamentally important as it is about the administration informing the board about the organization's condition.

Focusing on Strategic Issues

The notion of strategy can be made far more complicated than it needs to be. In addition to the guidance offered by Richard Chait in Chapter Nine of this volume, the literature on this subject offers the following definition that helps to clarify strategy for purposes of this discussion: "Strategic issues are . . . associated with effectiveness in . . . the few areas which are critical to the success of the institution. The key . . . for most organizations is to focus their most limited resources—the time of trustees and top administrators—on those issues which really make the difference between success and failure" (Taylor, Meyerson, Moffell, and Park, 1991).

Religious organizations want to focus on strategic issues of special interest to them. The following list, although by no means exhaustive, suggests the range of such issues that might be of concern to the board of a seminary (Fletcher, 1983; Schuth, 1989; Wilkes, 1990).

SERVICE MIX

I. Decreasing applicant pool and enrollments
   A. Pressure to diversify into new curricular offerings and vocational training options (such as the rise in clinical pastoral education)
   B. Increased need to incorporate adult learning into the curriculum to accommodate older students
II. Decreased interest in the ordained ministry as a vocation; increased interest in lay ministry
   A. Identifying sources of funding for lay ministry training
   B. Dealing with competition from secular educational institutions in training the laity, and from church-sponsored pastoral centers
   C. Affiliating with secular universities to protect fiscal viability; implications of this for maintaining theological integrity and institutional autonomy

    D. Maintaining the support of traditional seminary constituencies while broadening mission away from ordination

III. Coping with greater student lifestyle diversity (such as homosexuality) and cross-cultural interests (such as study of Eastern religious traditions)

IV. Role of the seminary in the continuing formation of ministers, priests, or rabbis; as centers for spiritual renewal, reflection, and prayer

  V. Implications of increasing numbers of women seminarians for
    A. Offsetting erosion in academic selectivity
    B. Ensuring meaningful vocational "field placement" in the face of conservative constituencies

SERVICE QUALITY

  VI. Pressure to reduce selectivity and academic standards as a consequence of decreasing applicant pool and waning interest in the ordained ministry

VII. Implications for the quality of theological research, the volume of scholarly output, and the climate of free academic inquiry posed by having productive but controversial faculty being drawn away to secular universities

VIII. Responsibility of the seminary with regard to increasing the spiritual dimension in the curriculum and in faculty and student life

RESOURCE ACQUISITION

  IX. Fundraising within constraints imposed by sponsors and the limited capacity of alumni

   X. Balancing the seminary's traditional heavy dependence on tuition with a need to keep tuition low enough to attract the best applicants and to reach out to the poor and minorities

RESOURCE MANAGEMENT

  XI. Aging physical plants; lack of capital for rebuilding and maintenance

XII. Finding alternative uses or sources of support for the rich legacy of architecturally and symbolically valuable—but expensive to maintain—facilities (such as churches and chapels)

How can specific elements in the BIS be designed to monitor and report on strategic issues such as these? The approach recommended in *Strategic Decision Making: Key Questions and Indicators for Trustees* (Frances, Huxel, Meyerson, and Park, 1987) is to define a set of indicators in each of ten critical areas for strategic decision making. Table 10.1 lists these decision areas and the strategic issues that fall within them.

Table 10.1. Strategic Decision-Making Framework of the Association of Governing Boards of Universities and Colleges.

I. Financial Affairs
  A. *Financial Performance*
    1. Assurance of sound financial management
    2. Positive financial performance
    3. Balanced sources of revenue
    4. Balanced expenditures
  B. *Financial Condition*
    5. Increase of institutional assets
    6. Prudent use of debt as leverage for needed assets
    7. Maintenance of strong financial condition
  C. *Endowment Management*
    8. Increasing total return on endowment
    9. Allocating return on endowment between current and future needs

II. Enrollment
  A. *Enrollment Planning*
    10. Choosing the optimum size of enrollment
    11. Influencing the selectivity of the institution
  B. *Tuition Pricing*
    12. Setting the right price for tuition
  C. *Student Financial Aid*
    13. Maximum leverage of financial aid to achieve targeted student mix and desired selectivity

III. Institutional Advancement
  A. *Development and Fundraising Programs*
    14. Sustaining the fundraising effort
    15. Managing development activities
    16. Launching a capital campaign
    17. Ensuring the development program supports the long-term needs of the institution's financial plans
  B. *Institutional Image and Advancement*
    18. Maintaining the support of constituents

IV. Human Resources
  A. *Faculty and Staff*
    19. Providing adequate support for faculty and staff
    20. Hiring and maintaining the right faculty and staff
    21. Maintaining equitable personnel policies and procedures
  B. *Governance, Management, and Morale*
    22. Participation in decision making
    23. Efficiency and effectiveness of management practices
  C. *Affirmative Action*
    24. Maintaining a healthy mix of faculty, staff, and students

Table 10.1. *(continued)*

V. **Academic Activities**
  A. *Instruction*
    25. A viable mix of academic programs
    26. Assurance of high-quality instruction
    27. Approval of new programs
    28. Discontinuance of existing programs
  B. *Research*
    29. Appropriate balance between instruction and research
  C. *Public Service*
    30. Appropriate public service activities
  D. *Academic Support Services*
    31. Adequacy of learning resources and computer support

VI. **Student Affairs**
  A. *Student Services*
    32. Quality of student life
  B. *Student Activities*
    33. Responsible expenditures of student activity fees

VII. **Intercollegiate Athletics**
  A. *Funding and Quality of Athletic Programs*
    34. Self-sufficiency of athletics
    35. Enhancement of institutional image and visibility through athletics

VIII. **Physical Plant and Equipment**
  A. *Physical Plant*
    36. Adequate and timely maintenance and renovation of the physical plant
    37. Allocation of space
    38. Controlling physical plant costs
  B. *Equipment*
    39. Effective management of equipment

IX. **Auxiliary Activities**
  A. *Auxiliary Services*
    40. Adequacy of administrative support services set up as auxiliaries
  B. *Auxiliary Enterprises*
    41. Utilization of auxiliary enterprises as sources of revenue

IX. **Institutional Mission**
  A. *Mission*
    42. Responsiveness of the mission to change in the external environment

Source: C. Frances, G. Huxel, J. Meyerson, and D. Park, *Strategic Decision Making: Key Questions and Indicators of Trustees.* Washington, D.C.: Association of Governing Boards of Universities and Colleges, 1987, pp. 8–10. Reprinted by permission.

Let us assume, for example, that a seminary board is motivated by two of the mission concerns referred to earlier: ordained ministry and high standards of scholarship. These concerns might lead the board to shine its mission spotlight on the strategic issue of a decreasing applicant pool and decreasing enrollments and their implications for maintaining a focus on ordination and a high level of selectivity. To better understand how these issues affect the organization, the board may choose to consider any number of possible indicators. Table 10.2 suggests several.

Some indicators are quantitative (such as popularity and admission drawing power indices), some are qualitative (such as surveys and image studies). The precise number and combination of indicators that will ensure effective monitoring of any particular issue will vary with each

Table 10.2. Strategic Issue 11: Influencing the Selectivity of the Institution.

Questions	Key Trends and Indicators
What is the image of the institution?	Self-selection among applicants
How popular is the institution among potential students?	Popularity Index (number of applicants per matriculating freshman or transfer)
How strong is the drawing power of the institution on students who have applied?	Admissions Drawing Power Index (matriculants as a percentage of admitted freshman and transfers)
	Surveys of students who decline admission
How successful is the institution in retaining students through graduation?	Retention Index (percentage of freshman who graduate)
What would be the impact on the applicant pool of changing student selectivity?	Projected number of qualified applicants based on SAT or ACT cutoff scores
What would be the impact on incoming student quality of more (or fewer) matriculants?	Projected SATs or ACTs of students based on different enrollments
Will the image of the institution help or hinder the recruitment of desired students?	Image studies among potential and random students
How effective are the institution's recruitment materials and plans in stimulating applications and matriculations?	Communications audits of recruitment materials and plans

board's level of concern and with the institution's capacity to produce or access the requisite information.

Integrating a Mission and Strategy Focus into the BIS

Once it has identified indicators of mission-sensitive or strategic performance, how might a board go about integrating them into the BIS? In addition to building them directly into the DashBoard and committee reports, as discussed earlier, several other techniques have been found effective.

• *The midlevel document.* Frequently an organization's formal mission statement is expressed in such lofty terms that it loses any power to serve as a guide for decision making. In these situations one might need to find—or create—more useful statements. Whether they are called statements of mission imperatives, corporate intents, strategic directions, strategic initiatives, or simply vision statements, such midlevel documents reside somewhere between an overly general mission statement and an overly detailed strategic plan. Sometimes the strategic plan that exists on paper has emerged through a process that involved the board and explicitly made a connection with mission. Often, however, the board was not involved in any meaningful way or the mission connection was not clearly made. In these cases, undertaking a process of crafting such a midlevel document becomes an opportunity to go back and make that connection. In so doing, language emerges that more readily lends itself to creating measurable, mission-sensitive performance indicators.

• *Linking strategy to budgets.* Even when boards have had some prior involvement in the strategic planning process, they appreciate an effort to deconstruct or recast the strategic plan in the somewhat broader midlevel terms appropriate to the governance perspective. Such an effort is particularly valuable if it takes the next step and links strategic goals with the operating budget. The budget is perhaps the most important tool that boards use in monitoring institutional performance. Seeing the relationship between a mission-derived strategic plan and a multiyear budget completes the governance loop in an especially powerful way.

• *Mission and goal-related icons.* We have already discussed at some length the use of information graphics. There are, however, ways of using graphics that have a purpose other than making quantitative information more accessible. An example is the use of icons to create reminders of mission or big-picture goals. Figure 10.9 illustrates how this was done by a board through the use of a nine-diamond graphic icon that symbolically captured the organization's four core values and five institutional goals. The icon was used as an orienting device to remind the viewer of how each committee's area of responsibility related back to the basic concepts. Such devices not only speak to the spiritual dimension in a religious setting but could also apply to the way a religiously sponsored social service agency might relate to its clientele.

• *Intraboard dialogue.* The committee structure of one denominational board of trustees actually distinguishes between mission committees and operations committees, with the former adopting a mission-sensitive perspective toward each of three entities overseen by the board (one a seminary) and the latter adopting the more traditional functional perspective (such as finance, development, and education) across all three entities. Because each trustee is simultaneously a member of both types of committee, he or she is able to take turns adopting each perspective. This structure offers an opportunity to orchestrate a dialogue within the board itself between mission and operating committees. Even boards that do not structure their committees this way can still engage in an intentional exercise of raising mission-driven questions and concerns via the executive or some other committee or at designated times during full board sessions. Those questions that cannot be fully explored at a given meeting can be scheduled for follow-up at a subsequent board meeting or special retreat.

Enhancing Collective Understanding

"Some of us know a lot and some of us know very little. How can we all get up to speed so we can act collectively as a board?" asked another typical board member.

Creating and maintaining the base of shared knowledge that supports true collective deliberation is difficult at best. It is an even more challenging task the more complex the organization and its history are, the larger the board is, the higher the turnover in board membership is, and the more broadly representative the membership is. How can improvements in board information content and processing—such as including orientation techniques—help to promote this base of collective understanding?

Orientation

Boards vary considerably in the effort they expend and the success they achieve in orienting new board members and bringing them up to speed. Those that do a good job of it are willing to invest the time necessary to fully acquaint the new board member with the history and culture of the organization (and the board) and to convey clearly the responsibilities and expectations of board membership. Although it is not my intention here to discuss the orientation process in depth, I would simply mention a few practical ideas that have emerged from my research team's work.

THE BOARD HANDBOOK. It is useful to differentiate background or orientation information that tends not to change frequently from meeting-specific information and to organize and deliver it separately to all members of the board. One of the more effective ways to do this is in a handbook for board members. Typically this is a loose-leaf binder containing basic background information on the institution, such as the board's bylaws, trustee job descriptions, biographical data and photos of members and key staff, organization charts, institutional mission statement and strategic plan, historical time line of key institutional events, summary descriptions of key programs, major policies adopted by the board, the board and committee meeting calendar, and so on.

Available for reference at any time, such a regularly updated handbook serves as a common information base for the board as a whole, as an orientation resource for new board members, and as a way for established board members to refresh their memories without embarrassment. This last point deserves some emphasis.

Every board member—the veteran no less than the newcomer—needs continuing orientation. And because in many ways it can be more awkward for the veteran than for the newcomer to acknowledge his or her lack of understanding of some basic piece of background information, reminders that are routinely built into the board materials are greatly appreciated. One such method for maintaining an ongoing program of board orientation is to make available to individual board members on an as-needed basis a catalog of brief issue-specific summaries of minutes from past board meetings.

A linkage between the trustee handbook and the meeting book or pre-meeting information packet can be created by means of a set of pages in the meeting book that provides a glossary of terms and other summary descriptions that serve as orientation reminders, and by including tabbed sections in the handbook under which DashBoard and other summary pages from the meeting-specific board book can be inserted for safekeeping after the board meeting has taken place.

THE MEETING BOOK. The binders prepared for board meetings should employ one or more navigational aids to help focus board members' attention on key issues and pending decisions. Some examples are tables of

Figure 10.9. Graphic Icons Relating
Eastern School of Religion's Core Values and Goals.

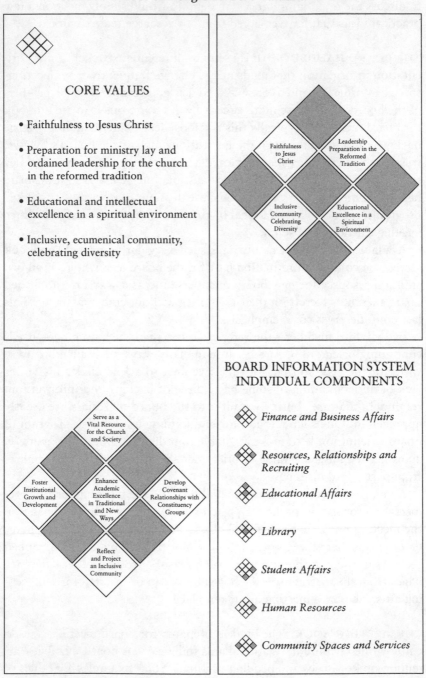

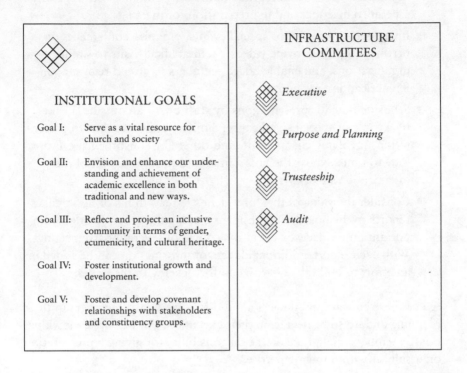

INSTITUTIONAL GOALS

Goal I: Serve as a vital resource for
           church and society

Goal II: Envision and enhance our under-
           standing and achievement of
           academic excellence in both
           traditional and new ways.

Goal III: Reflect and project an inclusive
           community in terms of gender,
           ecumenicity, and cultural heritage.

Goal IV: Foster institutional growth and
           development.

Goal V: Foster and develop covenant
           relationships with stakeholders
           and constituency groups.

INFRASTRUCTURE
COMMITEES

Executive

Purpose and Planning

Trusteeship

Audit

contents that are cross-referenced to the meeting agenda; agenda pages that highlight items that call for formal votes, other kinds of decisions, or general discussion; tabbed sections that are color-coded by committee or strategic theme; cover sheets under each tab that summarize key points in subsequent documents; paper stock of different colors that denote the relative urgency or significance of materials; and so on.

Education

Not all of a board's information needs can be met by these kinds of orientation materials or by the kinds of DashBoard and other performance reports described earlier. The board—no less than administration—must keep abreast of trends and issues in its area of responsibility and society in general. The following examples suggest the range of possibilities for conveying this more broadly educational information.

- Inform and update board members via mailings and faxes of newsletters, books and reprints of articles, both between regularly scheduled meetings and in preparation for meetings.

- Invite guest speakers for special events, organize conferences on pertinent topics, provide videos, facilitate field visits to similar organizations, and enable board members to attend relevant conferences and workshops.

- Set aside time for presentations by staff or for an outside speaker on a topic of special significance. Similarly, allocate time to presentations involving clients, staff, and other key constituencies. From time to time, expose the board firsthand to some aspect of the organization's work.

- Consider the value of the "president's letter." In his or her regular reports to the board, the president can lay the groundwork for important policy decisions over the course of several board meetings. With each report, additional layers of information can be added in an effort to build the board's comfort level with the issues.

All of these educational devices should involve board members in their planning and, to some degree, in their execution. For example, individual board members might take on the responsibility for giving a presentation on a subject within their expertise.

Conclusion

Many members of the boards of religious organizations are deeply concerned about how their desire to be of value through board service is often thwarted by information that is inadequate in the way it conveys meaning, supports their commitment to institutional mission, or empowers the board as a collective entity. We have seen how a broad array of techniques—a BIS—can address these concerns.

In themselves there is nothing magical about any of these techniques or in any set of reports, regardless of how well designed they are. Unless the messages they contain are heeded and used by the board to set policy or to guide administration more effectively, there is little purpose in an exercise to upgrade board information. Indeed, doing so without a real commitment to act on such information could have negative consequences for board and administration morale.

Herein lies the real challenge to boards. A commitment to improve the board's information is, in fact, a commitment by the board to engage itself—not just once, but on a continuing basis—with the entire spectrum of mission and strategy-related issues that arise in the life of the organization. In short, a commitment to better board information is a commitment to fully empowered governance.

REFERENCES

Association of Governing Boards of Universities and Colleges. *Exquisite Problems: The Role of Seminary Trustees.* Washington, D.C.: Association of Governing Boards of Universities and Colleges, 1989. Videotape sponsored by the Lilly Endowment, Inc.

Fletcher, J. C. *The Futures of Protestant Seminaries.* Washington, D.C.: Alban Institute, 1983.

Frances, C., Huxel, G., Meyerson, J., and Park, D. *Strategic Decision Making: Key Questions and Indicators for Trustees.* Washington, D.C.: Association of Governing Boards of Universities and Colleges, 1987.

Schuth, K. *Reason for the Hope: The Futures of Roman Catholic Theologates.* Wilmington, Del.: Michael Glazier, 1989.

Taylor, B., Meyerson, J., and Massey, L. *Strategic Indicators for Higher Education: Improving Performance.* Princeton, N.J.: Peterson's Guides, 1993.

Taylor, B., Meyerson, J., Moffell, L., and Park, D., Jr. *Strategic Analysis: Using Comparative Data to Understand Your Institution.* Washington, D.C.: Association of Governing Boards of Colleges and Universities, 1991.

Wilkes, P. "The Hands That Would Shape Our Souls: The Changing and Often Deeply Troubled World of America's Protestant, Catholic, and Jewish Seminaries." *Atlantic,* Dec. 1990, pp. 59–88.

CONCLUSION

TURNING TOWARD THE FUTURE

David C. Hester and Thomas P. Holland

THIS IS THE PLACE in a book like this for a conclusion. Rather than trying to bring this volume to an end with summary comments, drawing out what our authors have already said so well, we prefer to suggest here some "turning points." The author of the Hebrew Bible book of Ecclesiastes wisely noted, "For everything there is a season, and a time for every purpose under heaven" (3:1). With that, the wise writer held before his readers the boundary experiences of life, the magnetic poles of human being. It is not surprising, we suppose, that in God's scheme of things the biblical voice associated with the human search for meaning—that of the sage of Ecclesiastes—contains an echo of the Greek word adopted by early Christians for "church": *eccleisia*. Here is a reminder that the Christian Church was born—at a "purposeful time"—in search of understanding and in quest of meaning about Jesus, his ministry, and the linkage of person and work with messiahship. How is Jesus the Christ? may be a fair way of phrasing the question that confronted early Christians—a question out of which grew the four Gospels and, ultimately, the whole Christian Bible. A question of equal importance might be, What does Jesus being Christ mean for contemporary life, for the practice of love and justice, for the ordering of institutional and business practices, and for living with one another in human community? These two questions fill and fulfill the ages, generation after generation, even to now.

As she sang "Turn! Turn! Turn!" folk singer Judy Collins interpreted the wisdom of Ecclesiastes in the midst of a time filled with all the extremes that human community could endure without coming unraveled altogether yet promising "a time for every purpose under heaven." Her time included the ravages of the Vietnam War and the desperate struggle for human rights and civil rights throughout our nation. It included stark confrontation between generations—long-haired "radical" children turning their parents' values upside down. The writers of this volume work in a far different context. The present revolution focuses on information technology, the transformation of our national economy from an industrial to a service basis, corporate takeovers, leveraged buyouts, and the internationalization of business. Our society has become secular enough that the connections to the Bible's Ecclesiastes made by songwriter Pete Seeger in "Turn! Turn! Turn!" are no doubt lost on many.

This book demonstrates in myriad ways what the authors and editors believe: we are a part of a turning point under way in the practice of governance in religious institutions—from congregations to seminaries, from denominationally related colleges and universities to hospitals with a religious heritage and a public commitment that are fueled by public funds. Things are changing in the boardroom, in the vestry, and in the session or general council meeting. "High time, too," some say. If Talcott Parsons (1960) was right years ago to point to the inertia that inherently accompanies institutional life, those who work with religious institutions might offer to "double" Parsons's comment when it comes to institutions steeped in treasured and sacred traditions that are literally held in trust from a whole company of saints who now "from their labors rest."

Religious institutions, perhaps more than any other nonprofit group, are stretched between Ecclesiastes-like poles that rightly recognize a time for conserving tradition and a time for transforming tradition, and the tension is constant and must not be dissolved. For if it is dissolved, governance in religious institutions is not in good faith, because it is set adrift from its sacred past, with little other than instinct to avoid the shoals of an unknown future and the rocks of relativistic values and trendy decisions. Much in our contemporary life, as these chapters note, invites just that kind of quick-fix thinking on the part of busy boards or church leaders hurrying to keep up with the frenetic pace we as a culture have adopted for ourselves.

We hope that you have found these chapters an antidote to that kind of superficial problem solving and an inspiration to more constructive, well-informed, well-imagined, and faith-grounded thinking. We have called this latter kind of thinking "a search for practical wisdom" and "theological reflection," intending to underscore the absolute need for all of us in these days to ground the work of the boards on which we serve in the God-given mission the institution claims for itself.

"Mission awareness," represented in governance that is firmly and decisively located deeply within the commitments, values, beliefs, and purpose of the institution, is one of the turning points we've marked in this volume. *Mission* indeed captures the spirit of turning points as it points to how institutional past, present, and future are integrated in good governance. A mission statement is far more than a "factoid." In essence, it is an institutional community's expression of identity. As such, it must turn to the past, to the tradition of which it is now the trustee and advocate— or theologically speaking, a witness called to tell the institutional narrative truthfully. However, each board, session, or council is the creator of a new narrative that incorporates the past into the present, reading time through the unique perspective that is theirs. The mission statement, if it is to be useful as well as truthful, must be written in the language and through the vision of the present trustees. They also must guide the turning to its conclusion, pointing the mission statement toward the future.

Governance in the future is likely to confront some challenges that are different from those of the past, suggesting that a process of change will continue and that the exchange of good ideas will become even more important. The generation of trustees and leaders that emerged after the Second World War worked extensively to create and strengthen religious organizations, drawing on their understanding of the importance of structure and accountability. Corporate models of hierarchical organizations with order, stability, and long-term horizons were useful resources for many struggling organizations. Governing boards have been fully aware of their need to change in order to meet new challenges, such as financial crises, loss of critical leadership, decline in congregational membership, and loss of enrollment. In recent years, sparked by the need to respond constructively and creatively to rapid changes within and outside institutions, awareness of the importance of governing boards has grown, and many of them have begun asking for assistance in strengthening their performance. This volume offers a range of ideas and practices drawn from a number of the boards the authors have encountered. Further steps of sharing experiences and resources are needed in order to continue this process of improvement in the coming years.

Now those postwar leaders are moving into retirement and the next generation, the so-called baby boomers, have begun taking the mantle of leadership. Their experiences, values, and interests differ in many ways from those of their elders. Impatient with hierarchical structures, this next generation of leaders seems to be turning toward more collegial or horizontal linkages, flexibility, openness to extensive changes in the ways organizations operate, and concentration on short-term goals. The image of the leader as a charismatic figure managing up front is giving way to a concept of shared leadership in which leaders are servant-leaders. Their expectations about information have risen with the new technologies introduced in their lifetimes. Their experiences have led to changed perspectives on governance. Old structures are being replaced with ad hoc teams that focus on specific questions or objectives, bringing to bear a range of talents to solve a problem and then move on. Team composition is shuffled to meet the needs of the next issue. The carefully developed hierarchical structures of the board's predecessors are being dismantled and replaced with teams and matrix structures, allowing rapid change in approaches to dealing with diverse issues.

Each of these two generations may look at the other and wonder why they place such different emphases on how a board should work. But as soon as the boomers have reorganized boards to fit their new perspectives, they will be the ones moving into retirement and being replaced with the Generation X leaders. These young folks have grown up in a world that is as different from that of the boomers as the boomers' was from the world of their predecessors. Immediate access to information from anywhere in the world on any topic of interest has always been a part of the lives of Generation Xers. They will probably see organizational structures as irrelevant or even as obstacles. Recomposed teams will proceed on an even faster timetable as issues arise and are addressed far more quickly. As the pace of change accelerates, will the quality of decisions keep pace? Although every generation is optimistic about its own answers, each fears that the next will stumble and misuse the legacy so carefully put in place. "Turn! Turn! Turn! For everything a season, and a time for everything under heaven," to paraphrase Ecclesiastes.

The leaders and boards in this volume whose voices witness to their insights, complaints, hopes, and deep sense of calling to serve as agents of tradition and change have taught a great deal to those of us who have had the honor of working with them. Their ingenuity, honesty, and arguments in the context of the ambiguities of service attest to the living character of institutional boards and the lively nature of conversation about how boards become more effective in service to their mission.

Our purpose "under heaven" in this collection of chapters from authors who have worked with boards extensively and passionately over decades has been to hand on to you, the readers, what we have learned and the implications we see for improving the practice of faithful governance. As we noted in the preface, what we have said in these chapters may not, indeed cannot, fit your circumstances precisely. Now it is your turn to receive, reflect, and—most critical—revise and transform the narrative of these chapters into activity for the good that is described in your context and calling or purpose. Effective governing boards behave in certain characteristic ways. These have been discussed in this book from selected angles of vision. We know, for example, that effective, faithful governance requires a working mission statement that may serve as a foundation, informant, and measure of accomplishment. We have suggested ways to attend to making the mission statement a full conversation partner in decision making.

To take another example, we know that the flood of information that governing boards must sort through, organize, and interpret is fast becoming overwhelming. There is too much data and much of it is contradictory—that's the concern we heard widely from leaders and board members. The experts published here acknowledge that concern and address it in a variety of ways, including a very helpful strategy for developing a set of indicators of the health of the institution, which offers a way of sorting and organizing data that separates the wheat from the chaff.

Learning to receive the wisdom of the past as well as adapt the new ideas of the present and apply them all freshly and creatively to new and emerging problems is always a challenge. Certainly one of the benefits of the new technologies is that they make communication far easier than it was in the past. Whether this increasingly rapid transfer of data will actually be converted into wisdom remains to be seen. Governing boards will always need to renew and deepen their understanding of the implications of their faith commitments for the issues they confront. They will always need to learn from their own experiences as well as those of others in order to provide strong guidance to their organizations. Purposeful and sustained attention to the continuous improvement of the quality of their own work will be a never-ending responsibility of boards if they are to lead organizations successfully in future and different worlds of experience. The books and resources that extend and improve what has been offered in the present volume will be crucial to those efforts—which is to say, this closing marks an opening, another turning. We hope that this book, apart from the practical wisdom it contains, may also inspire. Inspiration involves literally being infused with spirit, and in the context of our writing, the Spirit we have in mind is Holy. Clearly this book alone cannot fulfill the work of inspiration; but the hope for inspiration can remind us that God's Spirit is already present to and for the governing work that leaders in religious institutions are about. The presence of the Holy Spirit enables the truth to be told about present circumstances, and encourages imagination toward creative and transformative change.

Finally, we hope that you will continue with us the conversation you've heard here. We invite and encourage you to tell us what you think about what has been said in this book. Tell us how it squares with your experience. Tell us, please, how useful the wisdom offered here may be to you in your service, and describe for us how you adapted what you received to your particular circumstances, especially in the context of congregational governance. We are quite serious about this last request; this is not a polite closing but a plea to keep the conversation going and not to leave us out of it!

"For everything there is a season." We hope that this book will help you consider the purpose under heaven that is faithful, effective governance of religious organizations.

REFERENCE

Parsons, T. *Structure and Process in Modern Societies*. New York: Free Press, 1960.

INDEX